THE
WOUNDED
SURGEON

THE
WOUNDED
SURGEON

Confession and Transformation
in Six American Poets

Robert Lowell
Elizabeth Bishop
John Berryman
Randall Jarrell
Delmore Schwartz
Sylvia Plath

ADAM KIRSCH

W. W. Norton & Company
New York London

Interior photographs: Lowell: AP Wide World; Bishop: AP Wide World; Berryman: Daniel
A. Lindley; Jarrell: Special Collections Department, Jackson Library, The University of
North Carolina at Greensboro; Schwartz: New Directions; Plath: AP Wide World

For information about permission to reproduce selections from this book, write to
Permissions, W. W. Norton & Company, Inc., 500 Fifth Avenue, New York, NY 10110

Manufacturing by RR Donnelley, Harrisonburg, VA
Book design by Chris Welch
Production manager: Andrew Marasia

Library of Congress Cataloging-in-Publication Data

Kirsch, Adam, 1976–
The wounded surgeon : confession and transformation in six American poets :
Robert Lowell, Elizabeth Bishop, John Berryman, Randall Jarrell, Delmore Schwartz,
and Sylvia Plath / Adam Kirsch.— 1st ed.
p. cm.
Includes bibliographical references and index.
ISBN 0-393-05197-8 (hardcover)
1. American poetry—20th century—History and criticism. 2. Confession in
literature. 3. Autobiography in literature. 4. Self in literature. I. Title.
PS310.C65K57 2005
813'.6—dc22

2004027970

W. W. Norton & Company, Inc., 500 Fifth Avenue, New York, N.Y. 10110
www.wwnorton.com

W. W. Norton & Company Ltd., Castle House, 75/76 Wells Street, London W1T 3QT

1 2 3 4 5 6 7 8 9 0

To Jonathan, Ann, and Jennifer Kirsch
and to Remy

CONTENTS

INTRODUCTION

The wounded surgeon plies the steel
That questions the distempered part
—*T. S. Eliot, "East Coker"*

The six writers discussed in this book make up one of the great constellations in the history of American poetry. From the 1940s through the 1970s, Robert Lowell, Elizabeth Bishop, John Berryman, Randall Jarrell, Delmore Schwartz, and Sylvia Plath not only wrote some of the most enduring poems in our literature; they redefined our notion of what it means for a poet to write honestly. Poems like Lowell's "Waking in the Blue" and Bishop's "In the Waiting Room," Schwartz's *Genesis* and Berryman's Dream Songs, made it possible for poets to put themselves at risk in their work in ways that would have been unthinkable a generation earlier.

Yet the achievement of this group of poets has always been easy to misunderstand. Almost immediately, the kind of self-exposure practiced by Lowell and Berryman, in particular, was labeled "confessional." Ever since, the confessional style has been one of the most popular, and most easily ridiculed, in American poetry. But the usefulness of criticism depends on its metaphors, and in confession it found a bad metaphor for what the most gifted of these poets were doing. The motive for confession is penitential or therapeutic—by speaking openly about his guilt and suffering, the poet hopes to make them easier to bear. Another possible motive is ethical: by refusing to join the conspiracy of polite silence around certain shameful subjects, he challenges us to shed light on our own dark places.

But the poets discussed in this book always approached their writing as artists, and their primary motive was aesthetic. When they turned to experiences like madness and despair and lust—as even Bishop and Jarrell, the least explicitly autobiographical of the six, sometimes did—they did so in order to make effective works of art, not in order to cure themselves or shatter taboos. To treat their poems mainly as documents of personal experience is not just to diminish their achievement, but to ignore their unanimous disdain for the idea of confessional poetry. Plath scorned the notion of poetry as "some kind of therapeutic public purge or excretion"; Berryman insisted that "the speaker [of a poem] can never be the actual writer," that there is always "an abyss between [the poet's] person and his persona"; Bishop deplored the trend toward "more and more anguish and less and less poetry"; Lowell explained that even in *Life Studies*, usually considered the first masterpiece of confessional poetry, "the whole balance of the poem was something invented."

In order to reclaim the true achievement of these six poets, a new metaphor is needed. This is what the title of *The Wounded Surgeon* hopes to supply: T. S. Eliot's image evokes the resolve, not to say heroism, that these poets displayed by submitting their most intimate and painful experiences to the objective discipline of art. (As Berryman wrote, perhaps with Eliot's lines in mind: "I am obliged to perform in complete darkness / operations of great delicacy / on my self.") Thanks to a flood of biographies and memoirs, the psychic wounds of Lowell, Schwartz, Plath, and the rest have been probed at great length; and because life is easier to talk about than art, there is a danger that they will become known mainly for their wounds. But the suffering that afflicted this group of poets becomes significant only because they examined it with the surgeon's rigor, detachment, and skill.

Poetry has its own life, with only an ambiguous connection to the life of the person who writes it; set down that these poets were mentally ill, or alcoholic, or suicidal—as all of them were, in some combination or degree—and you still have not come anywhere near to explaining why they wrote as they did. That is why I have written, for each of these six poets, what might be called a brief biography of their poetry. I have tried to explore the inner structure and logic of their work: how the questions raised in one poem are answered in another; how the limits of an early style are transcended in a later one; or, conversely, how strengths can eventually turn into weaknesses. By looking at the whole range of each poet's work, and by closely reading some of their most significant poems, I aim to shed light on what they were trying to do, and how far they succeeded.

From this perspective, what unites these six poets is not a style or subject, but a common starting point. Robert Lowell, Elizabeth Bishop, John Berryman, Delmore Schwartz, and Randall Jarrell were all born between 1911 and 1917, and came to maturity during the triumphant age of Modernist poetry. (Sylvia Plath, born in 1932, represents something of a special case.) All of them knew that the Modernists had achieved something epochal. "The generation of American poets that included Frost, Stevens, Eliot, Pound, Williams, Marianne Moore, Ransom," Jarrell wrote, "would establish once and for all the style and tone of American poetry." Lowell agreed that "never before or since have there been so many good poets in America; nor in England—unless we go back more than two hundred and fifty years."

To write in the wake of such giants was a mixed blessing. The Modernists had restored poetry to the position of a serious art, one that could—as Lowell wrote—"take a man's full weight and . . . bear his complete intelligence, passion, and subtlety." But at the same time, their huge success left the younger generation at a disadvantage. A young poet in the 1930s was faced with a body of poetry and criticism so authoritative that it took courage, and ingenuity, simply to avoid being crushed by it.

The Modernists were an extremely diverse group, and they certainly had no program in common. But the critical interpretation of Modernism that held sway in America from the 1930s through the 1950s—what is known as the New Criticism—did present a certain influential vision of what poetry should be; and the best poets of the younger generation were educated, on the page and in the classroom, by New Critics like Allen Tate and John Crowe Ransom. Jarrell was Ransom's student; Lowell went to Kenyon College specifically to study with Ransom, and later lived as a guest of Allen Tate; Berryman was introduced to Tate through Mark Van Doren, his mentor at Columbia; Schwartz entered into eager correspondence and debate with all of these senior figures. Bishop was adopted into Modernism by a different route, through her close friendship with Marianne Moore. Plath—the last of these poets to be born, and the first to die—studied with Lowell at Boston University (and was the subject of elegies by Lowell and Berryman).

The New Criticism was a complex body of thought, but its basic principle was drawn from T. S. Eliot, whose criticism was its central inspiration. In the famous essay "Tradition and the Individual Talent," Eliot set the tone for an era when he proclaimed that poetry must be impersonal. The poet has, Eliot claimed, "not a 'personality' to express, but a particular medium . . . in which impressions and experiences combine in peculiar and unexpected ways." The purpose of this argument was to shift attention away from the figure of "the poet," as a uniquely interesting and gifted individual, and toward poems themselves, which the poet creates only as a catalyst produces chemical reactions, or as a craftsman produces objects. "The emotion in . . . poetry will be a very complex thing," Eliot wrote, but the poet's own emotions are not "in any way remarkable . . . emotions which he has never experienced will serve his turn as well as those familiar to him." In short, poetry "is not the expression of personality, but an escape from personality."

By the 1950s, leading academic critics had turned Eliot's elusive insight into a doctrine. In *The Well Wrought Urn*, Cleanth Brooks declared that "the poet is a maker, not a communicator"; it followed that a poem was not, as Wordsworth taught, "a man speaking to men," but "a structure of meanings, evaluations, and interpretations," "a pattern of resolved stresses." Similarly, W. K. Wimsatt wrote in *The Verbal Icon* that "Judging a poem is like judging a pudding or a machine. One demands that it work." It makes no more sense to ask what a poet means by his lines than what a chef means by his ingredients: "we have no excuse for inquiring what part [of a poem] is intended or meant." Tate, Lowell recalled, pronounced that "a good poem . . . was simply a piece of craftsmanship, an intelligible or *cognitive* object."

The poets discussed in this book—again, with the partial exception of Plath—began to write in this literary climate, and at first they ardently embraced the principles of their teachers. With varying degrees of skill, they wrote poems that were ambiguous, allusive, symbolic, and impersonal—brilliantly so in the case of Lowell, lifelessly in the case of Berryman. But what unites them as a group is that each eventually rebelled against the New Critical understanding of poetry. In their very different ways, they attempted to break free of the styles and subjects that Modernism had considered suitable.

In Jarrell's dramatic monologues and Schwartz's family epic, Bishop's tense plainspokenness and Berryman's jagged comedy, the values of Modernism are tested, resisted, and transcended. As Schwartz wrote in 1954, "What the [old] literary methods . . . exclude from all but the privacy of the journal or the letter is brought to the surface and exposed to direct examination by the new method." A few years later, Berryman denigrated Eliot's "amusing theory of the impersonality of the artist," and championed instead Whitman's vision of the "poet not as *maker* but as spiritual historian." Eliot had declared that "the more perfect the artist, the more completely separate in him will be the man who suffers and the mind which creates"; Berryman and Lowell each published poems in which they included their home address.

Yet if it seems ironic to turn to Eliot for the title of a book about his rebellious heirs, the irony is an appropriate one. For while these six poets broke with some of his major precepts, in the end all of them would have agreed with Eliot's definition of a poem as "a verbal equivalent for states of mind and feeling." A verbal equivalent is not a record, transcript, or confession; it means using language in a deliberately artful and artificial way, in order to communicate to the reader not facts about the poet's life, but the inner truth of his or her experience. The peculiar strength of these poets came from the way they treated new, intimate subjects with the discipline, seriousness, and technical sophistication they had learned from the Modernists. As Lowell insisted, "The kind of poet I am was largely determined by the fact that I grew up in the heyday of the New Criticism."

In the chapters that follow, then, I am especially interested in the techniques that these poets used to make such verbal equivalents, or what Eliot famously called "objective correlatives." When their attempts to transform experience into art failed, as of course they sometimes did, I look for the other motives that interfered with the aesthetic one. Above all, I hope that this book will help readers return to the work of these six poets with renewed pleasure and appreciation. At a time when American poetry often seems split into two streams—one serious but abstract and theoretical, the other populist but banal and unchallenging—the example of these poets, who put their whole humanity into their art, is more valuable than ever.

THE
WOUNDED
SURGEON

ROBERT LOWELL

My heart, beat faster, faster

hat does it mean for a poet to tell the truth about
himself? For American poets of the last half century, the answer has been found above all in a
single book: Robert Lowell's *Life Studies*, published in 1959.
Before *Life Studies*, the standard account has it, poets of
Lowell's generation were strapped in a corset of critical orthodoxy; after its revelations of mental illness and family trauma,
they could breathe freely. Confessional poetry, as it came to be
known, learned from Lowell that Modernist allusions and ambiguities are less important than simple, searing honesty. For many

poets, indeed, Lowell's example was too potent, and led to the intoxication of narcissism; much of the worst American poetry of the 1960s and 1970s, as well as much of the best, can be traced back to his example.

To appreciate Lowell's real poetic stature, however, it is necessary to challenge this view of *Life Studies* and its effects. In fact, when Lowell is read alongside his most gifted peers, it becomes clear that he was hardly the first poet to bridle at the severe Modernist ideal of impersonality. Delmore Schwartz's *Genesis*, published in 1943, and John Berryman's "Sonnets to Chris," written in 1947 (though not published for another two decades), both pioneered a new level of autobiographical exposure. Nor did *Life Studies* offer the only way to treat the most highly charged and painful subjects in verse: the mythmaking of Sylvia Plath and the reticent observation of Elizabeth Bishop both showed that candor is not the only form of poetic honesty.

Most important, however, the word "confession" obscures much more than it reveals about Lowell's own work. Before he wrote *Life Studies*, Lowell was already a major poet of a very different kind, not personal and memoiristic but allegorical and cosmological; after *Life Studies*, much of his best writing engaged with large historical and political questions. And in his late poems, Lowell demonstrated the perils of self-exposure, just as he had earlier proved its potential. What unites all of Lowell's work, and makes him the best American poet born in the twentieth century, is something deeper than autobiography. It is the artistic personality that is revealed in his rhythms and his metaphors, his language and his thought. Even when he seems most directly confessional, it is Lowell's artistry—which is also to say, his artificiality—that makes him a great poet.

That Lowell set out to be a great poet, no one could ever doubt. Edmund Wilson wrote that, in the second half of the twentieth century, only Lowell and W. H. Auden had forged poetic careers "on the old nineteenth-century scale"; for Lowell, even when he was first starting out, being a poet meant earning a place in what he called "the line from King David to Hart Crane." The dimensions of his ambition were already evident when, as a twenty-year-old student, he literally staked a claim to the leading American poet-critic of his day, Allen Tate. Mistaking a brush-off for a serious invitation, Lowell pitched a tent on the lawn of Tate's Tennessee home and lived in it for three months.

It was a characteristic act for a young man already known for his heedlessness: all his life Lowell was called by his teenage nickname, Cal, after the debauched Roman emperor Caligula. He had come to Tennessee in flight from academic and romantic chaos in his native Boston, where a hurried engagement to a woman his parents disliked led to a fistfight with his father—an episode he wrote about again and again. It was in the aftermath of this crisis that Lowell quit Harvard, where his Boston Brahmin family had sent its sons for generations, and went South to study with Tate and his fellow New Critic John Crowe Ransom. It was a practical decision, but also a symbolic one: casting off his family's expectations, Lowell declared his determination to become a poet.

Given this background, it is not hard to believe his recollection of himself at the time as being "full of Miltonic, vaguely piratical ambitions." The adjectives are typically Lowellian in their provocative disjunction—nothing is more characteristic of his work than his largesse with adjectives, often dispensed three at a time. But they are also typically keen and revealing. For the "piratical"—a heedless energy, a doubtfully heroic violence—is the most commanding element in Lowell's poetry, from beginning to end. It is this rhythmic and linguistic energy, more than even the most personal subject matter, that makes his poems immediately recognizable. And in his early work, a "Miltonic" style—baroque, allusive, relentless—seems the fitting vehicle for that energy. When he wrote, in a late sonnet, about the life-changing quarrel with his father, he remembered "saying the start of *Lycidas* to myself / fevering my mind and cooling my hot nerves": poetry, especially Milton, was for the young Lowell a matter of chaotic power under rigid control.

In addition to Milton, the style of Lowell's early poetry was most influenced by Tate. "When I began to publish," he later recalled, "I wrote literally under the rooftree of Allen Tate. When I imitated him, I believed I was imitating the muse of poetry." And for the young Lowell, as for many of his peers, that muse spoke in a highly self-conscious, elaborately artificial voice: "poetry must be burly, must be courteous, must be tinkered with and recast until one's eyes pop out of one's head." In that formulation, from a 1959 memoir of Tate, Lowell speaks with the irony of a disciple who has already defected to a new, more natural-sounding style. But his earliest verse is burly and artificial without apology; Tate himself praised its "intellectual style compounded of brilliant puns and shifts of tone." And by the time of his first mature book—*Lord Weary's Castle*, published in 1946—he had made these qualities the foundation of a magnificent poetry. The only way to understand the sophistication of Lowell's seemingly transparent middle style, including *Life Studies*, is to see how it emerged from the baroque ruthlessness of *Lord Weary's Castle*.

But in 1944, two years before that official debut—which won the Pulitzer Prize and established Lowell as the leading poet of his generation—came a smaller, privately printed collection, *Land of Unlikeness*. Because he never republished this volume, choosing instead to cannibalize several of its poems for *Lord Weary's Castle*, it is best read as a rough draft for its triumphant successor. In fact, the sureness of Lowell's revisions—he discarded all the weakest and most confused poems in the book—makes clear that he himself understood the problems with his early work.

The chief problem is Lowell's use of Catholicism, to which he had converted in 1941, as a source of myth and moral authority. Written at the height of the Second World War, many poems in *Land of Unlikeness* do not so much observe or sympathize with the universal catastrophe as pass lofty judgment on it. Lowell uses the timeless myths of Christianity to enforce an ironic contempt for the travails of the present. But his poems more often read like parodies of the religious verse of the Renaissance, right down to its tropes and forms, than genuine successors; and his judgmental Catholicism seems like a corresponding parody, a trying on of an essentially foreign worldview.

Indeed, the most powerful poems in *Land of Unlikeness* have a grotesque violence whose source is far from Christian humility or pity. In "Christ for Sale," the traditional notion that mankind is redeemed in Christ's blood is given a repulsive turn: the sacred blood is compared to alcohol, gall, and bilge, and Lowell invokes the "drippings of the Lamb" and "the Savior's mangled mouth." Instead of making fallen mankind an object of horror, so as to glorify the redemptive power of Christ, the poem actually makes the sacrament itself revolting. It is hard to explain this on theological grounds; it seems more symptomatic than deliberate, as though Lowell's "piratical" energy, his aggressive disgust, has bled into every subject he touches.

In transforming *Land of Unlikeness* into *Lord Weary's Castle*, however, Lowell did not set about purifying and elevating his religious poetry, trying to make himself into a true devotional poet. Instead he took the opposite course, omitting "Christ for Sale" and most of his other overtly Catholic poems. What remained was the anger, the denunciatory impulse, which had sought expression within the frail machinery of Christian allegory. In *Lord Weary's Castle*, this violence becomes both a personal aesthetic—the rhythmic and musical signature that makes Lowell already an unmistakable voice—and a cosmic principle.

IN 1957, WHILE gestating the poems that would become *Life Studies*, Lowell wrote a prose memoir of his childhood titled "Antebellum Boston." It is a portrait of an unhappy household, where his own infantile anger can find no outlet other than sheer movement: "I used to lie on my back, hold my knees, and vibrate. '*Stop rocking*,' my nurse or Mother would say. I remember this trembling fury, but I do not know its reason." In *Lord Weary's Castle*, Lowell raises this vibration to the level of art:

> *Here the jack-hammer jabs into the ocean;*
> *My heart, you race and stagger and demand*
> *More blood-gangs for your nigger-brass percussions,*
> *Till I, the stunned machine of your devotion,*
> *Clanging upon this cymbal of a hand,*
> *Am rattled screw and footloose.*

In these opening lines of "Colloquy in Black Rock," Lowell shows how far he has transcended his early satire. He is no longer standing outside a violent spectacle and condemning it. The violence now comes from within, from a heart whose erratic fury is a source of both fear and exultation: "My heart, beat faster, faster" is the poem's refrain. And the poem is itself a "stunned machine," full of gagging consonants and syncopated vowels: the flat "a" is drummed over and over, in "jack," "hammer," "jabs," "stagger," "demand," "brass." (It even seems likely that Lowell used the word "nigger," indifferent to its offensiveness, simply for the sake of another hard double "g.") It is an aural portrait of a man coming unhinged, and shows that a poet is revealed less in his subject matter, however personal, than in his rhythms—just as a painter is most truly revealed in his brushstroke. That is why "Colloquy in Black Rock," though it does not give a diaristic account of mental illness like some of the *Life Studies* poems, is an equally effective expression of Lowell's inner tumult.

It is only after evoking a mind and a world in chaos that the poem turns to Christianity for a possible cure. Lowell imagines Christ as "the kingfisher," and proposes him as an escape from the encroaching "mud":

> *the mud*
> *Flies from his hunching wings and beak—my heart,*
> *The blue kingfisher dives on you in fire.*

These lines seem to be confidently proposing a belief in Christian redemption. But the whole atmosphere of the poem works against this proposition; instead, Lowell's kingfisher seems just another bodying forth of his turbulence. For while it is ostensibly an image of salvation, it also sounds very much like an attack, as though the "heart" were being dive-bombed by Christ. The kingfisher is less the cure for Lowell's percussive agony than its culmination.

The strength of *Lord Weary's Castle* is that it subverts its own religious symbols in this way. The kingfisher, like the mud and the jack-hammer, is something at once less commanding and more credible than a religious icon: it is what T. S. Eliot called an "objective correlative," an image that evokes a definite emotion. In poem after poem, Lowell commandeers the names and properties of Christian tradition in order to put them at the service of his own, essentially heretical art.

"In Memory of Arthur Winslow" offers examples of both the success and the failure of this method. This four-part elegy for Lowell's maternal grandfather is the most substantial poem carried over, with revisions, from *Land of Unlikeness*. In the first section, Lowell describes his grandfather wasting away in the hospital, in a highly self-conscious allegory: cancer becomes "wrestling with the crab," death is "longshoreman Charon." In this context, when Jesus himself appears, he seems just one more name from ancient mythology:

> the ghost
> *Of risen Jesus walks the waves to run*
> *Arthur upon a trumpeting black swan*
> *Beyond Charles River to the Acheron. . . .*

There is a certain daring involved in putting the Charles River, the Acheron, and Jesus together in one image; it is the sort of thing that, in Dante, succeeds in making each element both contemporary and supernatural. Here, however, it only seems willful, a wrenching of literary symbols out of their proper contexts.

In the fourth part of the poem, however, Lowell overcomes the artificiality of his Christian symbolism, not by moderating it, but by jolting it into motion with his savage energy. Like the "blue kingfisher," the Virgin Mary is turned into a grotesque redeemer, whose grace is indistinguishable from assault:

> *O Mother, I implore*
> *Your scorched, blue thunderbreasts of love to pour*
> *Buckets of blessings on my burning head*
> *Until I rise like Lazarus from the dead:*
> Lavabis nos et super nivem dealbabor.

The audacity of "thunderbreasts" is still greater than that of Jesus walking on the Charles River; but here the element of absurdity is dissolved in the power and conviction of the verse. What comes from Mary's "scorched" breasts seems not milk but a lightning bolt, and it is hard to imagine that such blessings could quench the poet's "burning" head; they would be more likely to incinerate him. The logic of Lowell's images contradicts his overt religious message; he cannot imagine salvation except in terms of exacerbation to the point of destruction. This gives a strange pathos to his concluding prayer, a Latin verse from the Book of Psalms that means "Wash us and we will be whiter than snow": in Lowell's poem, to be washed is to be scorched, to be saved is to be punished. The reader is convinced, not by the poet's God, but by the suffering of the poet who could imagine such a God.

That is why Lowell's grandest and most convincing expression of religious imagination comes in one of his least orthodox poems, "The Quaker Graveyard in Nantucket." In only one of the poem's seven sections does Lowell return to his conventional Marian imagery, when he invokes the peaceful shrine of "Our Lady of Walsingham." But this is the poem's only glimpse of land, where "hedgerows file / Slowly along the munching English lane." Otherwise "Quaker Graveyard," dedicated to Lowell's cousin "Warren Winslow, dead at sea," is obsessively devoted to the Atlantic Ocean, which is transformed by magnificent rhetoric into a pagan god: "the earth-shaker, green, unwearied, chaste / In his steel scales." And the poem's first section describes a human sacrifice to that god, a drowned sailor who "grappled at the net / With the coiled, hurdling muscles of his thighs."

This dead man has none of the peace of death: he seems like someone still paralyzed by terror, wrestling with an unseen enemy. The ocean has been transformed into a supernatural force of mindless violence, which only desires man's destruction. Inevitably, this idea is reminiscent of *Moby-Dick*, and Lowell embraces the echoes, invoking "the Pequod's sea wings" and "the whited monster." But for Lowell, as for Melville, this evil god seems to have no place in the Christian cosmology. At one daring moment, Lowell even seems to cast doubt on "God himself":

> *In the sperm-whale's slick*
> *I see the Quakers drown and hear their cry:*
> *"If God himself had not been on our side,*
> *If God himself had not been on our side,*
> *When the Atlantic rose against us, why,*
> *Then it had swallowed us up quick."*

The Quakers are affirming the protective power of God, but in fact they are about to drown. The only conclusion the poet allows us to draw is that God was not "on their side," since He did allow the ocean to swallow them. To set sail, in this vision, is only to seek one's death: death is "the end of the whaleroad and the whale," where all sailors end up.

And not just sailors. For just as Lowell, in "Colloquy in Black Rock," imagined the whole world consumed by mud, so "Quaker Graveyard" fuses Ahab's white whale and the biblical sea monster Leviathan into a figure of universal apocalypse. He imagines the end times, "When the whale's viscera go and the roll / Of its corruption overruns this world." In Lowell's version of Revelations, the "ash-pit of Jehoshaphat"—where, according to the Book of Joel, the Judgment Day will take place—becomes a nightmare out of *Moby-Dick*, where resurrected sailors butcher the white whale:

> *The fat flukes arch and whack about its ears,*
> *The death-lance churns into the sanctuary, tears*
> *The gun-blue swingle, heaving like a flail,*
> *And hacks the coiling life out: it works and drags*
> *And rips the sperm-whale's midriff into rags,*
> *Gobbets of blubber spill to wind and weather. . . .*

Here the grotesque rhetoric that seemed out of place in "Christ for Sale" has found its proper home. And it is because "Quaker Graveyard" is essentially pagan, rather than Christian, that Lowell's style is able to flourish. Violence is what the poet knows best, and in "Quaker Graveyard" he has remade the universe in the image of his violence.

No wonder that, in the poem's last lines, Lowell rewrites the story of Creation so that man is formed, not from earth, but from "sea's slime"; the change encapsulates the way Lowell has revised the essential spirit of his faith, making Catholicism the vehicle for a bloodthirsty Melvillean nihilism. It is in this sense that the poem's famously ambiguous last line can be understood: "The Lord survives the rainbow of His will." In Genesis, God created the rainbow as a pledge to mankind not to repeat the Flood. But at the conclusion of this poem, which began with a drowning, Lowell suggests that God's power to annihilate "survives" his voluntary renunciation. God withholds his destructive power only at his "will"—and one day He might change his mind. Lowell himself looks forward to that day with appalled fascination.

Along with his religious sensibility, Lowell's understanding of the American past grows darker and more complex in *Lord Weary's Castle*. Lowell had the ambiguous good luck to be born into one of America's oldest and most accomplished families— his relatives included the poets James Russell Lowell and Amy Lowell, as well as the astronomer Percival Lowell and A. Lawrence Lowell, a president of Harvard. In *Land of Unlikeness*, he had used this legacy in a predictable rhetoric of American decline, contrasting New England's illustrious past with its degraded present. "Salem" asks forlornly, "Where was it that New England bred the men / Who quartered the Leviathan's fat flanks / And fought the British lion to his knees?"

But while "Salem" is carried over into *Lord Weary's Castle*, other new poems make a more provocative use of American history. Lowell ceases to enlist his forebears as spokesmen for a lost virtue. Instead, he begins to see them as "sensuous and passionate" like Milton; as he wrote of Colonial Boston in a late essay, "Wasn't the Jamaican rum drunk there spiced with gunpowder to burn the tongue?" Certainly he finds in the Puritan religious sensibility a faith as sensational as his own in "Quaker Graveyard"—a faith not reassuringly conventional, but frightening and strange. "After the Surprising Conversions" is heavily indebted to Jonathan Edwards's famous account of a religious revival in Northampton, Massachusetts, in the early eighteenth century. Edwards was

Colonial America's leading theologian and a hellfire preacher of terrifying force, and Lowell's poem focuses on the psychic casualties of his Calvinism. One of Edwards's parishioners cuts his throat in despair, and soon there is an epidemic of suicidal terror:

> *The multitude, once unconcerned with doubt,*
> *Once neither callous, curious nor devout,*
> *Jumped at broad noon, as though some peddler groaned*
> *At it in its familiar twang: "My friend,*
> *Cut your own throat. Cut your own throat. Now! Now!"*

There is a clear line of descent from Edwards's God, who "holds you to the pit of hell / Much as one holds a spider," to Lowell's Manichean deity in "Quaker Graveyard." Indeed, the last word in *Lord Weary's Castle* belongs to "Where the Rainbow Ends," a vision of the Last Judgment just like those Edwards and his fellow preachers employed to terrorize the faithful: "I saw my city in the Scales, the pans / Of judgment rising and descending." Ordinarily, the title phrase means a land of enchantment, where the pot of gold is found; but in Lowell's ironic twist, it refers (as at the end of "Quaker Graveyard") to the biblical rainbow. When that pledge of God's mercy "ends," his wrath will be unleashed and the world will be destroyed. In the face of this prospect, Lowell dutifully exhorts himself to "Stand and live." But all his poetic passion goes into the vision of destruction, when the corruption at the heart of things will be consummated and purged. In a book saturated with Christian symbols, Lowell's verse always seems most authentic when he is imagining such annihilation. What gives *Lord Weary's Castle* poetic life is not its language of borrowed authority, but the intensely personal vibration, the angry hum, that is Lowell's rhythmic and emotional signature: "this skipping heart that shakes my house."

LORD WEARY'S CASTLE brought to perfection the violent, denunciatory strain of Lowell's early poetry. But the book also contains hints of several other possibilities for his verse, poems in which the prophetic rhetoric of "Quaker Graveyard" and "Where the Rainbow Ends" gives way to reminiscence and narrative. Amid the surrounding turbulence, a poem like "Buttercups" seems almost startling in its quietness and novelistic detail: Lowell conjures up his Boston childhood, with "our brassy sailor coats" and "the huge cobwebbed print of Waterloo." But the driving rhythms and formal symbolism of his style are ill suited to these subjects, and in several poems he begins with a humble anecdote only to swerve awkwardly into allegory. In "Mary Winslow," a companion elegy to "In Memory of Arthur Winslow," he begins with concrete details of his grandmother's illness, when "Her Irish maids could never spoon out mush / Or orange-juice enough"; but death seems to Lowell to demand a higher style, and soon enough Charon is back on the scene.

The limits of Lowell's style in dealing directly with personal experience are best seen in "Rebellion," his first attempt to write a poem about the traumatic fistfight with his father. Cast as an address to his father, the poem begins with Lowell describing the immediate aftermath of his Oedipal attack: "you hove backward, rammed / Into your heirlooms." But while there is no doubt that the poet is the one who dealt the blow, "Rebellion" begins in the passive mood: "There was rebellion," Lowell declares, as if it were something that happened to the poet and his father equally. And after the incident is described, Lowell immediately retreats into the symbolism of "Quaker Graveyard," invoking "Behemoth and Leviathan." The reader's inevitable questions—what were the reasons for this quarrel? what were its effects on father and son?—are left unanswered. This kind of intimate experience, "Rebellion" shows, cannot be dealt with in the visionary allegory Lowell had perfected in *Lord Weary's Castle*. Here, if nowhere else in the book, mythology seems evasive, because it is so closely juxtaposed with autobiography. And with the instinctive courage of a great poet, Lowell recognized that just this failure pointed his way forward. By the time of *Life Studies*, a decade later, he had invented a style in which the most private experience could be written about convincingly.

First, however, Lowell would follow a different thread out of *Lord Weary's Castle*. Two of the longer poems in the book are dramatic monologues, whose clumsy narrative exposition is far less impressive than their vague evocation of sexual dread. "The Death of the Sheriff" is spoken by a man who seems to be involved in an incestuous affair with his sister, while "Between the Porch and the Altar" concerns a young man trapped by guilty lust and Oedipal terror. The gruesome sexuality of these poems ("When we try to kiss, / Our eyes are slits and cringing, and we hiss") is obscure but effective, and suggests a new, more personal motive for Lowell's violence.

That baffled urgency became the keynote of Lowell's next book. *The Mills of the Kavanaughs*, published in 1951, shows that Lowell has followed some of his own best qualities into a dead end; the music and rhetoric of *Lord Weary's Castle* have become clotted and inert. This style can still produce passages of splendid strangeness, but it is highly unsuited to the task of telling stories, which requires more suppleness and objectivity. Yet this is just what Lowell asks it to do: the book contains seven dramatic monologues, including the very long title poem, all of them concerned in various ways with the intersection of religion and madness. The themes are a natural development from *Lord Weary's Castle*, which seems at times on the verge of its own kind of religious mania. But the way they are presented in *The Mills of the Kavanaughs*, embodied in extremely peculiar characters and situations, seems less like an expression than a concealment.

At over six hundred lines, "The Mills of the Kavanaughs" is by far the longest single poem Lowell ever wrote, yet its action can be summarized in a sentence: Anne Kavanaugh, a young widow in Maine, remembers the decline of her husband Harry into insanity and death. What fills the poem, and gives it its meandering, dreamlike shape, are the odd turns and associations of Anne's memory: her childhood, the history of the Kavanaugh family, and Harry's jealous rage are braided with symbolic visions of the goddess Persephone. All of these subjects, with their wildly different registers—ranging from savage sexual drama to intellectual reverie—are not so much united as yoked together in Lowell's couplets and quatrains.

The poem is full of verbal magic, and offers a wider range of natural description than Lowell had attempted before: "the perching frogs / Chirred to the greener sizzle of a rain"; "torn / Into a thousand globules by that horn / Or whorl of river." But there is only one successfully dramatic moment, when Anne talks in her sleep to an imaginary lover, provoking Harry to attack her. Anne's address to her dream-lover shows both the suggestive strangeness of Lowell's verse, and its utter incredibility as speech:

> *"You have gored me black and blue.*
> *I am all prickle-tickle like the stars;*

I am a sleepy-foot, a dogfish skin
Rubbed backwards, wrongways; you have made my hide
Split snakey, Bad one—one!"

It comes as no surprise to learn that this episode was based on a similar confrontation between Lowell and his then-wife Jean Stafford; as in "Rebellion," the pressure of personal experience makes the poem's mythological scheme seem labored and abstract by comparison.

If the shorter dramatic monologues in the book lack the personal charge of "The Mills of the Kavanaughs," they also avoid its longueurs. "Falling Asleep over the Aeneid" and "Mother Marie Therese" compensate for their far-fetched, implausible premises with sheer musical virtuosity. "Falling Asleep" follows the stream of consciousness of an aged American scholar as he drifts off and dreams himself into the exotic world of Virgil:

The elephants of Carthage hold those snows,
Turms of Numidian horse unsling their bows,
The flaming turkey-feathered arrows swarm
Beyond the Alps.

Only at the end of the poem does the reverie dissolve, as he awakens to his staid Concord parlor. Like the nun who speaks in "Mother Marie Therese," he is less a character than an occasion for brilliant rhetorical performance, the rococo style polished to a dazzle.

But as the word "rococo" suggests, *The Mills of the Kavanaughs* represented the decadence of Lowell's early style. He had developed his verbal and rhythmic strength so far that he became poetically musclebound. If he was to explore other ranges of tone and subject, his very language would have to be remade. And his willingness to undertake that task, to break down one fully developed style and create another, is one measure of Lowell's greatness as an artist. If there is a morality in art, it lies here, in the artist's commitment to expressing what he finds most necessary, even when it requires the destruction of his own cherished means of expression.

After the publication of *The Mills of the Kavanaughs*, Lowell entered a long silence that in retrospect seems a kind of hibernation, a gathering of resources. As he later remembered, he produced only "five messy poems in five years," and his correspondence in the early and mid-1950s shows his frustration: "It's hell finding a new style or rather finding that your old style won't say any of the things that you want to."

What he wanted to be able to say is suggested by where he went looking. In 1952, Lowell wrote to William Carlos Williams "I wish rather in vain that I could absorb something of your way of writing into mine." Williams, whose deliberately informal, anti-intellectual, and precisely observed poems stood at the opposite pole from Tate's, seemed like an antidote to the maladies of the New Critical style. Indeed, the sudden rise of Williams's reputation around this time was owed largely to the desire of younger poets for a more natural and demotic version of Modernism. Around the time Lowell was turning into a Williams disciple, Randall Jarrell praised Williams in an important essay for being "spontaneous, open, impulsive, emotional, observant"— just the qualities that would distinguish *Life Studies* from *Lord Weary's Castle*.

Lowell was confirmed in his turn toward informality by the experience of a reading tour on the West Coast, where the Beat poets had developed their populist performance style. Next to the

Beats, Lowell later recalled, his own poems "seemed distant, symbol-ridden, and willfully difficult . . . like prehistoric monsters dragged down into the bog and death by their ponderous armor." Later generations of readers have taken this ironic comment all too seriously; but while it seems to flatter the formlessness of much confessional poetry, it is far from doing justice to what Lowell had actually accomplished in *Lord Weary's Castle*. What sets Lowell apart from the other poets of his generation is precisely the fact that his own early New Critical poems, however difficult and ambiguous they may be, are not inert; if they are monsters, they are monstrously alive. What Lowell's self-criticism really signifies is not the weakness of his early style, but the fact that he had reached the end of that style's usefulness.

To escape it, he turned from poetry to prose, and from myth to autobiography. In several prose memoirs—one published in *Life Studies*, two others only posthumously in his *Collected Prose*—Lowell practiced quieter strategies for capturing "human richness in simple descriptive language." His prose is anything but simple—it is fertile in metaphor and adjective, and displays great psychological and sociological sophistication. But prose gave Lowell a humility before the actual, a way of seeing and remembering faithfully, that his early verse, so willfully magnificent, could not:

And Uncle Devereux stood behind me. His face was putty. His blue coat and white-flannel trousers grew straighter and straighter, as though he were in a clothes press. His trousers were like solid cream from the top of the bottle. His coat was like a blue jay's tail feather. He was animated, hieratic. His glasses were like Harold Lloyd's glasses. He was dying of the incurable Hodgkin's disease.

. . .

IN 1959, LOWELL published his first book since *The Mills of the Kavanaughs* eight years earlier: *Life Studies*. The book was named after the sequence of poems that makes up its last section, a sequence that begins with "My Last Afternoon with Uncle Devereux Winslow":

> *His face was putty.*
> *His blue coat and white trousers*
> *grew sharper and straighter.*
> *His coat was a blue jay's tail,*
> *his trousers were solid cream from the top of the bottle.*
> *He was animated, hierarchical,*
> *like a gingersnap man in a clothes-press.*
> *He was dying of the incurable Hodgkin's disease. . . .*

In turning his prose into verse, Lowell changed similes to metaphors and rearranged some of the details. More important, however, is the way verse changes the pacing and weight of the passage: one detail in each line, the shape of the poem hewing closely to the contours of its subject. This is an entirely different approach to writing poetry from the domineering music of his early work. Yet, crucially, the discipline of that music still informs Lowell's free verse: his lines are still sonically dense, full of rich vowels, demanding to be heard rather than just read. What makes *Life Studies* one of Lowell's greatest achievements, and sets it apart from the thousands of confessional poems it inspired, is the way that even the most personal subjects are thoroughly transformed by Lowell's art. As the title suggests, these poems do not aspire to the artless sincerity of the photograph, but the interpretive shaping of the portrait.

Lowell's innovation is clearest in the "Life Studies" sequence, which forms the heart of the book; but there are hints of a changed style from the very beginning. "Beyond the Alps," the first poem in the collection, combines something of his early magniloquence with a much more natural diction and word order. The poem manages first-person narration more gracefully than "The Mills of the Kavanaughs" ever could, presenting a clear situation: the poet is on a train from Rome to Paris, reading the newspaper, observing the stewards and the landscape. Yet out of this ordinary beginning Lowell's language accelerates into harshness, perfectly reflecting the pace of his anxious thought:

> Pilgrims still kissed Saint Peter's brazen sandal.
> The Duce's lynched, bare, booted skull still spoke.
> God herded his people to the coup de grâce—
> the costumed Switzers sloped their pikes to push,
> O Pius, through the monstrous human crush. . . .

As this address to the pope suggests, Lowell is once again concerned with Catholicism; but this time his approach is neither prophetic nor clinical. Rather, it becomes clear that the journey from Catholic Rome to secular Paris is also a final symbolic renunciation of Lowell's faith: "Much against my will / I left the City of God where it belongs." Still more important, for the reader, is the poetic renunciation that this entails. The idiosyncratic Catholicism of Lord Weary's Castle was a myth Lowell created in his own image, an objective correlative of his temperament and experience. Now that he can no longer project that experience outward, Lowell has no choice but to turn inward, to follow his myths back to their sources.

Another kind of rupture is reflected in the book's second section, which turns unexpectedly from verse to prose. "91 Revere Street" is a long extract from the memoirs Lowell began writing in the mid-1950s. The title is the address of his childhood home in Boston, and the piece is an oblique inquest into the sources of his adult personality. But while there is no doubt of the misery at the center of Lowell's childhood, he does not write as an accuser. The pace is leisurely, the language rich and observant:

> He looked like a human ash-heap. Cigar ashes buried the heraldic hedgehog on the ash tray beside him; cigar ashes spilled over and tarnished the golden stork embroidered on the table-cover; cigar ashes littered his own shiny blue-black uniform.

The precision of detail, remembered from thirty years earlier, is evidence of a deep and deliberate trawl through memory, and the charged anecdotes Lowell presents suggest the controlled remembering of psychoanalysis. Certainly the family romance that emerges is classically Oedipal. Even as a boy, Lowell writes, he recognized his mother's excessive interest in him as a reflection on his father, whom she despised. Robert Lowell Senior was a retired navy officer who failed in civilian life: "Without drama, his earnings more or less decreased from year to year." Still more important, he was unable to satisfy his willful wife: "She had been married nine or ten years and still suspected that her husband was savorless, unmasterful, merely considerate." As a result, she half-consciously plays the son against his father: "She said, 'Oh Bobby, it's such a comfort to have a man in the house.' 'I am not a man,' I said, 'I am a boy.'"

It is this constellation of manipulative mother, weak father and guilty child that makes Lowell the kind of boy he is: "churlish, disloyal . . . thick-witted, narcissistic, thuggish." Yet if we look beneath this harsh judgment, we can immediately recognize in the Bobby of "91 Revere Street" the poet Lowell later became. His rebellious anger seems to resonate in the charging verse of *Lord Weary's Castle*: just as the child "used to look forward to the nights when my bedroom walls would once again vibrate, when I would awake with rapture to the rhythm of my parents arguing," so the adult would make his own verse vibrate with fury.

What this means is that "91 Revere Street," in some important sense, unwrites Lowell's early poetry. Instead of translating personal experience and emotion into the objective correlative of symbol, as Modernism demanded, he now excavates the autobiographical roots of his symbols, giving them a local habitation and a name. It would be a mistake to call Lowell's new approach more honest; after all, telling the truth, especially if it is disagreeable, was a central commandment of Modernism. (It was W. B. Yeats who declared, some forty-five years before *Life Studies*, that "there's more enterprise / in walking naked.") What Lowell achieved was, rather, a revolution in our sense of what poetic truthfulness sounds like. After *Life Studies*, it seemed that a poet who exposed less than Lowell wanted to risk less; and it is the risk, not the exposure, that makes a poem live.

After the clearance work of "91 Revere Street," Lowell could return to verse with a new vulnerability of both form and subject. The first three poems in the "Life Studies" sequence are devoted to Lowell's early childhood, and focus on his grandfather, whose home offered a refuge from his own parents. This is the same Arthur Winslow who Lowell mourned in *Lord Weary's Castle*, but the distance from that formal, allegorical elegy to this loving reminiscence is immense:

> *it seemed spontaneous and proper*
> *for Mr. MacDonald, the farmer,*
> *Karl, the chauffeur, and even my Grandmother*
> *to say: "your Father." They meant my Grandfather.*

> *He was my Father. I was his son.*

"Dunbarton," along with "My Last Afternoon with Uncle Devereux Winslow" and "Grandparents," demonstrates Lowell's new style but doesn't yet make the most of it. The verse is free, the diction is prosaic and natural; the first word of each line is no longer capitalized, helping to emphasize the sentence over the line. Only on closer examination does Lowell's patterning reveal itself: in the first stanza of "My Last Afternoon," lines end with "water," "Father's," "dinner," "summer" and "poplars," creating an undercurrent of half-rhymes. The real activity in the language, however, comes from the adjectives, as Lowell creates a friction among mismatched pairs and triplets: "Diamond-pointed, athirst and Norman"; "ingenu and porcine"; "neurasthenic, scarlet and wild"; "throw-away and shaggy." Instead of the concentrated attack of his early verse, he offers local eruptions of energy.

These three poems offer a great deal of detail about Lowell's childhood, and "Grandparents" in particular is a moving evocation of childish love. But they are lifted above private reminiscence, they gain a dramatic background and context, only if read alongside the prose memoir: the sweetness of life "at my Grand-father's farm" is mainly significant as a contrast to the bitterness of life at 91 Revere Street. And even with this supplement, the poems threaten to remain merely private and sentimental; they run the risk of committing the narcissistic fallacy of confessional poetry, the illusion that what is interesting to the poet will be equally interesting to the reader.

To counter this danger, Lowell seems to depend, consciously or otherwise, on the reader's curiosity about the illustrious family name and the gilded settings ("the farm, entitled *Char-de-sa* / in the Social Register"). Elizabeth Bishop envied, and perhaps implicitly criticized, this strategy in a letter to Lowell: "I feel I could write in as much detail about my uncle Artie, say—but what would be the significance? Nothing at all. . . . Whereas all you have to do is put down the names! And . . . it seems signifi-cant, illustrative, American etc." Lowell doesn't just put down the names, but he is aware that the names he puts down have an unusual potency.

The next four poems in the "Life Studies" sequence—"Com-mander Lowell," "Terminal Days at Beverly Farms," "Father's Bedroom," and "For Sale"—turn from grandfather to father, and from affection to mockery. The satire on Lowell's father is less direct than in the prose memoir, but no less cutting; Lowell's restrained, objective description forces the reader to draw his own devastating conclusions. In "Father's Bedroom," for instance, Lowell describes a "warped," "punished" old book of his father's:

In the flyleaf:
"Robbie from Mother."
Years later in the same hand:

*"This book has had hard usage
on the Yangtze River, China.
It was left under an open
porthole in a storm."*

It is left to the reader to wonder what kind of man could return from military adventure in China and submit to such prim maternal discipline, still under the thumb of "the same hand." Similarly, Lowell remarks on his father's inability to play golf or sail, his "piker speculations" on the stock market, and his fatuous pride in his specially ordered black Chevrolet. Even in death, Lowell writes with evident scorn, his father was unable to rise to the eloquence of tragedy: "After a morning of anxious, repetitive smiling, / his last words to Mother were: / 'I feel awful.'"

But if his father's death only seems the last stage of a lifelong futility, the death of his mother comes as a life-altering shock. "Sailing Home from Rapallo" recounts Lowell's voyage accompanying his mother's corpse back from Italy to the family graveyard in New Hampshire. He begins by speaking directly to his mother, describing how he learned of her death, as though the facts had to be blurted out. Only then does the poem seem to gather itself and begin again in a more eloquent vein:

*When I embarked from Italy with my Mother's body,
the whole shoreline of the* Golfo di Genova
was breaking into fiery flower.

. . . .

*Mother travelled first-class in the hold;
her* Risorgimento *black and gold casket
was like Napoleon's at the* Invalides. . . .

Against this heroic image of his mother, lying in state like an emperor in the Italian spring, Lowell sets "our family cemetery in Dunbarton," where it is still a New England winter, "Dour and dark against the blinding snowdrifts." His mother is heading inexorably to the same frozen earth, just as she is leaving life for death, and Italy for America: they are all parts of a journey to the underworld. But it is a measure of Lowell's poetic evolution that this symbolic scheme, which would have been explicit and allegorical in an earlier poem, remains tacit and metaphorical here. Charon makes no appearance in "Sailing Home from Rapallo," as he did in "In Memory of Arthur Winslow." And finally Lowell undermines the grandeur imparted to the journey by his own language, when he insists on telling the ridiculous truth: "In the grandiloquent lettering on Mother's coffin, / *Lowell* had been misspelled *LOVEL*." For a poet so conscious of his family name, this is an especially telling assertion of brute fact against symbol, of the way things are against the way they should be. And this makes it another token of the poetic revolution of *Life Studies*: when "risen Jesus" came to claim Arthur Winslow and carry him to the Acheron, there were no such imperfections to mar the scene.

In the emotional trajectory of the "Life Studies" sequence, the death of the poet's mother marks an abrupt shift. The poem that follows, "During Fever," shows us the child of "Dunbarton" now a parent himself. Looking after his sick daughter begins to move him to a new compassion for his own parents: "'Sorry,' she mumbles like her dim-bulb father, 'sorry.'" For the first time, Lowell expresses regret at the way he and his mother would sit "rehashing Father's character," just as he has been doing in these poems.

But the explosive change comes in the next poem in the

sequence, "Waking in the Blue." The poem's setting seems all the more terrible because of the casual way it is introduced:

> *My heart grows tense*
> *as though a harpoon were sparring for the kill.*
> *(This is the house for the "mentally ill.")*

The rhyme gains tremendously in dramatic power because full rhyme has become scarce in these poems: Lowell literally links his mental illness with a sense of impending doom. "Waking in the Blue" rewrites two of Lowell's early themes—madness and the decline of the American aristocracy—no longer as satire or dramatic monologue, but as memoir. The mental hospital is full of ruling-class WASP madmen, Harvard alumni reduced to brutes: there is Stanley, "more cut off from words than a seal," and Bobbie, "redolent and roly-poly as a sperm whale." Returning to one of the themes of *Land of Unlikeness*, Lowell sees these madmen as emblematic of the decline of a whole class: "(There are no Mayflower / screwballs in the Catholic Church.)" Yet the aside has a double irony: for Lowell himself was once a Catholic, and now he is revealed as another "Mayflower screwball." The poem ends with a terribly pregnant acknowledgment of Lowell's kinship with these other "thoroughbred mental cases": "We are all old-timers, / each of us holds a locked razor."

The razor is locked, of course, to prevent suicide; the matter-of-fact detail shows us just how seriously ill the poet is. In fact, Lowell suffered all his life from severe manic depression, and was hospitalized almost annually for decades. Thanks to his biographers, the details of his manic episodes—when he would talk wildly about Hitler, or start new love affairs, or turn violent and end up in jail—are well known, and form no small part of his legend. "Waking in the Blue" is remarkable for the candor with which the poet reveals himself at one of his most frightening and shameful moments. But even today, when such candor is no longer novel and madness has become a commonplace of confessional poetry (and memoir in general), Lowell's poem keeps its power—and not simply because he was one of the first to break this ground. Its effectiveness is emphatically literary, a matter of deliberate manipulation of tone and language.

The discipline of indirection that Lowell learned from writing his prose memoir, the skill at letting details tell their own story, comes to fruition in "Waking in the Blue." Lowell's observations are almost always ironic and reserved, from the "B.U. sophomore" who falls asleep reading the absurdly titled *The Meaning of Meaning*," to the patient who "swashbuckles about in his birthday suit." At times Lowell's irony is almost jaunty, as when he uses the deliberately banal adjective "hearty" to describe his breakfast. It is left to the reader to understand that, in describing his fellow patients, Lowell is also telling us about his own state, and asking us to supply the pity and terror that he suppresses.

In just the same way, the reader is meant to understand where Lowell is coming home from in "Home After Three Months Away." The domesticity of the scene—the infant daughter who "dabs her cheeks / to start me shaving"—seems fragile only in juxtaposition to the terrors Lowell has left behind. Yet he does not mention the words "mentally ill" in this poem, and his fears for himself are transferred, in an ingenious but immediately legible image, to the tulips in his yard: "Bushed by the late spring snow, / they cannot meet / another year's snowballing enervation." The poem, and the first half of the "Life Studies" sequence, ends on this note of anxious doubt. It is a moving admission of vulnerability from a poet who once seemed able to contemplate the Apocalypse itself with grim satisfaction.

The sequence concludes with a shorter second section, containing four poems that do not fit neatly into the "plot" of the first section. "Memories of West Street and Lepke" turns to Lowell's brief incarceration in a New York City jail, after he refused on religious grounds to serve in World War II. As in "Waking in the Blue," Lowell sketches the other denizens of the institution. But because he is not essentially one of them, not a criminal in the way that he is mentally ill, the tone of this poem is much closer to comedy—starting with the suggestion that, in Lowell's Boston neighborhood, "even the man / scavenging filth in the back alley trash cans" is a " 'young Republican.' " The poem darkens only at the end, when the prospect of going mad is raised by the sight of the notorious gangster Louis Lepke—"Flabby, bald, lobotomized . . . hanging like an oasis in his air / of lost connections. . . ."

But the major poem of this group, and one of the greatest Lowell ever wrote, is "Skunk Hour." Its power comes from the way it subjects the meandering, novelistic style of the earlier "Life Studies" poems to a formal heightening and compression: what we have here is not simply another anecdote, but a symbolic action. Yet it is a symbol in ordinary dress, refusing to call attention to itself, and gaining in power from its modesty and indirection.

"Skunk Hour" proceeds in free, irregularly rhymed six-line stanzas, a form that channels the poem's movement without constraining it. It opens with a leisurely portrait of the residents of a small New England village: the heiress, the summer millionaire, the decorator. Yet all these sketches quietly suggest that something has gone awry. The heiress is a "hermit," and buys up houses only to let them "fall"; the millionaire seems to have gone broke and has auctioned off his boat; the decorator complains "there is no money in his work." It is a portrait of a village in decline, a summer resort where "the season's ill."

Only in the fifth stanza does Lowell shift his attention to himself, as the language takes a more urgent turn. It is "One dark night," an uninsistent but deliberate reminder of the "dark night of the soul" of St. John of the Cross. The poet's car "climbed the hill's skull," invoking Golgotha, the Hill of Skulls where Jesus was crucified. He is there in the ambiguous role of voyeur, watching for "love-cars"; but even the lovemaking couples are tainted by the presence of "the graveyard" nearby. As in "Sailing Home from Rapallo," Lowell subdues the overt symbolism of his early work into hints and allusions, and thus demands a greater alertness from the reader.

Finally, in the last line of the stanza, the poet declares what these hints have already made clear: "My mind's not right." The simple admission gains its power from what is not said: reading "Skunk Hour" after the other poems in the sequence, we know just how badly wrong Lowell's mind can go, and we share his fear that this may be the beginning of another spell of madness. That fear builds with appalling quickness:

> *I hear*
> *my ill-spirit sob in each blood cell,*
> *as if my hand were at its throat. . . .*
> *I myself am hell;*
> *nobody's here—*

It is one of the heights of Lowell's poetry, every word chosen with absolute precision. The "ill-spirit" is forcibly joined to the "blood cell," uniting the spiritual and chemical dimensions of insanity. The simple pronoun "its" in the next line gives a complete sense of the poet's mental vacancy, his separation from his own body— his throat belongs more to his hand than to himself, and the suicidal gesture seems to have nothing to do with him. After all this, "I myself am hell" seems such a natural utterance that one realizes with a shock that it is also an allusion, to some of the most famous lines in English poetry. "Why, this is hell, nor am I out of it," says the Devil in Marlowe's *Doctor Faustus;* "The mind is its own place, and of itself / Can make a heaven of hell, a hell of heaven," says Satan in Milton's *Paradise Lost.* With bold simplicity, Lowell identifies himself with these devils.

After this terrible zero point, it would seem impossible for Lowell to offer any consolation without sounding like a liar. And here Lowell's use of novelistic detail is again vital. Instead of denying that "nobody's here," and claiming to recognize some saving divine or human presence, Lowell allows the negation to echo through the stanza break, and then modifies it: "only skunks, that search / in the moonlight for a bite to eat." No person is here, that is, only "a mother skunk with her column of kittens" rummaging through the trash. Yet this most comical of animals resolves the poem as no more noble creature could:

> *She jabs her wedge-head in a cup*
> *of sour cream, drops her ostrich tail,*
> *and will not scare.*

It is mere brutish persistence, and Lowell does not suggest that it is anything more. But the strong beat of the final line—three stressed syllables in a row—hints at the defiance, the survivor's will, that the skunk embodies and offers up. From the "blue king-fisher" and "trumpeting black swan" of *Lord Weary's Castle* to the garbage-swilling skunk of *Life Studies*: this is how daringly far Lowell's poetry has come.

WHEN ALLEN TATE first read the poems of *Life Studies* in manuscript, he recognized that Lowell had made a profound break with his early style and principles, and he was appalled. "*All* the poems about your family," he wrote Lowell, ". . . are definitely *bad*. I do not think you ought to publish them . . . the poems are composed of unassimilated details, terribly intimate, and coldly noted, which might well have been transferred from the notes from your autobiography without change. . . . Quite bluntly, these details, presented in *causerie* and at random, are of interest only to you."

Tate had guessed correctly—many details in the poems were "transferred" directly from Lowell's prose memoir. But the very features of *Life Studies* that he found distasteful and antipoetic— the private subjects, the prosaic diction—have proved to be of far more interest to readers than the formal symbolism of Lowell's early verse. Today Lowell is certainly best known as the founder of "confessional" poetry, and *Life Studies* is the book on which that reputation rests.

Yet just as Marx was not a Marxist, so Lowell was not a confessional poet. What gives the poems of *Life Studies* their enduring value is not their honesty about Lowell's personal life, but their artistic form; the poet's experiences are not simply revealed but shaped, through rhythm and symbol and tone, into works of art. Lowell could not have written poems like "Waking in the Blue" and "Sailing Home from Rapallo" without the formal mastery he acquired during his rigorous New Critical training. As Lowell wrote as late as 1974, "The kind of poet I am was largely determined by the fact that I grew up in the heyday of the New Criticism." Later poets who lacked such training would make confessional poetry a byword for limp self-infatuation.

What's more, Lowell acknowledged that even the effect of total honesty in *Life Studies* is just that—an effect, based on deliberate manipulation. As he told an interviewer, "You leave out a lot, and emphasize this and not that. Your actual experience is a complete flux. I've invented facts and changed things, and the whole balance of the poem was something invented." In confessional poetry, the reason for treating private subjects is either ethical—honesty requires that the poet confront what is most painful—or therapeutic—writing about trauma will help the poet (and the reader) overcome trauma. Lowell's motive, however, was always aesthetic; *Life Studies* just takes a new approach to his old goal of creating a self-sufficient work of art. Even Lowell's apparently total honesty was at bottom an artistic technique, designed to evoke a particular response: "you want the reader to say, This is true . . . the reader was to believe he was getting the *real* Robert Lowell." Whether we are, in fact, getting the real Robert Lowell—whether such a thing is even possible—is not finally important.

In fact, as Lowell's work went on to show, the balance between directness and artlessness is easily upset. The unrepeatable triumph of *Life Studies* was owed to its use of long-meditated biographical material and to its sense of deliberately loosened form—many of the poems began in couplets or other strict forms and retained traces of their rhymes even after they were picked apart. In *For the Union Dead* (1964), on the other hand, Lowell is less deliberate: most of the poems are presented as first-person utterances in immediate reaction to experience, as though we were hearing the poet in real time. The form is correspondingly stripped down, and tries to impart a sense of drama through repeated questions and exclamations. The result is a thinner and less powerful collection, which gives the impression of a convalescence after the exertions of *Life Studies*.

In fact, "Middle Age" would have been a more appropriate title poem for the book than "For the Union Dead." As he enters his late forties, Lowell feels sickly and irritable: "New York / drills through my nerves"; "my muscles cramp"; "my five senses clenched / their teeth." This sense gathers to a peak in "Eye and Tooth," where everything seems intent on rubbing the nerves raw: the "cut cornea," the rain that falls "in pinpricks," even the "sharp-shinned hawk." In "Fall 1961," Lowell daringly extends this inward feeling to the entire world: "All autumn, the chafe and jar / of nuclear war," he writes, as though war were the expression on a global scale of the same irritability. Most painful of all is the poet's sense that he has exhausted his credit in complaint: "I am tired. Everyone's tired of my turmoil." It is a moving evocation of age and illness, but also seems to allude to *Life Studies* and the way Lowell has insisted on bringing his turmoil to the world's attention.

As the present becomes too wearing to endure, the poet's mind begins to turn backward—not in the strenuous memory-work of *Life Studies*, but with something closer to simple nostalgia. "Remember?" Lowell asks in "Water," the first poem in the volume; "Remember our lists of birds?" in "The Old Flame"; "Remember summer?" in "The Public Garden." Lowell is writing directly to his companion in memory, and counts on the reader eagerly assuming the role of eavesdropper. But as in the least successful poems in *Life Studies*, the pathos of Lowell's memories often leaves him too little concerned with whether the reader will share his feeling.

Even in the less personal poems there is a certain complacency and discursiveness, the poet versifying what he knows instead of transforming it. "Jonathan Edwards in Western Massachusetts" suffers by comparison to the Edwards poems in *Lord Weary's Castle*, stuffed with biographical data and at times almost condescending in its direct address to Edwards: "Poor country Berkeley at Yale, / you saw the world was soul. . . ." Yet the contrast also shows how Lowell's sensibility has changed in the intervening years. "Mr. Edwards and the Spider" delighted in ventriloquizing a perverse Puritan violence; "Jonathan Edwards in Western Massachusetts" pays less attention to what Edwards says than to what he is, the middle-aged man behind the preacher:

> *I love you faded,*
> *old, exiled and afraid . . .*
> . . . .
> *afraid to leave*
> *all your writing, writing, writing. . . .*

For the Union Dead is exceptionally aware of this disjunction between the man and the writing, and the very thinness of the writing seems a deliberate effort to bring the man forward. Perhaps the best case to be made for this sort of poetry is the one Lowell makes in "Night Sweat," where art is at once the purgative and the waste product of life:

> *Sweet salt embalms me and my head is wet,*
> *everything streams and tells me this is right;*

my life's fever is soaking in night sweat—
one life, one writing!

THE GREAT EXCEPTION in *For the Union Dead*, ironically enough, is the title poem. It was written in 1960, early enough to appear for the first time in the paperback edition of *Life Studies*. But by putting it at the end of *For the Union Dead*, Lowell seems to draw a line under the private poems that have come before. Thematically, if not chronologically, "For the Union Dead" marks a transition away from private subjects and toward the public statement of his next book, *Near the Ocean*.

"For the Union Dead" was a public poem not just in subject but in occasion: Lowell read it at an arts festival in 1960, to a crowd gathered on the very Boston Common that is the poem's setting. But as he told that audience, he chose to approach his historical subject through "early personal memories because I wanted to avoid the fixed, brazen tone of the set-piece and official ode." It is this synthesis that makes "For the Union Dead" one of the very few American poems that can inspire genuine, unrhetorical patriotic emotion: Lowell treats history not as something official, but as a private possession. The same tendency, carried to more audacious lengths, would later produce the poems of *History*.

Like "Beyond the Alps" and "Skunk Hour," "For the Union Dead" plots a symbolic action without ever resorting to explicit allegory; through a chain of concrete observations, Lowell laments the decline of Boston and its best traditions. He begins with a homely example of decline: the "old South Boston Aquarium," which he visited as a child, is now deserted, its water replaced by "a Sahara of snow." Without ever saying so directly, Lowell goes on to suggest that the aquarium is empty because its "dark downward and vegetating kingdom," filled with "cowed, compliant fish," has been projected outward onto the city itself. Just as he once stared through the glass of the aquarium, so now he presses "against the new barbed and galvanized / fence on the Boston Common," where the "yellow dinosaur steamshovels" seem like monsters in captivity feeding on the "mush and grass" of the Common.

This park, the historic heart of Boston, is being undermined, torn up from below to make room for a parking garage. The city is being judged in this image, as surely as in "Where the Rainbow Ends"; but where the earlier poem invoked a traditional icon, "the pans / Of judgment rising and descending," now Lowell turns reality itself into a legible symbol. By the sixth stanza, the destruction has reached the famous Saint-Gaudens monument to Colonel Robert Gould Shaw, which stands literally at the north end of the Common, and figuratively for the highest ideals of the North in the Civil War. The monument depicts Shaw with his regiment of African-American soldiers, one of the only black outfits to see combat in the war: as Lowell writes, "half the regiment" was slaughtered at Fort Wagner, South Carolina, in 1863. They have become what T. S. Eliot called "a symbol perfected in death," an embodiment of the racial equality for which the war was fought. But just as the city takes no care to preserve the monument from "the garage's earthquake," so the America of 1960 is heedless of "the drained faces of Negro school-children" that the poet sees on television.

What most appeals to Lowell in the Shaw monument, however, is not just its nobility but its rebarbativeness. Shaw is a scandal and an offense to a city that allows its Common to be destroyed, and to a country that allows its schools to remain segregated. Lowell returns to the opening stanzas' fish imagery to make the point: the monument "sticks like a fishbone / in the city's throat." The twentieth century cannot accommodate Shaw's kind of individual heroism; even its great crusade, the Second World War, produces "no statues," only the terrifying image of "Hiroshima boiling," a destruction so massive as to be humanly void. And modern Boston is now the seat, not of Shaw's "vigilance," but of "a savage servility." In the poem's final stanza, Lowell delicately suggests the return of the Aquarium's "cowed, compliant fish," in the form of 1950s-style "giant finned cars." It is a quietly ominous reprise of Lowell's early apocalyptic vision, only now, instead of invoking Leviathan, he evokes it through a careful orchestration of symbols. The city itself, rather than the poet, seems to pronounce the terrible judgment.

If "For the Union Dead" speaks of America's lost republican virtue, the poems of *Near the Ocean* (1967) observe a country in its imperial phase, military might concealing spiritual crisis. Yet Lowell avoids the bombast of the political orator; these are in no sense protest poems, though they display an unmistakable fear and disappointment about the direction of the country in the 1960s. Instead, the opening sequence of five poems mingles the political with the personal, the disorders of each realm contaminating the other. And in the second half of the book, Lowell simply translates from Latin poetry, leaving the reader to make the connection— which his prefatory note pretends is "a mystery to me"—between America and "Rome, the greatness and horror of her Empire."

If the decadence of Rome is a warning to America, it presents Lowell himself with a challenge and an opportunity. "The Ruins of Time," a group of four sonnets translated from Spanish, dwells on the transience of power and the permanence of art:

O Rome! From all your palms, dominion, bronze
and beauty, what was firm has fled. What once
was fugitive maintains its permanence.

What was "fugitive" is the poetry that now constitutes our only living memory of Rome. "Waking Early Sunday Morning," Lowell's own poem from the heart of American empire, embraces this paradox: it seeks to commemorate a phase of history, not by deliberately setting out to preserve it, but by recording its effects on the poet's own life. In fact, the world of politics appears in the poem only according to the terms of Lowell's ingenious metaphor:

I watch a glass of water wet
with a fine fuzz of icy sweat,
silvery colors touched with sky,
serene in their neutrality—
yet if I shift, or change my mood,
I see some object made of wood,
background behind it of brown grain,
to darken it, but not to stain.

O that the spirit could remain
tinged but untarnished by its strain!

Unlike the glass, which is simply transparent, the spirit is not just colored but "tarnished" by its surroundings. And from the beginning, Lowell gives an unmistakable sense of his own troubled spirit. The heavily enjambed, fast-paced iambic tetrameter creates a perfectly mimetic rhythm, the sound of a mind racing to keep up with itself. Lowell draws an implicit contrast between this ragged verse and the authoritative "stiff quatrains" of the Protestant hymnbook. He sees the stolid hymn meter as a token of spiritual confidence: "they gave darkness some control / and left a loophole for the soul." But the poet is not at church on this Sunday morning, and his poem leaves no such hopeful loophole. The "Faithful," even the New England Puritans with their dark faith, inhabited a universe where humankind had dignity and purpose. Lowell's poem, on the other hand, is forced to "put old clothes on" and putter among the "dregs and dreck" of the modern, secular mind. Emblems of Christianity remain in the New England landscape, but without their old power to inspire; they are merely, in one of Lowell's brilliantly unaccountable metaphors, "old white china doorknobs, sad, / slight, useless things to calm the mad."

It is only at this mention of madness that the poem begins to attend to the public, political world. Its nervous rhythm is transposed, without warning, into a new martial key, a "Hammering military splendor." Lowell does not explicitly connect this new chain of thoughts to what has come before, but the ease of the transition makes clear that violence and war—"elephant and phalanx moving / with the times and still improving"—have underlain the poem from the beginning; war is the "brown grain" that stains the poet's mind.

Specifically, it is the Vietnam War that haunts "Waking Early Sunday Morning." Lowell daringly identifies his own manic mood with that of Lyndon Johnson: "elated as the President / girdled by his establishment / this Sunday morning." The violence that Lowell can only imagine, Johnson can actually inflict; and by describing Johnson as "elated," rather than merely bloodthirsty,

Lowell declares his own shameful sympathy with that elation. But finally, this deeply ambiguous joy must give way to pity, as the poem ends with a hopeless vision of America's future, and the world's: "peace to our children when they fall / in small war on the heels of small / war—until the end of time. . . ." Lowell's double perspective, confessing his secret fascination with violence while mourning its effect on the planet, does not offer the reader the satisfaction of being on the "right side" of the Vietnam War. Instead, Lowell demands that we join him in acknowledging our own complicity with violence, not just political but spiritual. That same balance of horror and fascination would become the keynote of his late masterpiece, *History*.

HISTORY WAS PUBLISHED in 1973, but its origins lie in 1967, when Lowell began to write in a new form—an over-packed, unrhymed sonnet. Lowell's stanza shows the influence of John Berryman's Dream Songs, whose irregularly rhymed, eighteen-line lyrics can also be thought of as modified sonnets. When they were first published, in 1964, Lowell was uncertain about the Dream Songs, but he soon became an enthusiastic champion; Berryman, he realized, had achieved the unpredictable freedom that he wanted for his own poems, a form that can "say almost anything conversation or correspondence can." More than Berryman, however, Lowell takes advantage of the episodic structure of the traditional sonnet sequence. Instead of trying to say everything about a subject in one perfectly achieved poem, he can revisit it again and again, changing mood and approach each time. This freedom both encouraged and suited a sudden, unprecedented fertility: "I did nothing but write; I was thinking lines even when teaching or playing tennis. . . . Ideas sprang from the bushes, my head; five or six sonnets started or reworked in a day. . . . If I saw something one day, I wrote it that day, or the next, or the next."

Because each sonnet was just a cell in a larger structure, Lowell felt even less hesitation than usual about revising individual poems. Ever since *Land of Unlikeness* was transformed into *Lord Weary's Castle*, revision and rewriting had always been a central part of his process of composition: as he said, "I don't believe I've ever written a poem in meter where I've kept a single one of the original lines." But now even publication did not terminate Lowell's revisions; individual poems and whole books continued to evolve after they appeared. Poems from *Notebook 1967–68* (published in 1969) returned in the expanded *Notebook* (1970), and again in two of the three books of sonnets Lowell issued in 1973, *History* and *For Lizzie and Harriet*.

As the title suggests, *Notebook 1967–68* emphasized the freedom and provisionality of Lowell's sonnets: a notebook is where an artist keeps his work before it is completed. Lowell's "afterthought" to *Notebook* refers to it as one long poem, whose "time is a summer, an autumn, a winter, a spring, another summer." Yet this does not mean that the years 1967–68 are exactly recorded, as in a "chronicle or almanac": a notebook is not a diary. Instead, Lowell simply wrote what he wanted to, or had to: "Accident threw up subjects, and the plot swallowed them."

The resulting volume gives an intimate sense of the poet's mind at work. Poems and groups of poems tethered to the calendar— "Long Summer," "October and November"—are interrupted by decades-old memories. Current events—the assassination of Martin Luther King Jr. in "Two Walls," the Democratic convention in Chicago—are intertwined with meditations on Attila the Hun and the battle of Bosworth Field. As in "Waking Early Sunday Morning," but on a much larger scale, Lowell portrays the age not with a journalist's objectivity, but only as it leaves scars and impressions on his own life.

In splitting *Notebook* into *History* and *For Lizzie and Harriet*, and adding a third, coordinate volume in *The Dolphin*, Lowell deliberately sacrificed this immediacy in the name of shape and coherence: "I hope this jumble or jungle is cleared—that I have cut the waste marble from the figure." But even in their revised form, plot is still not central to Lowell's sonnets; the coherence he achieves is not narrative but thematic. In *History*, he reflects on the history of the world and his own personal history, each in the light of the other; in the other two books, he tells the story of his recent past, centered on his divorce and remarriage. *History* is the more intellectually adventurous and poetically successful book. The personal sonnets of *For Lizzie and Harriet* and especially *The Dolphin*, on the other hand, are more scandalous and unsettled, with an intimacy that pushes the confessional impulse to new and problematic lengths.

The sheer number of sonnets in *History*—there are more than 350—has a fissiparous effect, tending to turn the volume into a huge picture gallery. Certainly it can be read simply as a collection of episodes and portraits, and much of its interest comes from the reader's curiosity about how Lowell will approach each of his incredibly wide-ranging subjects. At one moment he depicts himself rummaging through the vast storeroom of his reading:

> *It's somewhere, somewhere, thought beats stupidly—*
> *a scarlet patch of Tacitus or the Bible,*
> *Pound's Cantos lost in the rockslide of history?*

But while the *Cantos* return again and again to a few favored periods and personalities, Lowell takes all of history for his province. The sonnets are arranged in chronological order according to subject, beginning with prehistoric times, then moving through the Old Testament, Greek myth and history, Rome, the Middle Ages, the Renaissance, the eighteenth century in England, France and America, and the nineteenth century, with a particular emphasis on writers from Goethe to Mallarmé. The advent of the poet's own lifetime occasions no break in the form: Lowell simply continues to slot the events of his life into the same mold, from a schoolboy crush in "First Love" through "Remembrance Day, London 1970's."

History, in other words, is deliberately conceived as an intellectual feat, and Lowell's ambition would seem arrogant if it were not so astonishingly vindicated. He is able to find a fruitful approach to nearly every subject, and his language is constantly vigorous and inventive. The signal quality of the verse in *History* is its freedom, or what might more pointedly be called its unaccountability: Lowell refuses to be bound by the expectation that each sonnet will be a unity, or even that every line will make perfect sense. In "Painter," Lowell's unnamed speaker praises Constable's "sketches more finished than his oils," and the same provisional aesthetic is at work in *History*. It gives the impression of an artist so assured of his power that he works without premeditation, seizing images and lines as they come and fixing them to the page. As with many artists' late styles, coherence is to be found not in the individual works, but in the sensibility behind them all.

Certainly *History* could be plundered for an anthology of brilliant lines:

Stephen Decatur, spyglass screwed to raking
the cannonspout-smashed Bay of Tripoli

the white glittering inertia of the iceberg

he haws on the gristle of a Flemish word

the ant's cool, amber, hyperthyroid eye

As even these few examples suggest, the building block of Lowell's verse is still the adjective, often two or three lashed together in unexpected combinations. The sonnet's traditional iambic pentameter is packed with unstressed syllables, so that each line seems to strain to hold everything Lowell puts in. Together with the abundant adjectives, the effect is of an overflowing richness. This is not, however, the baroque richness of *The Mills of the Kavanaughs*, deforming its subject in its own image. Lowell's eloquence has become so natural that it seems more like an accent, elevating everything it touches.

If the language of *History* is constantly surprising, so too is the angle of vision. Seldom can a sonnet's contents be predicted from its title; Lowell's freedom extends to the way he sneaks up on his subject. "Judith," for instance, only reaches the story of Judith and Holofernes in its last three lines. It begins as an utterly contemporary monologue—in quotation marks, like many of the sonnets, but with only a conjectural speaker:

"The Jews were much like Arabs, I learned at Radcliffe,
decay of infeud scattered our bright clans;
now ours is an airier aristocracy:

professors, solons, new art, old, New York
where only Jews can write an English sentence. . . . "

What we are hearing, as the reference to Radcliffe shows, is a young Jewish woman in twentieth-century America, whose pride and aggressive irony are proposed as equivalents for the murderous patriotism of Judith: "for Judith, knowing / Holofernes was like knocking out a lightweight." If we understand this woman, Lowell suggests, we will understand Judith as well.

This vision of correspondences is what holds together the sonnets of *History*. Lowell sees everything he writes about under two aspects, as both intimate and historical. For Lowell, to go out toward the past is to draw the past inward, to interpret it by consulting his own experiences, feelings, and thoughts. This double vision allows Lowell to traverse huge stretches of history without giving the impression of miscellaneity or mere curiosity. Wherever he casts his eye he sees not just an alien surface but a familiar essence.

More precisely, he finds a few basic types, of which the past offers endlessly repeated examples. That is why his poem on "Mohammed" begins "Like Henry VIII, Mohammed got religion / in the dangerous years"; and his poem on Attila the Hun is titled "Attila, Hitler"; and his poem on Richard II is titled "Coleridge and Richard II." Each time, Lowell moves from the token to the type, and then proceeds from the type to another token, distant in time but essentially identical: the religious fanatic, the nihilistic tyrant, the indecisive intellectual.

The implication of this view of history is a savage Nietzschean fatalism: instead of progress, Lowell sees the eternal return of the same. Nietzsche wrote that the only noble response to such a fate is to embrace it, to do joyously what one is condemned to do in any case; the ability to make this affirmation is what separates the superman from the masses. And Lowell implicitly accepts this notion when he comes to judge historical figures. For in *History* there are not really heroes and villains; there are only the famous and the insignificant. We remember illustrious men and women, Lowell suggests, because of the intensity of their self-affirmation, no matter whether their actions are good or evil. In this, the artist, the hero, and the tyrant are united: Lowell could say of all of them, as he says of Stalin, "What raised him / was an unusual lust to break the icon, / joke cruelly, seriously, and be himself." Everyone else is simply forgotten and may as well not have existed, as he writes in "Fame":

> We bleed for people, so independent and selfsuspecting,
>   if the door is locked, they come back tomorrow, instead of
>   knocking—
> hearts scarred by complaints they would not breathe . . .
> . . . .
> Timur said something like: "The drop of water
> that fails to become a river is food for the dust."

Perhaps there can be heard in this superb contempt an echo of Lowell's attitude toward his father's "anxious, repetitive smiling." From the very beginning, Lowell expressed his determination to escape that meekness—to be "piratical," even, was better than to be insignificant. In *History*, he praises Alexander the Great in exactly the same terms:

> No one was like him. Terrible were his crimes—
> but if you wish to blackguard the Great King,

think how mean, obscure and dull you are,
your labors lowly and your merits less. . . .

Lowell fearlessly pursues this insight into the darkness where it leads. Just as, in "Waking Early Sunday Morning," he shares President Johnson's destructive "elation," so in *History* he writes with impassioned sympathy about wars, crimes, and murders. He is Orestes killing Clytemnestra: "He knew the monster must be guillotined. / He saw her knees tremble and he enjoyed the sight." He is Richard III: "What does he care for Thomas More and Shakespeare / pointing fingers at his polio'd body; / for the moment, he is king." Writing about Napoleon, Lowell asks mockingly, "Dare we say, he had no moral center?" For the lack of a "moral center" is, he proposes, the prerequisite for any historical achievement: "a blindman looking for gold / in a heap of dust must take the dust with the gold. . . ."

But such carelessness of individual life, easy enough to contemplate in poetry, is far more dubious when it comes to actual politics. And Lowell was, in fact, a prominent liberal, famous for publicly opposing the Vietnam War. In *History*, he reflects on the chaos of the late 1960s with scrupulous moral concern: we see him marching on the Pentagon, campaigning for Eugene McCarthy, and mourning Nixon's election. In "Women, Children, Babies, Cows, Cats," he writes in stark protest of the My Lai massacre, assuming the voice of an ignorant soldier ordered "to burn and kill." Yet this is the same poet who takes brutal delight in ventriloquizing Achilles at Troy: "You must die / and die and die and die and die."

This tension drives many of the later poems in *History*, where Lowell turns to his own life and times. He cannot and does not reconcile the opposite imperatives of life and art, ethics and aesthetics. Instead, he gives voice to this division, and to the self-contempt it engenders. When he marches on the Pentagon to protest the Vietnam War, Lowell acknowledges, he cuts a foolish figure, "unlocking to keep my wet glasses from slipping." Caught between the savagery of the state and the barbarism of the counterculture, Lowell feels the precariousness of the liberal, who "bites his own lip to warm his icy tooth, / and faces all vicissitudes with calmness. / That's why there are none, that's why we're none. . . ." In his willingness to make this admission, Lowell moves beyond the self-righteous pieties of most American political poetry. True to the logic of *History*, he sees the eternal types and forces still at work in his own day, and in his own soul.

FOR LIZZIE AND Harriet and *The Dolphin* share the sonnet form of *History*, but to read them is a very different experience. Instead of treating public themes in a personal manner, Lowell now takes private events and makes them public. For the subject of the two books is Lowell's estrangement and divorce from his second wife, Elizabeth Hardwick, after more than twenty years of marriage, and his remarriage to Caroline Blackwood. Since less than a year elapsed between Lowell's divorce and the publication of his poems about it, these books are more radically confessional than even *Life Studies*, which carefully reconstructed events sometimes decades in the past. Lowell is interpreting the ideal of "Night Sweat"—"one life, one writing"—in the most literal sense; and in doing so, he demonstrates the aesthetic and ethical dangers to which confessional poetry is vulnerable.

"History has to live with what was here," begins the first poem in *History*. In *For Lizzie and Harriet*, the definition is significantly revised: "What is history? What you cannot touch." The emphasis in this brief collection of sonnets, extracted from *Notebook* and revised, is no longer on the presence of the past, but on its absence. In particular, it chronicles the painful slipping away of the poet's life in New York with his wife and daughter, who are named in the title. The sonnets chart the unpredictable progress of Lowell's relationships, with his family and several unnamed lovers, over about a year. But their inevitable destination is the death of the marriage, announced in the last poem, "Obit": "Our love will not come back on fortune's wheel."

For Lizzie and Harriet is thus designed as a prelude to *The Dolphin*, published the same year, which portrays the divorce foretold in "Obit" and Lowell's creation of a new life and family in England. But while the whole story is not hard to follow—it is what Lowell himself calls "one man, two women, the common novel plot"—the events behind any particular sonnet must often be deduced, or even conjectured. Finally, what matters is not the week-to-week progress of the lovers' triangle, with its ruptures and reconciliations, but the poet's mood, which remains largely static: a compound of joy at his late-life romance and guilt over leaving his wife and daughter.

In *For Lizzie and Harriet*, the first baleful glimpse of Lowell's marriage comes in "Summer 3. Elizabeth":

An unaccustomed ripeness in the wood;
move but an inch and moldy splinters fall
in sawdust from the walls' aluminum-paint,
once loud and fresh, now aged to weathered wood.

It is an indirect but blunt metaphor for the marriage, aged past ripeness into rot and mold. And while the plot of *For Lizzie and*

Harriet is not resolved until *The Dolphin*, Lowell's persistently hostile treatment of "Elizabeth" leaves no doubt that the marriage is doomed. In later sonnets, she is the "prickly hedgehog of the hearth," or a "Dr. Johnson" eloquent in reproach; groups of poems about her are titled "No Hearing" and "Dear Sorrow."

On the other hand, Lowell's mistresses—there seem to be at least two, both much younger than he is—call forth a saccharine lyricism:

> *shouldn't I ask to hold to you forever,*
> *body of a dolphin, breast of cloud?*
> *You rival the renewal of the day,*
> *clearing the puddles with your green sack of books.*

In *For Lizzie and Harriet*, however, Lowell shows himself still constrained in his adulteries by guilt. One variety of guilt has to do simply with the age difference between him and his lovers: "Woman, so small, if one could trust appearance, / I might be in trouble with the law." A more substantial reservation is expressed in "Our Twentieth Wedding Anniversary 2": "By setting limits, man has withdrawn from the monsters; / a metal rod and then another metal rod. . . ." To leave his marriage, Lowell implies, would be to run roughshod over those limits, to reduce himself to a monster, or a buffoon: "the soul groans and laughs at its lack of stature." The most eloquent and convincing moments in the book come when Lowell shows himself painfully caught between desire and conscience, unable to tip either way:

> all flesh is grass, and like the flower of the grass—
> *no! lips, breasts, eyes, hands, lips, hair—*

the overworked central heating bangs the frame,
as the milkhorse in childhood would clang the morning milkcan.

In *The Dolphin*, the balance finally does tip. From the beginning it is clear that Lowell, now living in England with the writer Caroline Blackwood, is embarked on a permanent attachment, very different from the ones in *For Lizzie and Harriet*. But since Lowell seems certain finally to leave one wife for the next, the book can evoke little suspense from its melodramatic premise. The vacillations that form its only plot seem more like a period of penance, which the poet requires himself to undergo before he earns the right to divorce and remarry. Again and again, Lowell deploys his eloquence against himself: "I draw a card I wished to leave unchosen, / and discard the one card I had sworn to hold." He compares himself to the tomcats that "find their kittens and chew off their breakable heads," to the wasps that "drop in the beercans, clamber, buzz / debating like us whether to stay and drown, / or, by losing legs and wings, take flight." It is in this context that Lowell's decision to incorporate letters from Hardwick, seemingly verbatim, must be understood. His intention is not to betray her but to make the most damning case against himself, as in "Records":

> *"I got the letter*
> *this morning, the letter you wrote me Saturday.*
> *I thought my heart would break a thousand times . . .*
> *. . . . .*
> *you doomed to know what I have known with you,*
> *lying with someone fighting unreality—*
> *love vanquished by his mysterious carelessness."*

Yet it is the reader's very awareness of Lowell's motives that obtrudes upon and ultimately damages the poetry. If *For Lizzie and Harriet* and *The Dolphin* are less satisfying books than *History*, the reason is not stylistic. The verse is equally accomplished, though transposed to a different register: less grand and violent, more delicate and meditative, often occupied with natural description. But the sonnet form does seem unsatisfactory in these poems as it does not in *History*. The leaps and buried associations that propel the sonnets are much better suited to imitating thought than to recounting events, especially when real people are involved and fidelity to fact seems imperative.

In this way, the problem of form becomes entangled with the problem of substance. Ever since it was published, *The Dolphin* has been subjected to harsh criticism on ethical grounds; by turning his abandonment of his family into verse, at the very time it was happening, Lowell knowingly risked the charge of shamelessness. Still worse, in the eyes of many critics at the time and since, was Lowell's use of Hardwick's painfully intimate letters. Elizabeth Bishop, who made reticence the cornerstone of her poetry, was especially troubled by this violation of privacy. "One can use one's life as material," Bishop wrote Lowell, "but these letters—aren't you violating a trust? . . . *art just isn't worth that much.*"

This objection to confessional poetry does raise a serious ethical question. Indeed, Lowell himself was ready, even eager, to acknowledge it, apologizing in *The Dolphin*'s final sonnet for "not avoiding injury to others, / not avoiding injury to myself." What is more easily overlooked, however, is the injury that such naked confession inflicts on the poems themselves. The morality of Lowell's actions will cease to trouble readers in time; after all, no one today is much scandalized by *Modern Love*, George Meredith's Victorian sonnet sequence about adultery and divorce. But the aesthetic repercussions of Lowell's confessions run deeper, and exact a more permanent cost.

The problem, in this sense, is not how much Lowell is willing to reveal, but the way he reveals it. For no matter how candid he is about his own actions, Lowell cannot truly abdicate his interest in how those actions will be understood and judged by the reader. Humble, even self-abasing when it comes to embarrassing facts, Lowell remains tyrannical when it comes to interpretations. And just as Keats famously warned, because Lowell's designs on the reader's sympathy are so palpable, he eventually forfeits the reader's trust.

In part, Lowell's untrustworthiness in *The Dolphin* is a simple question of omission: in the loose weave of the sonnets, much crucial information is lost. The exact chronology of events, the identities of lovers and friends, the speakers of certain passages, can only be guessed at. And it is impossible to be sure if Lowell has made such omissions on artistic grounds, or in order to present a more flattering picture of himself. More generally, by presenting the events of his life in the genre of lyric rather than narrative, Lowell takes it upon himself to speak for everyone involved. It is impossible to know what "Lizzie," "Harriet," and "Caroline" think of each situation, except when Lowell chooses to quote them—or misquote them, for all the reader knows. This is exactly why they must be referred to in quotation marks; though they share the names of real people, what we meet in the poems are literary characters.

But when the poem is evidently unfair to these other characters, it is not just an ethical but primarily an aesthetic demand to want to know their side of the story. In "During a Transatlantic

Call," for instance, Lowell suggests that Hardwick wants him to return home out of mere greed: "They tell me to stop, they mustn't lose my money." But because Lowell is not only the narrator of this conversation but also a participant, it is impossible for the reader to have confidence in his report. He is an unreliable narrator claiming the authority of an omniscient one.

This is where *The Dolphin*—like the late, self-abasing poems of John Berryman—brushes up against the limits of confessional poetry. The rock on which confession founders is not honesty but vanity, the incurable human need to present oneself in the best possible light. In most lyric poetry, the conventional distinction between author and speaker is sufficient to free the poet from the demands of the ego. Even in some confessional poetry, the "I" being described is sufficiently distant in time from the "I" doing the writing that, with an impressive effort of selflessness and much narrative deliberation, the poet can seem impartial toward himself. But to exert aesthetic mastery over an experience going on at the time of writing, especially when that experience is discreditable, is probably impossible. Like a microphone that tries to listen to itself, the result is a whine of feedback:

> *Do I romanticize if I think that I*
> *can be as selfish a father as Karl Marx,*
> *Milton, Dickens, Trotsky, Freud, James Mill,*
> *or George II, a bad son and worse father—*
> *the great lions needed a free cage to roar in.* . . .

Such unappealing, unconvincing justification is inevitable when self-exposure collides with self-love. *The Dolphin* is full of reflective asides about the ethics of confessional poetry: "the fiction I colored with first-hand evidence, / letters and talk I marketed as fiction." But it is the aesthetic, not the ethical pitfall that traps Lowell; and *The Dolphin* is finally unable to extricate itself from that "eelnet made by man for the eel fighting."

DEATH CAN GIVE an artist's last work the imposing sense of a destination. But this effect can just as easily be spurious, and death merely the accidental truncation of something still growing. It is difficult to say in which category Lowell's last book, *Day by Day*, belongs. Certainly it is consumed with thoughts of age and dying:

> *Less than ever I expect to be alive*
> *six months from now—*
> 1976,
> *a date I dare not affix to my grave.*

In this poem, "Home," Lowell was off by just one year: he died at the age of sixty in 1977, the year *Day by Day* was published. The book seems to be preparing for death by deliberately stripping bare, casting off not just the endless proficiency of the sonnets but any kind of form. The process can be seen in "Phillips House Revisited," in which the poet returns, himself now a patient, to the hospital where his grandfather died in "In Memory of Arthur Winslow." In that early, heavily symbolic poem, cancer was euphemized as "the crab"; now Lowell returns to the same image, only to reduce it to pathetic homeliness:

> *But these forty years grandfather would insist*
> *have turned the world on its head—*
> *their point was*
> *to extinguish him like a stranded crab.*

Arthur Winslow is no longer a hieratic figure, but a small doomed animal. In just the same way, in *Day by Day* Lowell is concerned no longer with his power, as artist or lover, but with his vulnerability. The change extends to his style. The book's long, narrow stanzas of free verse remain recognizably Lowellian, especially in their layered adjectives. But the language is less wrenched and composed than ever before, and even those adjectives have become less surprising, more conventional and Latinate: the River Liffey is "torrential," pain is "unspecified, unlimited." For the first time, these seem like words a poet other than Lowell could have chosen.

In their subjects, too, the poems of *Day by Day* seem unpremeditated, starting directly from their inner or outer occasions. "Joy of standing up my dentist," begins "Bright Day in Boston"; "Leaving a taxi at Victoria, / I saw my own face," begins "Our Afterlife II." As a result, these poems seem less like separate compositions than installments in an ongoing monologue. Fortified by his fame in the assumption that the reader is already familiar with the cast and settings of his life, Lowell simply sets down episodes: here again are Caroline, Elizabeth and Harriet, the New York apartment and the English country house. In writing so unemphatically about his personal life, Lowell offers not the explosive intimacy of *The Dolphin*, but a leisurely familiarity, descending sometimes to mere trivia.

Whatever his subjects—the insults he endured as a schoolboy, or having dinner with a Rothschild, or simply a summer day— Lowell's theme is always age. But he writes with neither the indignation nor the serenity of the great poets of old age. *Day by Day* is dominated by quieter emotions: nostalgia, exhaustion, resignation. Sometimes, indeed, Lowell can sound simply valetudinar-

ian, recording his symptoms and frailties: "What is won by surviving, / if two glasses of red wine are poison?" In most of these
poems, the inconsequential stream of observation and anecdote
is only occasionally enlivened by a sudden compression into wit:

> *We are things thrown in the air*
> *alive in flight . . .*
> *our rust the color of the chameleon.*
>
> *we learn the spirit is very willing to give up,*
> *but the body is not weak and will not die.*
>
> *if we see a light at the end of the tunnel,*
> *it's the light of an oncoming train.*

Such islands of eloquence stand out from the prevailing casual-
ness, making *Day by Day* most memorable as a collection of scattered epigrams.

In the book's last poem, however, Lowell seems to make a
greater claim for *Day by Day*, and for its style. Because of its terminal position in Lowell's body of work, "Epilogue" has often
been read as a sort of *credo* for Lowell's art, and for confessional
poetry in general:

> *But sometimes everything I write*
> *with the threadbare art of my eye*
> *seems a snapshot,*
> *lurid, rapid, garish, grouped,*
> *heightened from life,*
> *yet paralyzed by fact.*

All's misalliance.
Yet why not say what happened? . . .
We are poor passing facts,
warned by that to give
each figure in the photograph
his living name.

It is easy to pass lightly over Lowell's reservations and land heavily on his apologia: the transitoriness of human life demands a testimonial art, in which eloquence is less important than accuracy. This is an apt description of the aesthetic behind *Day by Day*, whose "threadbare art" seems appropriate to the theme of mortality. But it would be a mistake to ignore Lowell's artistic decline in *Day by Day*, or to forget that his art was not always "rapid, garish, grouped." Other poems in the book make the same admission in ways that are harder to ignore. In "Ten Minutes," Lowell laments that "there's no truth in this processing of words"; in "Shifting Colors," he regrets his "description without significance, / transcribed verbatim by my eye," and longs for something higher: "I would write only in response to the gods."

If Lowell is considered primarily as a confessional poet, *Day by Day* seems like the logical conclusion of his artistic evolution, from *Life Studies* through *The Dolphin*. But while Lowell joined his generation in writing more freely than ever before about private life, this is not what distinguishes him as a great artist and a major American poet. His best poetry is personal, not in the way of a diary entry, but in the way of a work of art: it expresses him essentially but indirectly. The violent and surging eloquence of *Lord Weary's Castle* belongs recognizably to the same poet who wrote the gaily terrible sonnets of *History*. Even the most revealing poems of *Life Studies* remain memorable, when a thousand other poems of the madhouse do not, because of the controlled and canalized force of Lowell's language.

There is an art of restraint and witness, which many poets of the late twentieth century found to be the appropriate response to their time. But Lowell's art is one of power and grandeur, assertion and transformation. It is this that makes him the natural heir and companion to the classic English poets, starting with his beloved Milton; it is this that gave him the confidence to write so magnificently in so many different styles. And it is this, rather than "poor passing facts," that survives when, as Lowell writes in "Endings," "the immortal / is scraped unconsenting from the mortal."

ELIZABETH BISHOP

Everything only connected by "and" and "and"

The most surprising moment in the hundreds of pages of Elizabeth Bishop's published correspondence comes on November 16, 1953, when she learns of the death of Dylan Thomas. To all outward appearances, there could be no more perfect opposites, in their lives and their work, than Bishop and Thomas. Thomas had burst into print as a teenager, with passionately obscure poems in which the life force itself seems to be speaking; and that same "force that through the green fuse drives the flower" consumed the poet, in a series of legendary debaucheries. He was the Dionysus of twentieth-century poetry, the heir to charismatically dissolute poets from Villon to Hart Crane, and alcohol killed him at the age of thirty-nine. By the time Thomas died, Bishop, who didn't publish her first book until she was thirty-five, had already begun to develop the reputation she enjoys to this day as the most reticent and meticulous of poets, always deflecting emotion with careful strokes of description.

Yet when Bishop met Thomas in 1949, she immediately felt drawn to him: "I have met few people in my life I felt such an instantaneous sympathy and pity for," she recalled. And news of his death released a flood of grief in which, to borrow a phrase from her poem "The Map," "emotion too far exceeds its cause": "The first time I met Dylan . . . even after knowing him for three or four hours, I felt frightened for him and depressed. Yet I found him tremendously sympathetic at the same time . . . in my own minor way I know enough about drink & destruction."

Bishop, it is clear, saw in Thomas a sorcerer's apprentice who succumbed to forces that she herself could only barely control. During her lifetime, only her closest friends knew about the "drink & destruction" that are now amply chronicled in biographies, memoirs, and letters. Bishop's life, like those of so many poets of her generation, was shadowed by mental illness: when she was four years old, her mother was committed to an insane asylum. Since her father died when she was an infant, Bishop effectively grew up as an orphan, shuttled between relatives' homes. As an adult, she continued her nervous peregrination, living in Nova Scotia, New York, Paris, Key West, Brazil, San Francisco, and Boston, with many shorter stops along the way. And "destruction" shadowed Bishop's romantic life, as well: her great love, Lota de Macedo Soares, died by suicide, overdosing on tranquilizers while Bishop slept downstairs.

For another kind of writer, such a life could have fuelled a poetry of brutal confession; similar traumas in the lives of Robert Lowell and John Berryman were incorporated directly into their work. But Bishop never explicitly mentioned her griefs in her poems, and she often reprehended those who did. "In general, I deplore the 'confessional,' " she wrote to Lowell in 1972. "Now— ye gods—anything goes, and I am so sick of poems about . . . mothers and fathers and sex lives and so on." As her instinctive sympathy for Dylan Thomas shows, however, what separated Bishop from her peers was not the inner experience of "destruction," but the aesthetic and ethical strategies with which she simultaneously revealed and concealed it. Her poems are experiments in control, constantly testing how much she can dare to feel or express. And her great poetry demonstrates that experience channeled into symbol, sublimated into landscape, embodied in rhythm and image, can be both more effective and more honest than simple confession. Vision, in Bishop's passionately visual work, is not the pure receptivity of Emerson's "transparent eyeball," but the most delicate form of self-revelation. As her friend Mary McCarthy observed, Bishop allows herself to be known in her poems only as an " 'I' counting up to a hundred waiting to be found."

With the first poem in her first book, Bishop began her lifelong exploration of the connections between observation and emotion, seeing and feeling. "The Map," which leads off *North & South* (1946), is Bishop's variation on a favorite theme of Wallace Stevens, one of her most important early influences: the relation between reality and its representation. But while the subject is Stevensian, the technique of "The Map" is already distinctively Bishop's: precise metaphors, plain diction, irregular meter, and the illusion of a speaking voice. Equally characteristic is Bishop's concern with the difference between two ways of looking at the world, which she identifies as the "map-makers' " and the "historians'."

The map-maker, as Bishop describes him, is a kind of artist, replacing geographic reality with a stilled and attractive abstraction: "We can stroke these lovely bays, / under a glass as if they were expected to blossom." Bishop dwells lovingly on the map's greens and tans and yellows, whimsically asking, "can the countries pick their colors?" And in the poem's last line, she appears to endorse the map-maker's kind of artistry, which is "more quiet" and "more delicate" than the reality that the historian portrays. But as "The Map" also suggests, there is a danger in this way of seeing: it can lead to mere aestheticism, an interest only in "lovely" surfaces for their own sake. And while Bishop will always be painstaking in her description of surfaces, her mature poetry shows her to be anything but an aesthete. Seeing, for her, is not a luxurious pleasure, but a means of escape, and finally an ordeal.

A quarter of a century after writing "The Map," Bishop would deliberately repudiate its idealized, "unperturbed" vision. In "Primer Class," a prose memoir, she recounts a memory from her schooldays in Nova Scotia that seems clearly linked to the poem:

When they had a geography lesson, Miss Morash pulled down one or both of these maps [of Canada and of the world], like window shades. They were on cloth, very limp, with a shiny surface, and in pale colors—tan, pink, yellow, and green—surrounded by the blue that was the ocean. The light coming in from their windows, falling on the glazed, crackly surface, made it hard for me to see them properly from where I sat. . . .

> I got the general impression . . . that in the world and Canada
> the sun was always shining and everything was dry and glitter-
> ing. At the same time, I knew perfectly well that this was not
> true.

What the child knew, the poet of "The Map" only hints at: the beautiful colors of the map can make it impossible to "see prop-erly." In reality, the sun is not always shining.

In a sense, the achievement of Bishop's generation of poets was to win through from the map-maker's way of seeing to the histo-rian's. And for Bishop, as for her peers, this meant first casting off the influence of a grandly symbolic Modernism. Bishop was never as much under the spell of Modernist doctrine as Randall Jarrell or Robert Lowell, both of whom studied with leading New Critics. But Bishop, too, was initiated into the dominant poetic idiom of her time, through her own reading of the Modernists and the seventeenth-century Metaphysical poets they admired. Both Modernist and Metaphysical influences can be seen in the elaborate stanza forms and extended metaphors of Bishop's early poems, such as "Paris, 7 A.M.":

> *Time is an Etoile; the hours diverge*
> *so much that days are journeys round the suburbs,*
> *circles surrounding stars, overlapping circles.*

This is a classic example of a conceit, that staple of Metaphys-ical poetry: a metaphor extended so unexpectedly far that it gains startling implications. Bishop compares the clock to the hub-and-spokes of the star-shaped Etoile in Paris; by implication, the hours on the rim of the clock remain "suburbs," in permanent exile from the clock's unattainable center. And so that center becomes a symbol of the transcendence that can never be experienced within time, but seems to stand outside it. This sort of brilliantly contrived symbolism would, however, become increasingly uncommon in Bishop's mature work. Instead of metaphors that expand meaning like a telescope, she will mainly employ metaphors that focus and clarify it like a microscope.

Bishop's best early poems do not just employ symbolism—they are themselves symbols, of the kind that T. S. Eliot named objective correlatives. Poems like "The Man-Moth," "The Weed," and "The Unbeliever" express an emotion or experience not directly, in the first person, but obliquely, through the creation of an image that is its dramatic equivalent. In their combination of precision and uncanniness, Bishop's symbols also echo the parables of Kafka, whom she greatly admired.

The echo is especially strong in "The Man-Moth," the best poem of Bishop's early style. It was inspired, as her note reveals, by a newspaper misprint—"man-moth" for "mammoth"—but the notion of a human insect is also, inevitably, an allusion to Gregor Samsa in Kafka's "Metamorphosis." Bishop's man-moth is an exile from the city of men: he lives in hiding under a sidewalk, comes out only at night, and on the subway "always seats himself facing the wrong way." Like so many artistic misfits before him, he is marked out by his unusual sensitivity: he feels that "the sky [is] quite useless for protection," and the third rail strikes him as "a disease / he has inherited the susceptibility to." And like an artist, the man-moth transmutes his pain into a gift: his carefully guarded tear, "his only possession," is also a healing draught, "cool as from underground springs and pure enough to drink." Everything about him, but especially the protective pathos with which he is described, makes clear that the man-moth is an alter ego for the poet.

"The Man-Moth" shares with many of Bishop's early poems a sense of universal threat, of peculiar and seemingly inexplicable vulnerability. In "The Unbeliever," Bishop assumes the voice of a man asleep on top of a mast, who warns: "The spangled sea below wants me to fall. / It is hard as diamonds; it wants to destroy us all." In "Wading at Wellfleet," the poet regards the sea as "all a case of knives," and "Love Lies Sleeping" ends with the uncanny image of a man "whose head has fallen over the edge of his bed," either drunk or dead.

There is no mistaking the anxiety that pervades Bishop's best early poems. But so far, she is still attempting to represent that anxiety indirectly, by providing it with fables, symbols, objective correlatives. It is her own feeling only by implication, when we imagine what sort of poet would create such a world. Yet while Bishop's early poems are often brilliant exercises of the symbolizing imagination, she was to find, like all her peers, that this imagination was not truly hers. "The Man-Moth" remains an obviously literary parable; in her later work, emotion will be invested far more subtly in actual creatures and landscapes. Bishop's best symbols are found, not invented, and keep the stubborn particularity of the actual.

This development can already be seen taking place in the later poems of *North & South*, which strike a freer, more distinctive note. "Roosters" has a casual, aggressive motion far different from Bishop's earlier baroque stanzas, its loosely rhymed triplets propelling a wonderful satire on masculine egotism and violence. The poem has the freedom that comes from concentration on something concrete: Bishop noted that she began writing it early in the morning "with the roosters carrying on just as I said," and this "historian's" insistence on fact would become a cornerstone of her aesthetic. The roosters, unlike the man-moth, have a reassuring ordinariness, and inspire Bishop to a different sort of metaphor. When she writes that the rooster-crow "grates like a wet match," she does not want to allegorize the sound, but to allow the reader to hear it exactly. "Roosters" also has a public, even political bearing that is new to Bishop's poetry. The "green-gold medals" on the roosters' chests evoke the military uniforms much in evidence in the prewar year 1940, when the poem was written. And the "many wives / who lead hens' lives / of being courted and despised" are not just birds.

Bishop recognized that she had made an important advance in "Roosters," as can be seen from her argument with Marianne Moore about the poem. In 1934, while a senior at Vassar, Bishop had secured an introduction to Moore, who over the next six years would become her most important teacher—reading all her work, introducing her in an anthology of young writers, and sending out her poems to editors. As Bishop remembered years later, Moore offered her a role model of poetic integrity, inspiring her "to be good, to work harder, not to worry what other people thought." Moore also played for Bishop the role of Modernist mentor, which her male peers found in poet-critics like John Crowe Ransom and Allen Tate.

The difference goes some way toward explaining the freedom from New Critical conventions of even Bishop's earliest work. Instead of ambiguity and allusion, which feature so prominently in the early poems of Lowell and Berryman, Bishop learned from Moore the value of painstaking vision—not simply for its own sake, but as an ethical principle. In Moore's poems, elaborateness of description is a token of an honest, zealous, exacting mind. Bishop's movement away from overt symbolism and toward suggestive description, her sharp eye for landscape and creatures, are owed in large part to Moore's influence and example. These can be seen most obviously in Bishop's poem "Florida," which—with its archly observed "pelicans whose delight it is to clown," and its list of "fading shells: Job's Tear, the Chinese Alphabet, the scarce Junonia"—is practically a parody of Moore.

"Roosters," too, is significantly Moorean in its organization and construction. The bird acts as a magnet, drawing associations toward itself—first the military rooster, then the biblical rooster of Saint Peter—just as "The Plumet Basilisk" or "The Jerboa" did for Moore. Bishop's description of a battle map, marked out with "glass-headed pins, / oil-golds and copper greens, / anthracite blues, alizarins," is reminiscent of Moore's painstaking, parti-colored descriptions. Yet it makes sense that this poem should have been the occasion of Bishop's aesthetic declaration of independence from her mentor, since the essential spirit of "Roosters" is very unlike Moore. The older poet, who cultivated an eccentric prim-ness of manner and language, objected to Bishop's sordid details—the "dropping-plastered henhouse floor" and the "water-closet"—and urged her to change the poem's title to the more lit-erary (and unwittingly comic) "The Cock."

But Bishop knew that it was precisely the poem's directness and colloquial energy that made it a success. For "Roosters" is not, like a Moore poem, strictly a meditation on its subject. It is also the recollection of an experience that actually befell the poet at a particular moment in time; the very first line names the hour—"At four o'clock"—when the roosters began to crow. When Bishop wrote to Moore rejecting her changes and announcing "ELIZABETH KNOWS BEST," she was giving notice that, despite all she had learned, her artistic path would be very different from Moore's.

Still, the explicit social satire of "Roosters" remained a rarity for Bishop. More significant for the future of her work was "The Fish," one of her best known poems, which points the way from *North & South* to the major poems of her next book, *A Cold Spring*. Without being at all didactic or abstract—few poems could be more thoroughly concrete—"The Fish" suggests an entire aesthetic and ethic of observation, which would become central to Bishop's work.

The poem begins as a simple anecdote: "I caught a tremendous fish." But if the conventional fish story is a boast—the size of the catch proves the prowess of the hunter—Bishop immediately disavows any such heroism: "He hadn't fought at all," she admits. And once the fish is caught, the poet is drawn, as though helplessly, to a minute observation of her prey. For dozens of lines, Bishop devotes her skill entirely to describing the fish as it really is, so that she herself almost disappears from view. When the poem's "I" does appear, it is not to express an emotion or idea, but always to observe: "I looked," "I saw," "I stared and stared." This total attention allows such beautiful strokes of imagery as the skin "hung in strips / like ancient wallpaper," or the eyes like "tarnished tinfoil."

Those eyes are seen with wonderful precision, but as Bishop is at pains to acknowledge, they do not see back; she resolutely refuses to grant the fish any anthropomorphic feelings or symbolic significance, and insists that it is simply "an object." The fish has been preserved in its reticent composure: it has been seen, not used. And this respect for things seen is what motivates and justifies the poem's famous conclusion. The poet notices that the fish has old hooks in his jaw, evidence that he has eluded capture five times before. She has succeeded, that is, where other fishermen have failed; and at first it seems that she is willing to indulge the egotism of victory:

> *I stared and stared*
> *and victory filled up*
> *the little rented boat . . .*
> *. . . . .*
> *until everything*
> *was rainbow, rainbow, rainbow!*

If the poem ended here, then the meaning of "victory" would be unambiguous: it would mean her capture of the fish. Still more important, all of Bishop's careful description would be revealed as a more sophisticated form of predation. The poet would have "captured" the fish in her language as surely as she captured it with hook and line; she would be making it an opportunity for the display of her own skill. But with the swift, simple reversal of the last line, Bishop turns the poem into something entirely different: "And I let the fish go."

Bishop's "victory" has suddenly become a much richer and subtler thing. It is still the victory of having caught the fish, and of having so completely described it; but it is also, and still more, the victory of letting it go. To interpret this conclusion merely as a protest against cruelty to animals would be to miss Bishop's more valuable meaning (after all, it is safe to assume that she has kept and eaten many fish before this one). Rather, "The Fish" speaks on the level of aesthetic ethics—the responsibility of the poet to the things she sees. Bishop recognizes that to keep faith with the natural world means not to force our motives on it, not to take pride of ownership, but patiently to submit to its foreignness. If nature provokes an emotional response, even one as joyous as Bishop's "victory," the responsible writer must acknowledge that this emotion is hers, not nature's. By refusing to turn the fish to her own purposes, Bishop signals her rejection of the imperious, mythmaking imagination of the Modernist masters.

"THE FISH" INAUGURATES Elizabeth Bishop's major poetry, and in doing so raises a new set of problems and themes, which will dominate *A Cold Spring*. This small collection—when it was first published in 1955, it was combined with the poems of *North & South* to create a bulkier book—contains three of Bishop's major poems, "The Bight," "At the Fishhouses," and "Over 2,000 Illustrations and a Complete Concordance." With their careful visual description, conversational tone, and vast reserve, they define Bishop's middle style. At the same time, the volume contains several poems that show Bishop experimenting with a more direct and emotional kind of statement, almost but not quite of the kind associated with confessional poetry. Having achieved a mature, distinctive style, Bishop's poetic challenge would be to find the right balance between reserve and confession, observation and emotion.

The insight of "The Fish" was that description is most effective when it has no overt designs on the reader—when meaning is allowed to emerge indirectly, instead of being imposed in the manner of the objective correlative. But Bishop had also made clear, in her debate with Moore over "Roosters," that she would not be content with elaborating description to the point of baroqueness; her poems would be personal and historical, not timeless and abstract. The conflict of these impulses produces the poems of Bishop's middle period, giving them a remarkably fraught poise, but also occasionally tipping them over into sentimentality.

"The Bight" represents Bishop's furthest extreme of reserve. It is entirely composed of the kind of description that led Anne Stevenson, in one of the earliest critical studies of Bishop, to write that "In her long, descriptive poems, particularly, there are passages which are so exact that they seem to strain to be poetry at all." Of course, the illusion that the poet is not being literary is only made possible by a careful evasion of literariness—of her acquired sense of what poetry is supposed to sound like. Indeed, it took some of Bishop's contemporaries much longer to break free of those inherited expectations. But she is already a long way from "The Man-Moth," and from Marianne Moore, in "The Bight":

> At low tide like this how sheer the water is.
> White, crumbling ribs of marl protrude and glare
> and the boats are dry, the pilings dry as matches.
> Absorbing, rather than being absorbed,
> the water in the bight doesn't wet anything,
> the color of the gas flame turned as low as possible.

This is exact description from which the "I" has been purged: the poet simply notices. At least, that is the reader's first impression. On closer inspection, however, it is clear that Bishop's metaphors, though inconspicuous, are creating a definite emotional tone. The pilings "dry as matches" seem to be in perilous proximity to the water that resembles a "gas flame"; the water itself seems unnatural, dry instead of wet. The same quiet menace infects the animals in the scene, which are tagged with mechanical, violent verbs: the pelicans "crash" into the water "like pick-axes," the birds "open their tails like scissors." Yet Bishop refuses to take responsibility for this uncanniness by openly identifying herself as its source. She eludes the reader's grasp, leaving behind a world obscurely tainted with menace. The effect is similar to, but far subtler than, the surreal atmospherics of her early fables.

Bishop's strategy in "The Bight" is underscored by one of the rare literary allusions in her poetry, her seemingly gratuitous mention of Baudelaire: "One can smell it turning to gas; if one were Baudelaire / one could probably hear it turning to marimba music." This is a parody of the idea of synesthesia—the merging or unity of the senses, so that a smell can produce a sound, or a sound an image. Later on in the poem, Bishop again alludes to this idea, covertly, in the line: "The bight is littered with old correspondences." Ostensibly, this refers to the image of the previous lines, comparing boats wrecked in a storm to "torn-open, unanswered letters." But "correspondences" is also the title of the poem in which Baudelaire makes his classic statement of synesthesia, where "forests of symbols" address the poet with "confused words," and "perfumes, colors and sounds correspond." Baudelairean nature speaks, though confusedly; it makes sensual experience a code that the poet, in visionary moments, can half-understand. This is the foundation of the Symbolist poetics that inspired the Modernist generation, especially Yeats and Eliot, who created mystically eloquent symbols like the Rose and the Waste Land.

"The Bight," however, evacuates this Symbolist language through understatement and mockery. The "correspondences" Bishop sees in the bight are old, "worn-out"; they are "littered," like useless trash; and they fail to communicate, like "unanswered letters." And because the landscape says nothing itself, it can be made to say anything the observer wants, as Bishop wryly acknowledges in the poem's last lines:

All the untidy activity continues,
awful but cheerful.

Clearly Bishop has been making the bight seem awful, but at the last minute she admits that everything—the water, the birds, the boats—could just as well be called cheerful. The banality of the words—"awful," "cheerful"—is a form of self-mockery, exposing the threadbareness of the emotions we project onto a nature that knows nothing of them.

Nevertheless, "The Bight" chooses awful over cheerful; as though despite herself, Bishop is telling the reader something about her sickness of spirit. Indeed, the obliquity and indirectness of the poem are so extreme that the poet seems to be doing penance for hinting at her unhappiness at all. It is as though, to excuse herself for giving voice to inner experience, she must pay elaborate obeisance to the outer world.

Yet at the same time, Bishop makes in this very poem a recklessly sentimental personal statement, though it is scrupulously segregated from the poem proper. It is the subtitle, in small type and parentheses: "On my birthday." This little puncture threatens to collapse Bishop's whole structure of evasion, giving the suffering that "The Bight" barely expresses an all too banal cause: the ordinary grief of getting older. It is only because Bishop is usually so restrained that such a moment of self-exposure seems damaging, as it would not in a poet like Berryman. When self-pity invades Bishop's poetry, as it does in the subtitle of "The Bight" and at a few other significant moments, it carries the shock of the return of the repressed.

Another such moment comes at the end of "At the Fishhouses," the second major poem in *A Cold Spring*. Like "The Bight," it is a painstaking description of a landscape: in this case, the seaside fishermen's huts of Bishop's native Nova Scotia. The poem's first section carefully records the details of the scene: the codfish smell in the air, the peaked roofs of the fishhouses, the silver reflection of the sea. Once again, the poet's ego seems to have been stubbed out in the mass of details.

With the second stanza, however, "At the Fishhouses" takes on a more anxious motion:

> *Down at the water's edge, at the place*
> *where they haul up the boats, up the long ramp*
> *descending into the water, thin silver*
> *tree trunks are laid horizontally*
> *across the gray stones, down and down*
> *at intervals of four or five feet.*

Bishop has still not inserted herself into the poem. Yet as in "The Bight," but even more subtly, the landscape begins to tremble with her suppressed emotion. The prepositions in this passage are agitated: the poet's (and the reader's) gaze is first directed "down" to the water, then retreats "up the long ramp"; but the ramp itself repeats the downward motion, "descending into the water." The poem then turns away from the water again, to take note of the tree trunks laid across the ramp; but once again it travels "down and down," as though being pulled to the water's edge.

The poet's downward gaze connects with the water, shockingly, in the first line of the next stanza:

Cold dark deep and absolutely clear,
element bearable to no mortal,
to fish and to seals . . .

All at once, we understand the poet's reluctance to look at the water: it is, for her, the element of death. As if for self-protection, she immediately begins to withdraw from it once again; she reminds herself that the water is in fact bearable to some mortals, fish and seals, and goes off on a whimsical tangent about a seal she has seen in the water. Yet the deathly refrain returns, only to be fended off once again:

Cold dark deep and absolutely clear,
the clear gray icy water . . . Back, behind us,
the dignified tall firs begin.

That "back" is no longer just a preposition; it has become an imperative, a command breaking the poem's hypnotic focus on the water. Bishop seems to retreat from an encounter with her own overpowering feeling by grasping at the details of the outer world: the seal, the fir trees. Yet once again her attention is drawn back, obsessively, to the water, and this time the unspoken threat of drowning is allowed to come to consciousness: "If you tasted it, it would first taste bitter, / then briny, then surely burn your tongue."

The rhythm of the suicidal impulse, so quietly embodied in the poem, has built to a crescendo in which the suicide is imaginatively consummated. And yet all this has been done without a mention of the word "suicide," almost without a first-person pronoun: Bishop seems to hold her own words at a distance, thus increasing the sense that they are uttered out of an irresistible compulsion. The terror of "At the Fishhouses" is the terror of "The Unbeliever"—where the sea "wants to destroy us all"—muted and naturalized, and thus made all the more effective. Indeed, the poem's epigraph could be Bishop's remark, in her essay "Efforts at Affection," that "there is an element of mortal panic and fear underlying all works of art."

Only at the very end of the poem does Bishop break her careful spell. The passage is one of the most famous in Bishop's work, celebrated for its urgent eloquence:

> *It is like what we imagine knowledge to be:*
> *dark, salt, clear, moving, utterly free,*
> *drawn from the cold hard mouth*
> *of the world, derived from the rocky breasts*
> *forever, flowing and drawn, and since*
> *our knowledge is historical, flowing and flown.*

But while the lines make sense as detachable formulations, and provide a rhythmic climax to the poem, they do not finally provide an adequate conclusion to what has gone before. The sea, until these last lines, has been simply the sea, as indifferent and resistant to metaphor as the fish in "The Fish." If there is an insinuating terror in the "clear gray icy water," it is because the whole seascape has been colored by the poet's nearly hidden compulsion and dread. But now the sea is drafted into service as a metaphor for "knowledge," and neither knowledge nor the sea benefits from the comparison. Concretely, Bishop's description of the sea as "flown" and "drawn" seems inapt: a river flows, well water can be drawn, but the ocean simply repeats itself, and thus seems an awkward symbol for transitoriness. At the same time, the abstraction "knowledge" is not made more meaningful by assigning it two more abstractions, especially when they are as contradictory as "utterly free" and "historical." It is hard to avoid the conclusion that, in these plangent lines, Bishop is not resolving "At the Fishhouses" but actually refusing a resolution that might be too terrible to be portrayed.

"At the Fishhouses" is undoubtedly one of Bishop's best poems, but its doubtful conclusion—like the sentimental subtitle of "The Bight"—betrays the limits of her indirect, descriptive method. In each case, the suffering ego has been so rigorously excluded that there is no room for the cry it yearns to utter; to complete itself, the poem must betray itself. And Bishop was more than just conscious of this limitation of her style: she went so far as to make it the theme of the third major poem in *A Cold Spring*, "Over 2,000 Illustrations and a Complete Concordance."

Here Bishop links her concern with seeing, which has dominated her work since "The Fish," with the experience of travel, which will increasingly provide her subjects. By the early 1950s, Bishop was already an experienced traveler—she had spent several years in Europe in the 1930s, and shuttled between New York, Key West, Mexico, and elsewhere in the 1940s. In "Over 2,000 Illustrations," however, Bishop sounds the questioning note that will echo through all her poems on travel, culminating in the final disillusionment of "Crusoe in England." The title refers to a

picture book for children, full of mythological scenes from the
Bible and antiquity: the Seven Wonders of the World, the Sepul-
cher of Christ. These images, described in the poem's first section,
are essentially different from the mere "sights" that tourists
thoughtlessly consume; their importance is not just how they
look but what they mean. Indeed, the world itself, viewed
through a Christian lens, is a kind of book, whose author is God;
the biblical holy places are charged with meaning, marked with
"God's spreading fingerprint."

By comparison, Bishop complains, her own travels have been
lacking in weight, as the opening line suggests: "Thus should
have been our travels: / serious, engravable." Instead, as the
poem's second section goes on to detail, they are random and sordid. In Mexico there is a "dead man" surrounded by "dead volcanoes"; in Dingle harbor, the ships are "rotting hulks"; and in
Marrakesh the travelers are surrounded by "little pockmarked
prostitutes" begging for cigarettes. The poem names sights on
three continents, but their very abundance mocks their lack of
inner structure and meaning: "Everything only connected by
'and' and 'and.' " The empty accumulation of sightseeing has
become a metaphor for vision itself. It is in this sense that Bishop,
instinctively returning to the Christian imagery of this poem,
agreed with a correspondent decades later that "being so fearfully,
automatically 'observant' can be a 'Calvary.' "

The ordeal of vision could only be redeemed if, like Jesus's Calvary, it were part of a larger Providence. To be meaningful, the
world should not have the "and" logic of sight, but the "so that"
logic of narrative. Bishop had renounced that kind of symbolic
seeing as far back as "The Fish," and she proved the bleak power
of her own chastened vision in "The Bight" and "At the Fish-

houses." But in the final section of "Over 2,000 Illustrations," Bishop returns nostalgically to the mythic vision of the children's book, with its illustration of the Holy Family. "Why couldn't we have seen / this old Nativity . . . ?" she laments. Only a sight of such vast significance could have held and satisfied the poet's wandering gaze, as the last line implies: "and looked and looked our infant sight away." The inevitable secret wish of this consummate observer is to be freed of the burden of seeing.

IN LATE 1951, Bishop traveled to Rio de Janeiro on what was meant to be the first leg of a South American tour. Unexpectedly, however, she fell in love with a Brazilian woman, Lota de Macedo Soares, and began a fifteen-year residence in Brazil that would transform her writing. Bishop's new life had the effect of splitting her work into two streams. The shallower and more colorful of these is her poetry about Brazil, in which the country's landscape, people, and mythology are often charmingly displayed. But Bishop's Brazilian-themed poems usually exercise her gift for description without evoking the depths that, in "At the Fish-houses" or "The Bight," give the surfaces their intensity. She herself was aware of this danger, writing to Robert Lowell in 1960 that "I'm going to turn into solid cuteness in my poetry if I don't watch out—or if I do watch out."

There is also, in Bishop's poems about Brazil, frequently a tone of condescension toward the natives—never genuinely mean-spirited, but sufficient to mark out Bishop as an outsider among the people she describes. "Manuelzinho" and "House Guest" make fun of Brazilian servants in a way that would never pass muster if the poems had an American setting. And "Squatter's Children," a Wordsworthian lyric about desperately poor children caught in a storm, concludes on a complacent note that recalls the old joke about how, in a democracy, the rich and the poor are equally free to sleep under a bridge: "wet and beguiled, you stand among / the mansions you may choose / out of a bigger house than yours, / whose lawfulness endures."

As the title of her third book, *Questions of Travel* (1965), suggests, the best of Bishop's Brazil poems are those in which travel itself is the subject, rather than the things seen. "Arrival at Santos," dated January 1952—just after her ship docked in the Brazilian port—raises the question of whether this new voyage will offer any more lasting satisfaction than those catalogued in "Over 2,000 Illustrations": "Oh tourist, / is this how this country is going to answer you // and your immodest demands for a different world, / and a better life . . . ?" Landscape, Bishop suggests, even the gorgeous tropical landscape of Brazil, can never be essentially satisfying, no matter how carefully it is observed. In "Brazil, January 1, 1502," Bishop imagines that for the first European explorers, as for her, the "big leaves, little leaves, and giant leaves, / blue, blue-green, and olive" only conceal a country as elusive as its native Indians, "retreating, always retreating" from the newcomer.

Bishop's doubts are given their fullest statement in the book's title poem, "Questions of Travel." Here the questions that remained implicit in "Over 2,000 Illustrations" are brought into the open, in a conversational style that seems to be the poet's own speaking voice:

Should we have stayed at home and thought of here? . . .
. . . .
What childishness is it that while there's a breath of life

in our bodies, we are determined to rush
to see the sun the other way around?

In the second stanza, Bishop strengthens the case against travel by deliberately trivializing what Brazil has to offer into a Ripley's Believe It or Not of oddities, like "the tiniest green hummingbird in the world." The local "stonework" becomes a metaphor for all the sights available to the traveler: no matter how "delightful" it may be to look at, it remains permanently foreign, "impenetrable." Bishop then goes on to give the other side of the argument, making a list of the genuinely splendid things she has experienced in Brazil: the trees "robed in pink," the song of the "fat brown bird," the hours of rain followed by "sudden golden silence." And yet the most she finds it possible to say about these things is that "it would have been a pity" not to have seen them—a meager affirmation not far removed from apathy.

If the most exotic spectacles the world has to offer are just things that one might as well see, then the world is essentially barren. The race for novelty, Bishop suggests, is really a sign that the traveler is looking outside herself for something that only she can supply: it is not imagination but *lack of imagination that makes us come / to imagined places.* True imagination, as Bishop's early influence Wallace Stevens wrote in "Stars at Tallapoosa," resides in the eye that sees, not the objects that it looks at: "The body is no body to be seen / But is an eye that studies its black lid." And the black lid could just as easily be contemplated in Hartford as in Tallapoosa, in New York as in Rio de Janeiro.

This paradox explains why, living in Brazil, Bishop wrote her best poems and prose about Nova Scotia, her childhood home. "It is funny," she wrote, "to come to Brazil to experience total

recall about Nova Scotia." The readiness with which she abandoned America for Brazil suggests that Bishop's love of travel had
never been just a curiosity about new places, but also, more
painfully, a result of having no place to go. Now, thanks to Lota,
Bishop had found at the age of forty-one the safe harbor that was
denied her as a child. And this newfound security allowed her to
write about her painful early experiences more directly than ever
before. Starting in the early 1950s, and increasingly until her
death in 1979, Bishop would cast off the indirection, the intense
sublimation, of her middle period.

This development shows Bishop taking part in her generation's
common movement toward a more self-revelatory and autobiographical style. But in her letters and public statements, Bishop
never ceased to disapprove of confessional poetry, condemning
the trend toward "more and more anguish and less and less
poetry. Surely never in all the ages has poetry been so personal
and confessional—and I don't think it is what I like, really. . . ."
And Bishop was never to engage in the kind of confession where
the most shameful and painful experiences—madness, drunkenness, lust—are presented as the most authentic. Readers of her
poems would never know what readers of her letters and biographies have since discovered; her alcoholism, her sexual experiences, her bouts of severe depression never become subjects for
poetry. Yet the example of other poets—above all Lowell, who
was her close lifelong friend—was surely another factor in
encouraging Bishop to move from the indirection of "At the Fishhouses" to the childhood recollection of poems like "In the Waiting Room" and "First Death in Nova Scotia."

Bishop's first major work of recall was the story "In the Village." She wrote it in just two days and nights, a pace that suggests the sudden eruption of something just below the surface.

Typically for Bishop, however, even this almost completely autobiographical story is very oblique. Told from the point of view of a child, "In the Village" allows its central fact—the madness of the girl's mother—to appear only indirectly. The mother's periodic stays in a sanitarium are told in a childish shorthand: "First, she had come home, with her child. Then she had gone away again, alone, and left the child. Then she had come home. Then she had gone away again, with her sister; and now she was home again." And the terrifying fact of her madness is not so much depicted as symbolized in the single, unexplained scream the mother gives while trying on a dress: "The dress was all wrong. She screamed. The child vanishes." The child vanishes by leaving the room, but Bishop means more: in that scream and what it represents, her childhood itself vanished.

From the point of view of Bishop's development as a poet, the most significant moment in "In the Village" comes at the very end, after the narrator's mother has been sent away, finally, to an insane asylum. In a richly symbolic passage, Bishop counterpoints the memory of her mother's scream with the "clang" made by the kind blacksmith, Nate, hammering out horseshoes:

Clang.
Clang.
Nate is shaping a horseshoe.
Oh, beautiful pure sound!
It turns everything else to silence . . .
Now there is no scream. Once there was one and it settled slowly down to earth one hot summer afternoon; or did it float up, into that dark, too dark, blue sky? But surely it has gone away, forever.

The blacksmith, with his purposeful, constructive craft, is the only one capable of banishing the destructive chaos of the scream. In just the same way, Bishop's art had always striven to contain and sublimate feeling into conscious artistry: from the fables of "The Man-Moth" and "The Unbeliever" to the landscapes of "At the Fishhouses" and "The Bight," Bishop's poetry is a scream translated into a clang. The desperate quality of her attention makes even her quietest and most objective poems more dramatic than the confessional outpourings of other writers. She gives the perfect emblem of her technique in the modestly assured "Sandpiper":

> The world is a mist. And then the world is
> minute and vast and clear. The tide
> is higher or lower. He couldn't tell you which.
> His beak is focussed; he is preoccupied,
>
> looking for something, something, something.
> Poor bird, he is obsessed!
> The millions of grains are black, white, tan, and gray,
> mixed with quartz grains, rose and amethyst.

Whenever we encounter, in Bishop's most successful poems, a minute description of the sort she condenses here—the seemingly egoless observation of "black, white, tan, and gray"—we are also aware of the shattering alternations of the tide, which periodically threaten to drown the sandpiper-poet. Only her obsessive, ultimately hopeless attention to the outer world allows her to survive.

Appropriately, "In the Village" was published in the middle of *Questions of Travel*, dividing the first section, "Brazil," from the second, "Elsewhere." For the revelations of that story inaugurate a new direction for Bishop's work, from the "Elsewhere" poems to the nine poems of her brief last book, *Geography III*, and the posthumously published poems, including the brilliant "Sonnet." Freed by her new life and the changing times to be more directly personal—though always decorous, and by contrast to her contemporaries positively reticent—Bishop wrote the best poems of her final period.

Her characteristic method of revealing and concealing at once is demonstrated in "Sestina," whose very title is a deliberately neutral replacement for the original "Early Sorrow." The sestina, an elaborately patterned poem in which the last words of each line repeat themselves in a predetermined order, is one of the most complex forms in English verse. And it is to this elaborate artifice that Bishop turns for what might otherwise be an overwhelmingly sentimental poem, a vignette of an orphaned child with her weeping grandmother. Though Bishop never identifies the child—even its gender is not specified—reading "In the Village" makes it inevitable that we see it as the poet herself.

"Sestina" has the atmosphere of one of Bishop's earliest poems, uncanny quietness concealing an indistinct menace. We are left to deduce nearly everything about the child and the grandmother: the absence of parents suggests that the child is an orphan, as do the grandmother's unexplained tears. What is beyond doubt is the universal air of hopeless sorrow, which extends to inanimate objects: "*It was to be*, says the Marvel Stove. / *I know what I know*, says the almanac." In this atmosphere, even the child's drawing of a "rigid house" suggests that something has gone wrong, as though the rigidity were a sign of the child's desperate need for order. The excessively ordered form of the sestina, Bishop unmistakably suggests, is the same kind of rigidity, to which the grown child is forced to turn.

IN 1967, AFTER years of increasing discord, the refuge Bishop had found in Brazil finally collapsed with the suicide of Lota de Macedo Soares. For the last twelve years of her life, Bishop resumed her migrations, moving between San Francisco, Brazil, New York, Maine, and Seattle, until she finally settled in Boston as a teacher of creative writing at Harvard. Of course, none of these events appears directly in her poems; Bishop was not about to begin writing nakedly autobiographical poetry of the kind she detested when it came from her peers and students. In fact, the worst strain in her friendship with Robert Lowell came in the early 1970s, when she was appalled by Lowell's use of private letters in *The Dolphin*. Yet to know the painful facts of Bishop's life is to be all the more struck by the evolution of her verse. Her last poems are an unsparingly intimate, yet impersonal and immensely controlled, investigation of suffering.

The closest Bishop ever came to writing the sort of poem Lowell had perfected in *Life Studies* is "In the Waiting Room." Here we find the unambiguously autobiographical "I," the proper names and dates, and the fraught childhood experience that are standard in confessional poetry. Yet, characteristically, Bishop does not turn to a moment of degradation or madness, as in Lowell's "Waking in the Blue." Rather, she chronicles a moment of existential awakening, in which suffering is revealed to be not the result of an injury inflicted by fate or family, but a part of the very structure of human life.

The poem takes pains to ground its revelation in fact. The incident it describes is given a place—Worcester, Massachusetts—

and a date—February 5, 1918, three days before Bishop's seventh birthday. As though offering evidence, Bishop takes care to tell us what was in the *National Geographic* for that month. All of this detail sets the stage for the young girl's sudden eruption of self-consciousness, which is above all a consciousness of living in time:

> *I said to myself: three days*
> *and you'll be seven years old.*
> *I was saying it to stop*
> *the sensation of falling off*
> *the round, turning world*
> *into cold, blue-black space.*
> *But I felt: you are an* I,
> *you are an* Elizabeth,
> *you are one of* them. . . .

The setting helps to provoke this epiphany: the "horrifying" sexual images seen in the magazine and the aunt's cry of pain in the dentist's chair are both reminders of the grim facts of bodily existence. But what the young girl feels is not contingent on any particular injury: it is a knowledge that comes to every "I" simply because it is an "I." In spirit, then, "In the Waiting Room"—for all its diaristic accuracy—is actually anticonfessional. The poem does not claim to be significant because it tells of something that happened to Elizabeth Bishop; it is significant because what happened to Bishop happens to all of us.

"In the Waiting Room" appeared in *Geography III* (1976), Bishop's last and shortest book. The volume's spareness seems a fitting reflection of the general spareness of Bishop's work, just as its individual poems recapitulate the major themes of her entire career. Though she continued to write after it was published, and produced one of her best poems in the last year of her life, *Geography III* stands as Bishop's last statement on some of her major subjects: travel and vision, reticence and loss.

Robinson Crusoe, the classic lonely traveler, was a natural, even inevitable subject for Bishop. It is almost as though, knowing this, she deliberately saved it for the end of her life. For as early as 1934, staying in primitive quarters on Cuttyhunk Island, Massachusetts, Bishop was already thinking poetically about Crusoe:

> . . . it is fun to be in a difficult situation for a few hours, in which you have to make clothes out of barrells [sic], tie machinery together with strings, eat berries, etc. On an island you live all the time in this Robinson Crusoe atmosphere, making this do for that, and contriving and inventing. . . . A poem should be made about making things in a pinch—& how it looks sad when the emergency is over.

Bishop has made a Crusoe in her own image; his artistry becomes, like her own, a last-ditch response to an emergency. And when she came to write "Crusoe in England," more than thirty years later, this is exactly how Bishop approached the story: after the emergency is over, when the exhilaration of survival is gone and only the detritus remains. The poem is also an example of how circumspectly Bishop deploys her own life in verse: the parallel between Crusoe returned to England from his island and Bishop returned to America from Brazil is obvious, to those who know her biography, but it is nowhere mentioned in the poem itself.

The poem is spoken by Crusoe as he reminisces about his island, but it is the opposite of nostalgic. Just as in her earlier poems of landscape and travel, from "Over 2,000 Illustrations" through "Questions of Travel," Bishop deliberately deflates the things her narrator has seen. Crusoe's island has volcanoes, but they are "miserable, small"; the sky is "mostly overcast," a "dump" for "left-over clouds." Only the waterspouts earn a magical description—"flexible, attenuated, / sacerdotal beings of glass"— but even they are dismissed as "not much company." Once more, Bishop tells us that travel's promises are false, that it does not expand our horizons but narrows them:

> *The sun set in the sea; the same odd sun*
> *rose from the sea,*
> *and there was one of it and one of me.*

The central experience of Crusoe's travels is not adventure or beauty but loneliness. Bishop emphasizes the point with a literary joke, when Crusoe tries to recite Wordsworth's "Daffodils" but can't remember the words: " 'They flash upon that inward eye, / which is the bliss . . . ' The bliss of what?" Ironically, the missing word is "solitude": Bishop's poem is, among other things, a rebuttal of the Wordsworthian idealization of solitude. Far from being a blissful daydream, it is the dream of reason that produces monsters:

> *I'd have*
> *nightmares of other islands*
> *stretching away from mine, infinities*
> *of islands, islands spawning islands . . .*
> *. . . . .*

knowing that I had to live
on each and every one, eventually,
for ages, registering their flora,
their fauna, their geography.

Here again is the "Calvary" of being observant, "everything only connected by 'and' and 'and.' " The one thing that might conceivably break through this tedium is love, genuine contact with another human being. But Bishop is as reserved about Crusoe's love life as she is about her own. What the poem says about Friday, Crusoe's only companion, is virtually a parody of reticence: "Friday was nice. / Friday was nice, and we were friends." Any further revelation is instantly forestalled by Crusoe himself, who seems in a hurry to pass it over: "And then one day they came and took us off."

Just how empty the whole adventure has been only becomes clear when Crusoe returns to England, and realizes that there is no essential difference between the British Isles and his tiny desert island. The real source of Crusoe's isolation (the word derives from the Latin *isola*, island) was internal: "my brain / bred islands." As Milton's Satan knew, "The mind is its own place, and of itself / Can make a heaven of hell, a hell of heaven." And the artifacts of Crusoe's island sojourn—those things made "in a pinch," to which Bishop referred in 1934—are meaningless in retrospect: "The living soul has dribbled away." "Crusoe in England" is Bishop's reply to her own "question of travel"—"Should we have stayed at home and thought of here?"—and her answer is worse than "yes" or "no." It is that, finally, it doesn't matter.

And yet this is not quite the last word. "Poem," as its title suggests, is more than just another poem; it is the closest Bishop comes to a statement of her artistic aims. (To make the point clear, she changed the title to "Poem" from the more descriptive "Small Painting.") Like so many of Bishop's poems before it, "Poem" begins with a slow, careful description: in this case, of a painting by her great-uncle, "about the size of an old-style dollar bill," which depicts a Nova Scotia scene. Suddenly, Bishop realizes that she knows the scene: it is the same meadow and steeple that she also grew up seeing, generations later. And this coincidence suggests a motive for seeing that has never before entered Bishop's verse. Until now, Bishop has always considered vision a refuge from interiority—a temporary refuge that is doomed to fail. But the small painting offers another understanding:

> *Our visions coincided—"visions" is*
> *too serious a word—our looks, two looks:*
> *art "copying from life" and life itself,*
> *life and the memory of it so compressed*
> *they've turned into each other.*

Her great-uncle recorded what he saw so that she could one day share it; they are brought together, indirectly, but with surprising intimacy. In "Poem," for the first time, Bishop can understand her vision—or, to use her characteristically unpretentious word, her "look"—not as a self-defense or an escape, but as a witnessing and a gift. It is a beautiful conception, all the more moving for its emergence so late in Bishop's painful experience of seeing.

"Crusoe in England," "In the Waiting Room," and "Poem" are Bishop's ultimate statements on the themes that drove her art from the beginning. But there remain two poems, written in her last decade, which seem to transcend any period; they have a precision, economy, and inevitability that can be called classical. The first, "One Art," from *Geography III*, is probably her best-known poem; the other, "Sonnet," included in the posthumous *Complete Poems*, is her most surprisingly perfect.

Bishop's most characteristic poems are anxiously indirect, allowing her to evade the confessional mode while still harnessing its energies. But in "One Art," the usual opposition between personal and impersonal falls away, or simply fails to arise. The poem's "I" speaks forthrightly, and the details, as a reader familiar with Bishop's biography can tell, come straight from her own life. Yet the concision and confidence of Bishop's language, and the universality of her theme, make even these contingent details seem like symbols. The very form of the poem—it is a villanelle, like the sestina an extremely strict form—tends to evacuate self-expression in favor of a craftsman's discipline. In form, mood, and theme, "One Art" is an epitome of Bishop's work, so that the title takes on a double meaning: it refers not just to the "art of losing," but to Bishop's own unitary, consistent art, in which loss is controlled and redeemed.

"One Art" begins by seeming to deprecate the very notion of loss. The first line, which in accordance with the villanelle form will be repeated throughout the poem, proposes this theme: "The art of losing isn't hard to master." And the third line—whose last word will be repeated at the end of alternate stanzas—reaffirms that "loss is no disaster." Yet by placing the word "disaster" in this terminal position, Bishop ensures that it has to come back, again and again, throughout the poem—and what's more, that it will be the poem's literal last word. In its very form, then, "One Art" enacts its subject, and the subject of Bishop's best work throughout her life: the attempt to integrate "disaster" into the order of poetry.

Bishop creates a dramatic forward movement, within the repetitions of the villanelle, by steadily increasing the volume of loss from stanza to stanza. First it is merely the "fluster" of "lost door keys, the hour badly spent"; then the loss of words and memories, "places, and names." In the third stanza, the poem's urgency is ratcheted up by a sudden switch from the second person to the first: "I lost my mother's watch." With this, the scale of losses begins to shoot up alarmingly, like Alice in Wonderland: houses, cities, realms, rivers, a continent. All these "losses" can be interpreted biographically—the "three loved houses," for instance, are Bishop's residences in Samambaia, Rio de Janeiro, and Ouro Preto, Brazil—but the effect is as impersonal as a fairy tale. Yet through all these increasing losses, Bishop's deprecation of loss returns, as the form demands: "it wasn't a disaster."

The form demands, also, that the two refrains will be united in the last stanza. Bishop responds to this formal challenge by making her sense of loss itself redouble, and nearly—but not quite—burst the poem's composure. By placing the loss of "you" last in the poem's ascending series, Bishop implies that "losing you" will be a loss still worse than realms and continents; it is a paradox that movingly expresses the dearness of "you," and gives the reader the sense that the whole poem has been inevitably moving to just this point. But this loss, too, the poem promises to control, bringing back the same refrain, with a slight difference:

the art of losing's not too hard to master
though it may look like (Write it!) like disaster.

The loss of "you," alone of all the poem's losses, makes the speaker hesitate, and threaten to break off the poem in an excess of grief. The italics and parentheses of "*Write* it!" have the effect of an indrawn breath, a self-command; the poet is whipping herself over this last, nearly insuperable barrier, to complete the poem and the structure of endurance that it represents. Bishop's control of the villanelle form is so sure, and the form itself is so rigid, that this slight interjection produces a great dramatic effect. And yet the poem does resolve itself, and proceeds to its foreordained conclusion. Once again, Bishop suggests, she will contain loss in art, the scream in the clang—but only barely.

"One Art" is Bishop's most emblematic poem, but it does not have the privilege of the final word. That belongs to "Sonnet," the last of the finished, published poems in her *Complete Poems.* "Sonnet" is very unlike most of Bishop's work, in its truncated lines and compressed, Dickinsonian idiom, but still more in its delighted resolution. Starting with a simple, explosive "Caught," Bishop offers two symbols of constraint: the "bubble / in the spirit-level," permanently trapped, and the "compass needle / wobbling and wavering," never able to decide on a single course. These are fitting icons of Bishop's work: the bubble is trapped like the Unbeliever on his mast or Crusoe on his island, the needle is as uncertain as the Sandpiper.

But then "Sonnet" leaps away, with the single word "Freed," to a realm of unconstraint mostly unknown to Bishop's poetry. Here the emblems are the "broken / thermometer's mercury," spilled and freely flowing, and the "rainbow-bird" that escapes from the mirror—either because it has flown away out of sight, or, more mysteriously and somehow more appropriately, because the reflection itself has made its way out of the mirror. These are by no means placid images: once out of the thermometer mercury is useless and poisonous, while the bird escapes the mirror only through some uncanny sleight-of-hand. Unmistakably, these are symbols of the same type of freedom that the soul wins by leaving the body at death—a freedom that is also a loss.

But this ambivalence does not diminish the unexpected delight of the poem's last word: "gay." Of course, it would be a mistake to ignore the implication of homosexuality, in a writer so careful of nuance. For Bishop to pronounce the word "gay," as the last word of her last poem, is an affirmation of the lesbianism she almost never allowed to appear in her work. But the largest, the final meaning is the old-fashioned one: gaiety is the lightness of spirit so rarely evident in Bishop's serious poetry. The final exclamation point underlines her excitement at using the word, for the first and last time. At the very end of Bishop's life and work, we see clearly the saving joy of creation that she once described: "It seems to me *it's* the whole purpose of art, to the artist (not to the audience)—that rare feeling of control, illumination—life *is* all right, for the time being."

JOHN BERRYMAN

To become ourselves we are these wayward things

In 1960, John Berryman received an award for promising writers. To a forty-five-year-old poet who had been writing for a quarter of a century, this was a bittersweet honor: "it was far from agreeable to me to accept an award, in particular so publicly, as 'promising.' *Promising.* I did so," Berryman wrote with characteristic wry realism, "with many misgivings and much gall and a bitter smile, because I had to have the money." Twelve years later he would be dead, yet it is true that, in 1960, his significant work was still to come. As he himself later wrote:

my orders were sealed:
at forty nearly when I took them out
I gave a joyless shout.

Joyless because fulfillment came so late, after decades of frustrated ambition; but also because his great subject, when he found it, would be his own fears and failures. Even more than Lowell's or Plath's, Berryman's poetry is harrowingly intimate. Yet while he is usually considered one of the chief confessional poets, it is only in his flawed, very late work that he uses poetry simply to expose his traumas. In fact, Berryman's best poetry—especially the two volumes of *The Dream Songs*, published in 1964 and 1968—never simply mirrors his life, since his life was itself profoundly shaped by the demands of his poetry. None of his contemporaries better illustrates the deeply ambiguous relationship between a poet's private experience and the public language of art.

If no poet of Berryman's generation broke so violently with established poetic models, it is partly because none had such a long and dedicated apprenticeship in the dominant Modernist style. As a student at Columbia University, Berryman had the mixed fortune to come under the tutelage of highly influential poet-critics like Mark Van Doren and R. P. Blackmur. As a result, his fierce ambition was poured from the start into the rigorous and impersonal mold established by his teachers. As he wrote in the late, heavily ironic poem "Olympus," he made Blackmur in particular into a "Law-giver," a "prophet," copying in his own writing his master's "key terms / & even his sentence-structure wherever I could."

Berryman's idolatry reached its height when, as a student at Cambridge University from 1936 to 1938, he fell under the spell of W. B. Yeats. Yeats was at the end of his life—he died in 1939—

and the peak of his skill. On Berryman he had an effect that went beyond literary influence; as he was to write later, "I didn't so much wish to resemble as to *be*" Yeats. Sometimes this produced comic self-inflation, as when the twenty-two-year-old Berryman promised himself "to keep free from any struggle for an 'American literature' or a 'new state,' such as that which exhausted Yeats for twenty years." These might have been the concerns of an Irish writer in 1897; for an American in 1937 they were simply borrowed finery.

But there was a serious risk that the young poet would completely lose his own voice in his master's. In February 1937, Berryman—who managed to correspond with Yeats and had begun to think about writing his biography—had a symbolic vision of his idol:

I shut my eyes and an image rose before them, not clear but strong: I saw that it was the figure of Yeats, white-haired and tall, struggling laboriously to lift something dark which was on his right side and below the level on which he stood; as it came into my view, he lifting it with difficulty, I saw that it was a great piece of coal, irregular, black. He raised it high above his head, hair flying and with a set expression, brilliant eyes, dashed it to the ground at his feet, a polished ground that might have been a floor: the pieces rolled away silver.

Whether Berryman literally saw this vision, or was using poetic license to capture Yeats's significance for him, the image he hit on was precise. The transformation of coal to silver is Berryman's version of the Yeatsian idea that profoundly influenced him: what Yeats variously described as the mask, the image, or the anti-self.

Yeats developed an intricate private symbolism on these subjects, drawing in part on communications he believed he was receiving from the spirit world; but even without esoteric knowledge, it is possible to see what the mask meant for Yeats, and for Berryman. Simply put, it was the principle that the poet should strive to become, in his writing, the achieved opposite of what he is in life. Weakness, cowardice, and limitation are transformed through art into strength, courage, perfection. Thus poetry becomes an ethical discipline, an overcoming of the self: "As I look backward upon my own writing," Yeats wrote in *The Trembling of the Veil*, "I take pleasure alone in those verses where it seems to me I have found something hard and cold, some articulation of the Image which is the opposite of all that I am in my daily life."

It follows that a poetry conceived in this way will be, as Yeats's magnificently is, formal, symbolic, and highly artificial. "Style," he declared, is "a deliberate shaping of all things . . . never being swept away, whatever the emotion, into confusion or dullness." Life is not supposed to be represented in art, but transformed and elevated. Or, as Berryman's "Law-giver" Blackmur put it, Yeats "writes to express that which he is not and perforce, for completion or unity, desires to be."

For Berryman, this vision of life and art was dangerously seductive. Already in 1936, when he was twenty-one years old, Berryman wrote an essay for his college magazine on "The Ritual of W. B. Yeats" that demonstrates his perfect indoctrination by Yeats's ideas and Blackmur's rhetoric:

Let us take "ritual" to signify a code or form of ceremonies, the formal character imposed on any experience as it is given objective existence by the imagination working in craft; the experience attains independent aesthetic vitality precisely through and by its limitation.

All of Berryman's concepts—ritual, ceremony, form, limitation, objectivity—are different ways of saying the same thing: art is the transformation of life into something nobler and more deliberate. But as might be expected, when Berryman tried to put this creed into practice, he fell prey to its defects more easily than he mastered its possibilities.

The debilitating effect of Yeats on the young Berryman can be seen in "Homage to Film," a poem he wrote in October 1936 after seeing a movie called *The Prisoner of Shark Island:*

> *This night I have seen a film*
> *That would have startled Henry James*
> *Out of his massive calm*
> *Of disciplines or sent Donne*
> *Into tortuous passion, and all names*
> *Of crafty men flooded with the sun.*

What is striking is not just the pretentious incongruity between the B movie and Henry James; it is the immediate disappearance of Berryman's particular subject into conventional literariness. Seeing a movie, one of the ordinary experiences of twentieth-century life, is not allowed to dictate its own appropriate treatment; instead, it is anxiously redefined in terms of canonical literature. But the style and language of "Homage to Film" do not make us feel that the poet has really seen a film at all, and therefore Berryman cannot convincingly compare it to older arts. What the poem is really about is Berryman's own desire to be ranked with the masters he names, to share their "complexities" and "intensity." Its real question is asked unconsciously: how can the same life include both *The Prisoner of Shark Island* and "Sailing to Byzantium"? How can the demotic, everyday Berryman attain the remote perfection of Yeats?

It was not until he violently rejected the Yeatsian ideal, and took his own actual imperfection as his subject, that Berryman was able to write his major poems. As a novice poet, however, he eagerly accepted the principle that art must be segregated from life, the sacred from the profane. He reveled in the chance to exchange self for mask: "More and more I hate any studied appearance of literature except in formal, definite literature," he wrote. "In line with this separation of formal literary 'personality' . . . I've practically decided to use simply JOHN BERRYMAN for all verse or dramatic publications, and J. A. M. Berryman for everything else."

The result of this separation was that, in his early work, the "formal literary personality" is both the author and the subject of almost every poem. Berryman did not publish a full-length book until *The Dispossessed* in 1948—a long, painful delay for a man who wrote, as early as 1938, "Given life and tenacity in discipline, I shall be a great poet." But the poems in *The Dispossessed* are, with few exceptions, negligible, apprentice work, and were recognized as such; in his review, Randall Jarrell mocked their "slavishly Yeatsish grandiloquence." Paradoxically, by aiming straight for the tone of greatness, Berryman had missed the substance.

Again and again in *The Dispossessed*, Berryman raises himself up to a Yeatsian height, and then finds himself with nothing to say. Every poem becomes a paraphrase of its motive, the striving for literary greatness, which seems to be the only thing that sincerely interests the poet. In "The Statue," for example, Berryman uses the Central Park statue of the German scientist Alexander von Humboldt as an emblem of his aspiration, contrasting the statue's loftiness with the brute ignorance of the average man:

The lovers pass. Not one of them can know
Or care which Humboldt is immortalized.
If they glance up, they glance in passing,
An idle outcome of that pacing
That never stops, and proves them animal. . . .

But Berryman himself seems no more interested than the passing lovers in who Humboldt was or what he did: the reason for his "immortality" has been evacuated, and only the posture remains. This impasse, where Berryman's work stalled for many years, makes it easy to understand why he was so irritable about still being called "promising" as late as 1960. Promising and not delivering was the all-too-familiar situation of his poetry.

If Berryman had stopped writing after *The Dispossessed*, or continued to write in the same style, he would not be remembered at all today. Knowing what was to come, however, it is possible to see even in his early work faint intimations of his mature themes. Already in 1940, when he contributed (along with Jarrell) to an anthology of *Five Young American Poets*, Berryman was aware of the fault line, charged with destructive force, between his art and his life. In "Sanctuary," the refuge of art is menaced by sexuality:

An evening faultless interval when
Blood ran crescendo in the brain
And time lay as a poem clear

Falls from me now . . .

The insolent look a woman gave
Casually from a door one day
Leaves me not, on the other hand . . .

By describing the woman's provocative look as "insolent," Berryman is able to maintain an attitude of proud superiority; but the fact that this memory remains with him, when the pure aesthetic bliss of poetry has fled, suggests that the glance is also seductive. Sex, it seems, is the one force powerful enough to shatter the poetic mask. Berryman expands on this theme in "Desires of Men and Women," cleverly invoking the trope of the great house, the subject of some of Yeats's best poems. For Berryman, however, the noble mansion can only be a camouflage for his real, sordid desires:

Exasperated, worn, you conjure a mansion,
The absolute butlers in the spacious hall. . . .
. . . .
And none of us, my dears, would dream of you
The half-lit and lascivious apartments
That are in fact your goal, for which you'd do
Murder if you had not your cowardice
To prop the law. . . .

But Berryman is unwilling, for now, to take up residence in those half-lit apartments. At most, he pays a series of visits to them under borrowed names, in the series of poems he called "The Nervous Songs." In these modified sonnets, made up of three stanzas of six lines apiece, Berryman imitates a series of similar poems by Rainer Maria Rilke, which are spoken by various victims and outcasts—Rilke has a Dwarf's Song, a Blind Man's Song, and an Idiot's Song, among others. This example gave Berryman the opportunity to cast off his "formal literary personality" and try on exotic voices. "A Professor's Song" is comically pedantic; "Song of the Man Forsaken and Obsessed" is exotic and Gauguinesque; "The Pacifist's Song" is philosophical. But the most interesting are the truly nervous songs, where Berryman, like Rilke, sympathizes with the mad and wounded. The neurosis of his speakers allows him to experiment with illogic, bent grammar, and emotional extremity in ways new to his work. In "Young Woman's Song," for instance, there is the strange, sexually suggestive image: "I hate this something like a bobbing cork / Not going." In "The Song of the Bridegroom," Berryman voices the infantile desire "to be laid away / Felted in depths of caves."

In form and subject, "The Nervous Songs" foreshadow the Dream Songs that would be Berryman's major work. And the poems that follow them in *The Dispossessed* are notably stranger, as though "The Nervous Songs" had inaugurated a new period of experiment. None of these poems coheres or makes a very strong impression, but Berryman enjoys a new freedom to be odd and opaque, as in "The Long Home": "Whisked off, a voice, fainter, faint, a guise, / A gleam, pin of a, a. Nothing." Here the influences of Hopkins and E. E. Cummings seem to have disjointed the majestic syntax of Yeats. And there is a new openness to self-mockery, as when Berryman describes his friends as "Analysands all, and the rest ought to be"; or remembers a New Year's Eve party where "Somebody slapped / Somebody's second wife somewhere." At such moments there is a far more concrete and credible sense of Berryman's own time and place, and of his own personality, than in the more polished earlier poems. Indeed, the most hopeful thing about *The Dispossessed* is that, in its last section, Berryman's apprentice style is undergoing a visible decomposition. The question for readers in 1948 was what, if anything, would emerge.

IN FACT, THOUGH none of his readers could have known it, the first major breakthrough in Berryman's poetic style had already taken place. In 1947, in the fifth year of his first marriage, Berryman engaged in a passionate love affair with a married woman, and in the few months it lasted he wrote more than a hundred sonnets. The "Sonnets to Chris," as he called them, were mannered and slipshod, combining Elizabethan convention with undisguised personal details. They are far from Berryman's best work, but they marked a decisive advance on *The Dispossessed*. Indeed, it is hard to say which Berryman found more desirable, Chris herself or the poems she inspired. His then-wife Eileen interpreted the affair in terms of Berryman's comment on Yeats's lifelong, unrequited love for Maud Gonne: "If Miss Gonne had called Willie's bluff and gone to bed with him, she wouldn't have filled his days with misery. No misery, no poems. You can bet your life that what Yeats was after was *poems.*"

Berryman, who wanted to be a great poet earlier and more intensely than he wanted anything else, found the affair with Chris a similar incitement to writing. It was a time-honored occasion for verse, and in particular for a sonnet sequence. Berryman was an accomplished Shakespeare scholar—at the time of the affair he was at Princeton, working on a new critical edition of *King Lear*—and he wrote about Shakespeare's sonnets in terms that shed light on his own: they are "pieces of living," Berryman claimed, and "strike one as proceeding from a man more or less without a pose—roughly, naked." While this is a better description of his own sonnets than of Shakespeare's, it shows that—like Lowell and Jarrell at roughly the same time—Berryman was beginning to lose patience with the impersonal Modernism of his mentors. At this point in his development, to discard "a pose" was exactly what Berryman needed.

That the affair with Chris was illicit was, in literary terms, a double advantage. First, it constituted an excursion into those "half-lit and lascivious apartments" where Berryman's poetry had previously feared to go; it was a form of self-abasement, whose violence was necessary to dislodge him from his poetic elevation. Second, and more practically, their subject matter ensured that the sonnets could not be published or even widely circulated. Knowing that they would remain private enabled Berryman to take artistic risks that his "formal literary personality" would not allow. (Not until 1967, when the Dream Songs had made his name and he was on his third marriage, did Berryman publish them as *Berryman's Sonnets*, changing the name "Chris" to "Lise.")

The sonnets bear all the signs of having been written at great speed. Again, Berryman described Shakespeare in self-revealing terms: "the poet's effort differs wildly in degree, there is no steady attention to craft; numerous as they are, the best like the worst appear to be thrown off, impulsive." In fact, Berryman wrote as many as four sonnets a day, with the haste of a delinquent mind trying to elude its own internal censors. The poet who had praised ritual and craft as a young man was now, at age thirty-two, writing so fast there was no time for either. This would remain characteristic of Berryman's writing process: at moments of stylistic crisis—when he completed *Homage to Mistress Bradstreet*, when he began the Dream Songs, and when he turned to a new style with *Love & Fame*—he would write in hectic profusion.

The sonnets embroider on a simple plot. Meeting Chris in "the mild days of middle March," Berryman becomes infatuated with her, and soon they begin an affair. They are separated when Chris goes away with her family on summer vacation, then reunited; finally the affair gives way to guilt and recriminations. Virtually anything that happens during the course of the romance, Berryman finds a way of incorporating into the sequence. In Sonnet 9 the couple makes love in the back seat of a car; in Sonnet 13, while she is "five States away" with her family, he toasts her in a Princeton bar; in Sonnet 19, he escorts her home, drunk, to face her husband's reproaches. Other poems speculate about the future of their relationship: in Sonnet 82, Berryman wildly suggests that his wife and Chris's husband, "mild both," should fall in love, leaving them free to pair off. Still others draw on Berryman's reading, as Balzac, Kafka, and Stephen Crane are drafted to provide metaphors for the affair.

Throughout, Chris is seen in Berryman's double vision as both a love object and a poetic subject. Her importance in his life, Berryman allows us to suspect, is inseparable from her importance to the developing sonnet sequence. Certainly he offers little sense of her actual personality: by the bitter end, when he is calling her "the SS woman," the injustice is so palpable as to seem like sheer indifference to reality. Berryman treats Chris like a Galatea in reverse; as he tells her bluntly in Sonnet 27, "What you excite, / You are."

The fascination of the sonnets, then, is not their portrayal of the love affair—which in fact comes across as rather clichéd, with its tipsy secrecy and academic-suburban setting. It is, rather, the spectacle of the poet's willed disintegration, in both life and art. As the affair and the writing about the affair proceed, so entangled that they are essentially one experience, Berryman senses that he is becoming another person: lustful, proud, deceitful, extravagant, incontinent. Yet he sees this lower self as more genuine, and certainly more prolific, than his old one. And it is this simultaneous self-hatred and self-love that bring the sonnets to life.

Like his poetic personality, Berryman's style also moves away from the stilted formality of his early work. He uses plain local references to anchor his flights of Elizabethan rhetoric in the Princeton of 1947: "The Old Boys' blazers" seen at a college reunion, the martinis and daiquiris the lovers drink, Groucho Marx and Charlie Chaplin, station wagons, blue jeans. When a friend to whom he had shown the sonnets objected to such details, Berryman insisted that "the truth is . . . that it *is* the *Local* in them that is new, that is characteristic of them, and will I suppose be memorable if ever they are made public." Casual, accurate, unliterary detail is just what Berryman could not find a way to handle in "Homage to Film"; now he makes it the basic texture of the sonnets.

Berryman's language is an even greater affront to decorum. Writing at high speed, he teaches his old Yeatsian diction new tricks, many of them learned from Hopkins and Cummings: nouns used as verbs, joke rhymes, extravagant metaphors, singsong refrains, archaism, obscenity, slang. The result is an unruliness that exactly mirrors the unruliness of the affair. None of the sonnets is a perfectly finished poem, but they have an awkward vitality that shows a risk is being taken. As he writes in Sonnet 61:

Languid the songs I wish I willed . . . I try . . .
Smooth songs untroubled like a silver spoon
To pour your creamy beauty back, warm croon
Blind, soft . . . but I have something in my eye,
I see by fits, see what there, rapid and sly,
Difficult, so that it will be off soon,
I'd better fix *it! frantic as a loon,*
Smarting, world-churned, some convulsed song I cry.

Here, again, it seems that the "frantic" quality of the affair is just what allured Berryman; having exhausted the vein of "smooth songs," he was ready to try the "convulsed." What makes this change so fascinating is that, to effect it, Berryman needed to convulse his life as well. In fact, Berryman practices what might be called reverse confessionalism—he does not simply use poetry to reveal his life, but upsets his life in order to incite poetry. In sonnet after sonnet, Berryman surprises himself by embracing his lower nature. Like the sailors on Circe's island, he is a "swine- / enchanted lover, loafing in the abyss"; his desires are "mutinous" and "malignant"; he is like "a clown / Dancing upon a one-night hot-foot stage," with "my leer, my Groucho crouch and rush." Significantly, he equates his betrayal of his wife with his betrayal of his high poetic vocation: "Muffled in capes of waves my clear signs, torn, / Hitherto most clear—Loyalty and Art." The former "monk / Of Yeatsian order," as he calls himself in one sonnet, has become a debauchee, and finds that he is a better writer as a result. This ambiguous discovery, which would point the way to the still greater derangements of the Dream Songs, is the real burden and theme of the sonnets:

I am this strange thing I despised; you are.
To become ourselves we are these wayward things.

BY THE END of 1947, Berryman was finished with both the sonnets and the affair. He placed at the end of the sequence a biblical citation from the story of Samson: "But the hair of his head began to grow again after it had been shaved." The verse suggests that the Chris episode was a catastrophe safely passed, and looks forward to a period of penance and recuperation. In fact, its effects on Berryman's life and writing were only postponed. By 1953 he would be separated from his wife, and in 1955 he began writing the Dream Songs, which radically extended the techniques and subjects of the sonnets.

Before the Dream Songs, however, came Berryman's first critical success, and the work that he himself regarded as his first major achievement: *Homage to Mistress Bradstreet*. It, too, was written in a concentrated burst of activity, over two months at the beginning of 1953. Berryman declared that "I have never tried before so hard to control hysteria"; yet this was a joyful ordeal, for he felt sure he was producing his best work so far. "I have always failed," he wrote in a letter, "but I am not failing now."

The exact nature of *Bradstreet's* success can be gauged by its rapturous reception among Berryman's mentors. Allen Tate told him "You've never written any poetry before within six light years of this"; Edmund Wilson called it "the most distinguished long poem by an American since *The Waste Land*." One can sense their relief at being able to award their pupil his poetic doctorate, as it were. At last, Berryman had written something that satisfied his teachers' rigorous New Critical standards. But this also indicates *Bradstreet's* limitations; for it was not until he could transcend those standards, in the defiantly original Dream Songs, that Berryman became a truly great poet.

This is not to say that *Homage to Mistress Bradstreet* is grossly imitative, the way his earlier work had imitated Yeats; it was acclaimed precisely because it was written in a strenuously original style. Looking back on it in later years, Berryman claimed that he designed it as "something spectacularly NOT *The Waste Land*": he wanted "narrative, and at least one dominant personality, and no fragmentation." But in a wider perspective, *Bradstreet* clearly looks like an entry in the Modernist long-poem competition. It is a sustained dramatic monologue, like Eliot's "The Love Song of J. Alfred Prufrock" and "Gerontion"; it employs stream-of-consciousness narration, like Joyce and Woolf; it is frequently ambiguous in plot and syntax, as the New Criticism prescribed; it deals with a canonical, if minor, American writer, and evokes early American history. Even the eight-line stanza is based, as Berryman wrote, on "a lifetime's study" of Yeats's *ottava rima*. All of these things made *Bradstreet* critically acceptable, in a way that the unsteady exhilaration of the sonnets would not have been.

The poem begins with Berryman addressing, in his own voice, the shade of Anne Bradstreet: "I seem to see you pause here still." As Berryman's introductory note informs us, Bradstreet was an early American colonist, who came to Massachusetts in 1630 with her husband Simon. Berryman omits to mention that she is also known as the first American poet, though this clearly determined his choice of Bradstreet as a subject: "Both of our worlds unhanded us," he writes, suggesting their affinity as artists in commercial America. But Berryman is not interested in her as a writer, and goes out of his way to disparage her "bald / abstract didactic rime." She interests him, rather, as a woman, and the poem charts her progress through the phases of a woman's life: daughter, wife, mother, and finally "old woman." And in the poem's strangest and most interesting section, we see her as a lover, attracting Berryman himself across the space of centuries.

After four stanzas of "exordium," in which Berryman conjures Bradstreet and her world, the poem shifts without warning into Bradstreet's own voice: "By the week we landed we were, most, used up." And that voice is the real interest of the poem. By using archaic-sounding idioms and word order in the service of an opaque, telegraphic narration, Berryman achieves an ingenious fusion of antique and modern. The language of *Bradstreet* is not a period imitation, but the sound of a modern poet ventriloquizing the past.

While Berryman's skillful manipulation of diction and point of view are new in his poetry, the action, settings, and ideas of the poem are less surprising. In Berryman's telling, Bradstreet is a textbook example of Puritan psychology, oppressed by her over-active conscience. Even in the most celebrated passage in the poem, Bradstreet's narration of childbirth, there is something dutiful about Berryman's virtuosity:

> *No. No. Yes! everything down*
> *hardens I press with horrible joy down*
> *my back cracks like a wrist*
> *shame I am voiding oh behind it is too late*

This is impressive writing, a feat to be admired; but like the poem as a whole, it is not truly dramatic. *Homage to Mistress Bradstreet* does not put the poet or the reader at stake, as the sonnets do in their much less assured way.

The one exception comes in the middle stanzas, numbers 25–35 out of fifty-seven, when Berryman's own voice reenters the poem. This surprising development, violating the unity of plot and character, seems like a mistake on the poem's own terms. But for just that reason it raises the work's emotional temperature, making us feel that we are watching the poet act out an unseemly compulsion. For Berryman's purpose in barging into Anne's monologue is, bizarrely, to seduce her:

> —*I miss you, Anne,*
> *day or night weak as a child,*
> *tender & empty, doomed, quick to no tryst.*

This has nothing to do with the historical Anne Bradstreet, and little to do even with the character Berryman has been creating. Anne has become an "empty" vessel indeed, a version of the eternal-feminine who leads the poet onward: "You must not love me, but I do not bid you cease." Anne's Puritan guilt makes her hesitate, even makes her physically ill—"faintings black, rigour, chilling"—but finally she succumbs to Berryman's imploring. "Kiss me," she says, and "Talk to me," and finally: "I *want* to take you for my lover." But her surrender only seems to transfer her own guilt to Berryman, provoking a nightmare hallucination that is the poem's most surprising and memorable image:

> *I trundle the bodies, on the iron bars,*
> *over that fire backward & forth; they burn;*
> *bits fall. I wonder if*
> *I killed them. Women serve my turn.*

Suddenly the poem has taken a disturbing and highly personal swerve. The sexual anxiety and violence that has flickered through Berryman's work from the beginning leaps, momentarily, into full view, opening a gulf between the painstaking historical monologuist and the nightmare killer. But *Bradstreet* is not yet ready to cross it: after this eruption the lovers' dialogue peters out, and Anne's narrative resumes. Inevitably, the rest of the poem—chronicling her motherhood, age, illness, and death—is an anticlimax. Ten years later, when Berryman returned to this nightmare, in Dream Song #29, he would produce one of the best poems he ever wrote. In the meantime, he had *Bradstreet* as the credential of a style mastered, and the token of a style to come.

BETWEEN *HOMAGE TO* Mistress Bradstreet and *77 Dream Songs*, eleven years later, Berryman published only one short pamphlet of verse. But an attentive reader of Berryman's prose—his essays and reviews, introductions and lectures, and his full-length biography of Stephen Crane—could have detected a subterranean shift in his understanding of poetry. In 1940, the twenty-five-year-old poet was faithfully repeating the New Critical creed: "a poem means more than the abstract, banal statement of its theme; it means its imagery, the disparate parts and relations of it, its ambiguities, by extension the techniques which produced it and the emotions it legitimately produces." A poem, in other words, is not a communication from author to reader; it is a self-sufficient entity, a product of expert techniques, and its meaning lies not in what it says but how it says it.

By the late 1940s, however, Berryman was moving away from New Critical orthodoxy. In 1949 he published an essay on Ezra Pound, suggesting that the real subject of Pound's poetry is "the life of the modern poet," and that this fact has been ignored by critics "interested in craft, not personality and subject." This sounds like a deliberate repudiation of Berryman's erstwhile idol, R. P. Blackmur, whose 1933 essay "Masks of Ezra Pound" claimed that Pound was only a craftsman, "all surface and articulation." Critics like Blackmur, Berryman politely suggests, have been "blinded, perhaps, by the notion of the 'impersonality' of the poet. This perverse and valuable doctrine, associated in our time with Eliot's name," is suited to explaining some kinds of poetry, but "for most other poetry, including Pound's, it is somewhat paradoxical, and may disfigure more than it enlightens."

By insisting that the poet's actual life can be a valid subject for poetry, that personality is just as important as craft, Berryman was voicing the common feeling of his generation. The stern pursuit of "impersonality" was just what had drained his early poems of specificity and vigor; by abandoning his Yeatsian creed, Berryman was staking out the territory of his own best work. (Interestingly, this essay predates by four years the impersonal and elaborately crafted *Bradstreet*, another sign that that poem was more a summing up for Berryman than a new departure.) And as he grew more convinced of his artistic path, his condemnation of Eliotic impersonality grew more strident. In a 1957 essay, Eliot's theory has been demoted from "perverse and valuable" to "amusing," and by 1960 it has become "intolerable." In 1962 Berryman turns to sarcasm: "One thing critics not themselves writers of poetry occasionally forget is that poetry is composed by actual human beings, and tracts of it are very closely about them. When Shakespeare wrote 'Two loves I have,' reader, he was *not kidding*."

The essay that best reveals Berryman's changing ideas about poetry is his 1957 examination of Whitman, "Song of Myself: Intention and Substance." Whitman's poetry—profuse, excitable, personal—stands at the opposite pole to Eliot's, and for just this reason he becomes an important model for Berryman. The essay admiringly quotes Whitman's description of *Leaves of Grass* as "an attempt, from first to last, to put *a Person*, a human being (myself, in the latter part of the Nineteenth Century, in America), freely, fully and truly on record." This idea of the poet "not as *maker* but as spiritual historian" strikes Berryman as truer and "less pretentious" than the Modernist idea of impersonal craft. And it inspires his own, daringly primitive metaphor for the writing of poetry:

> The poet—one would say, a mere channel, but with its own ferocious difficulties—fills with experiences, a valve opens; he speaks them. I am obliged to remark that I prefer this theory of poetry to those that have ruled the critical quarterlies since I was an undergraduate twenty-five years ago.

Speaking out of necessity, under the "ferocious" pressure of personal experience, is just what Berryman fails to do in most of *The Dispossessed*. It is what he does only fleetingly in *Homage to Mistress Bradstreet*, when his own voice bursts into Anne's meticulously imagined story. But by the time Berryman wrote about Whitman, he had already spent two years writing poetry that brilliantly achieved his new ideal.

On October 25, 1954, his fortieth birthday, Berryman wrote a letter taking stock of his achievement so far: "If I take 1938 . . . I was nearly 24 and that was 16 years ago. I had done nothing up to then. In the 16 years since I've done very little, but something. I can imagine 16 years ahead, that is, to the age of 56 . . . and I can hardly fear doing less in the next 16 years than I did in the last." He was not to live much past his target age of fifty-six; but in the years remaining to him, he far surpassed everything he had written before.

This literary accounting, however, omits the fact that, in the previous year, Berryman's personal life had reached its nadir. His first wife left him after ten years of marriage; then he was fired from a job at the University of Iowa, after getting into a drunken brawl with his landlord and spending the night in jail. But just as with the sonnets, Berryman found that abjection was the prelude to inspiration. For it was in late 1954, just after this scandal, that he began the intensive process of recording and analyzing his dreams that would ultimately give birth to the Dream Songs.

"I am engaged in a sort of self-analysis, which is slow and difficult," he wrote at the beginning of December. But as with the sonnets and *Bradstreet*, Berryman had tapped a source of obsessive energy, and by the end of December he had catalogued thirty-eight dreams. "38 in two months would be *228 a year!* intolerable," he wrote. By the following summer he had reached 120: "I'm . . . literally out of the world, dealing solely with dreams . . . I am unblocking gradually, or rather in violent painful strides." But if this process was painful, it was also extremely fruitful: "Some of my simplest (in appearance) dreams have proved . . . more complex than any poem I ever read, a great deal to say; I have almost a new idea of the mind's strength, cunning, & beauty."

At first, Berryman thought about publishing the dream analyses themselves, under the title "St. Pancras' Braser," a phrase that came to him in a dream. This could have been an occult work not unlike Yeats's *A Vision*. But instead, he began to channel the energy and insights he gained from dream analysis into a new kind of poem. In the summer of 1955, returning to the form he had used in "The Nervous Songs," Berryman began to write poems made up of three six-line stanzas, with a loose meter and variable rhyme scheme.

These "Dream Songs," as he named them, are not simply versified accounts of his dream analyses. A few of them do recount dreams, or nightmares; but Berryman knew that nothing is less interesting than someone else's dreams. Rather, the connection between the dreams and the poems is suggested by a passage in Freud's "The Interpretation of Dreams":

> The reflective man makes use of his critical faculties, with the result that he rejects some of the thoughts which rise into consciousness after he has become aware of them, and abruptly interrupts others, so that he does not follow the lines of thought which they would otherwise open up for him; while in respect of yet other thoughts he is able to behave in such a manner that they do not become conscious at all—that is to say, they are suppressed before they are perceived. In self-observation, on the other hand, he has but one task—that of suppressing criticism; if he succeeds in doing this, an unlimited number of thoughts enter his consciousness which would otherwise have eluded his grasp.

This is exactly what Berryman had been groping toward in his poetry, and what the dream work allowed him to achieve: what Freud goes on to call, quoting Schiller, "the withdrawal of the watchers from the gates." His new poetry would record the uncensored consciousness, the freely rising ideas, before his artistic superego had a chance to tame them. By "suppressing criticism," he could allow the most discreditable thoughts and feelings to take up residence in his poetry.

Still, neither his dreams themselves, nor the psychic turmoil they embodied, were Berryman's real interest. As the Chris affair showed, his own life mattered to Berryman chiefly as a provocation to writing poetry. And the Dream Songs are intricately constructed poems, not psychoanalytic free association or automatic writing. Indeed, for Berryman to bring private experience, as never before, into the public realm of poetry required a long education in style. He could never have written about his "wayward" thoughts had he not begun, as early as the sonnets, to invent a language equally wayward. And he could not have handled the delicate ironies of the Dream Songs, or the subtle relationship between the author of the poems and their speakers and characters, without the training in manipulating point of view that *Bradstreet* had provided. After twenty years of writing, what Berryman had to say and the means he had to say it with finally came together.

FROM 1955 TO 1968, Berryman wrote Dream Songs almost exclusively. He produced hundreds before culling a selection for *77 Dream Songs* in 1964; he went on to write hundreds more before publishing a second and final volume, *His Toy, His Dream, His Rest*, in 1968. As a result, the two books, published together under the title *The Dream Songs* in 1969, incorporate work written over a long span of time, making it difficult to generalize about the evolution of Berryman's style. It is clear, however, that the first collection of Songs is generally stranger, denser, odder, and better than the second. As time went on, and especially after the first book made Berryman a literary celebrity, his idea of the

Songs' purpose evolved, not necessarily for the better. Therefore it makes sense to treat the two volumes of Dream Songs separately, even though they are parts of a single large work.

Exactly how to categorize the Dream Songs has always been a vexed question. In 1965, Berryman wrote that "editors and critics for years have been characterizing them as poems, but I do not quite see them as that; I see them as parts" of a single long poem. Yet this long poem, composed of 385 independent lyrics and divided into seven "books," is far from a continuous narrative. And while many critics have proposed interpretive schemes, it does not really have a clear thematic structure either. Perhaps the best description of the Dream Songs is Berryman's definition of what a long poem entails: "the construction of a world rather than the reliance upon one already existent which is available to a small poem."

At the center of the world constructed by the Dream Songs is the character of Henry, "a white American in early middle age." Henry, Berryman insisted in an introductory note, is "an imaginary character (not the poet, not me)," and he disclaimed responsibility for Henry's fantasies and adventures. Yet Henry shares many elements of his creator's history and personality; especially in the later Songs, they are often biographically identical. Nevertheless, it was crucial for Berryman to insist that Henry is not simply the historical John Berryman, but an imaginative surrogate, through whom he interprets his own experience. As he wrote in 1962, apropos of Robert Lowell's poem "Skunk Hour":

> the speaker can never be the actual writer, who is a person with an address, a Social Security number, debts, tastes, memories, expectations. . . . The necessity for the artist of selection opens

inevitably an abyss between his person and his persona. . . .
The persona looks across at the person and then sets about its
own work.

The Dream Songs do not so much abandon as triumphantly
invert Berryman's early ambition to become in his work, in Blackmur's phrase, "that which he is not and perforce, for completion
or unity, desires to be": Henry could be described as what Berryman is not and dreads he might become. As in his early work,
Berryman splits off his "literary personality" from his actual self;
but now, instead of making that personality an idealized fiction,
he makes it a polluted and sinful fiction.

The other major character in the Dream Songs is Henry's
friend, never named, who addresses him as "Mr. Bones." This
name, and the fact that the friend speaks in African-American
dialect, suggest that he is Henry's partner in a kind of minstrel
act, where Tambo and Bones were a standard pair of characters.
But more important, this friend is Henry's conscience, his superego, even his guardian angel. This makes him essential to the
poetic success of the Dream Songs, because his critical perspective
assures the reader that Berryman's authorial consciousness is
wider than the consciousness of Henry. Because he allows Berryman to judge and pity his creation, Henry's friend makes it possible for the reader to enjoy Henry's irresponsibility without
feeling that the Dream Songs are simply the confessions of an
irresponsible author.

Along with the characters, Berryman's language helps to create
the world of the Dream Songs. That language is so innovative and
various that it can only be defined negatively: it includes just
about every kind of diction, except the serious, elevated, literary

diction of Berryman's early poems. In place of what Jarrell had derided as "Yeatsish grandiloquence," Berryman makes use of baby talk, black slang, gangster talk from the movies, Cummingsesque wordplay, puns, bureaucratic jargon, and more. Sometimes grammar breaks down to such an extent that it is nearly impossible to say what a particular passage means. Yet, at the same time, Henry is clearly an intellectual, and he makes frequent allusions to literature and theology. As with Moses Herzog, the fictional surrogate of Berryman's close friend Saul Bellow, Henry's erudition contributes to his comic self-abasement: what he knows about books only emphasizes what he does not know about himself. The result of this manic polyphony is to give a remarkably convincing picture of Henry's unquiet spirit, which delights in degradation even as it aspires to salvation.

For it is Henry's fear and longing that finally unite the poem and create its world. In his introductory note, Berryman says that Henry has "suffered an irreversible loss," and this sense of grief is the ground note of the Dream Songs. It cannot be blamed on any one specific loss, though they abound: wives, friends, mentors. Above all, Henry mourns for his father—like Berryman, whose father, beset by marital and financial troubles, shot himself in the family's front yard when his son was eleven years old. Yet even this horror, which haunted Berryman for his whole life, cannot fully account for the inescapable sense that something has gone wrong, in Henry or in his world or both. Elegy runs through all of Henry's mockery, self-pity, lust, and despair. The first Dream Song introduces it:

All the world like a woolen lover
once did seem on Henry's side.

Then came a departure.
Thereafter nothing fell out as it might or ought.

This "departure" goes unnamed, but Berryman cleverly and economically characterizes it in the odd phrase "woolen lover." This name for the state of lost content combines the childish—a woolen blanket in the crib, thus a mother's love—with the sexual, adult sense of "lover"; Henry seems to be talking about an early and profound loss, like mankind's "departure" from the Garden of Eden, but also a recent romantic one. Certainly, one of Henry's most frequent pitfalls is lust: "hopeless inextricable lust, Henry's fate." His pursuit of women is compulsive, mechanical, and therefore, on one level, comic:

Love her he doesn't but the thought he puts
into that young woman
would launch a national product
complete with TV spots & skywriting. . . .

When he writes in this vein, Berryman's comedy is clever but conventional. It is the same tone in which he mocks safe targets like the IRS: "Bats have no bankers . . . and pay no tax / and, in general, bats have it made." In this telling, Henry is not so much guilty as helpless, bullied by internal and external powers.

But at other moments lust is a much more serious matter, the archetype of all of Henry's sins. Dream Song #4, which begins in the comic register with Henry ogling a woman in a restaurant, ends on a more ambiguous note:

The restaurant buzzes. She might as well be on Mars.
Where did it all go wrong? There ought to be a law against

> *Henry.*
> *—Mr. Bones: there is.*

Henry is mocking his own appetites, and his "there ought to be a law" is a stock phrase. But the response of his religious friend suggests to Henry, and the reader, that there really is a moral law; that Henry's lust is not a joke, but a sin that will be punished. In Dream Song #26, lust is seen as Henry's original sin, the cause of his "departure":

> *The glories of the world struck me, made me aria, once.*
> *—What happen then, Mr Bones?*
> *if be you cares to say.*
> *—Henry. Henry became interested in women's bodies,*
> *his loins were & were the scene of stupendous achievement.*

Here "Henry" seems like the name of a disease that afflicts the author. Or perhaps it is simply a name for adulthood, which begins with sexual awakening in puberty and continues through the rest of the travails this Song chronicles, until there is only one way out:

> *—What happen then, Mr Bones?*
> *—I had a most marvelous piece of luck. I died.*

Berryman's humor can always turn suddenly into horror: the language of the poem is like a radioactive substance, constantly threatening to decay. To borrow Berryman's own description of Isaac Babel, the Dream Songs are "tragic, yet funny, yet not funny."

That is why, when Berryman discards humor entirely and writes a poem as dark as Dream Song #29, the effect is almost shocking. One of the best Dream Songs, and one of the peaks of Berryman's entire work, this Song revisits the brief episode in *Bradstreet* where Berryman's guilt over seducing Anne gives rise to an image of sexual murder: "I wonder if / *I* killed them." Now Berryman expands this vision of lust as a hellish nightmare:

> *But never did Henry, as he thought he did,*
> *end anyone and hacks her body up*
> *and hide the pieces, where they may be found.*
> *He knows: he went over everyone, & nobody's missing.*
> *Often he reckons, in the dawn, them up.*
> *Nobody is ever missing.*

The ambiguity of this stanza is brilliantly handled, assuring us of Henry's innocence while distinctly implying his guilt. It begins by affirming that "never did Henry . . . end anyone," but as the sentence carries over to the third line, its meaning changes: he never ended anyone and hid "the pieces, where they may be found." That is, perhaps he did "end" someone but has covered up the deed so well that it will never be discovered. Likewise, in the second half of the stanza, Henry "reckons" up all his possible victims and assures himself that "nobody's missing." But the sinister repetition of the last line suggests the reverse interpretation: perhaps "Nobody is ever missing" from the list of his victims. It is moments like this, when the smallest nuance creates overpowering effects, that justify Berryman's boast: "I have a style now pared straight to the bone and can make the reader's nerves jump by moving my little finger."

Berryman moves naturally from lust to the second major theme of the Dream Songs, death and the fear of death. If lust is Henry's crime against the world, it is more than matched by the world's crime against Henry, his own inevitable death and the deaths of everyone he loves and admires. In *His Toy, His Dream, His Rest*, after the many poetic deaths of the mid-1960s, an increasing number of Songs would become elegies for individuals; already in *77 Dream Songs*, there are poems in memory of Theodore Roethke and Robert Frost. These are occasions for praise: Roethke is called "The Garden Master" for his poetry about flowers and plants, Frost is "the quirky medium of so many truths." But Berryman also resents the expanding dominion of death, guiltily insisting on his own right to keep living:

> *The high ones die, die. They die. You look up and who's there?*
> *—Easy, easy, Mr Bones. I is on your side.*
> *I smell your grief.*
> *—I sent my grief away. I cannot care*
> *forever. With them all again & again I died*
> *and cried, and I have to live.*
>
> *—Now there you exaggerate, Sah. We hafta die.*

Henry's friend, always the voice of reason, reminds him that he, too, is destined to die. Yet this is something Henry seldom forgets; his will to live is usually weak, and in danger of turning into its opposite. One of the most distinctive emotional tones of the Dream Songs is the combination of terror and longing with which Henry thinks about death. His childishness is especially effective here: Henry confronts with astonishment facts that ordinary adult discourse ignores or stoically takes for granted. In Dream Song #21, the very idea that everyone must die and be buried produces an outraged incomprehension:

Appalled: by all the dead: Henry brooded.
Without exception! All.
ALL.

Such disbelief goes hand in hand with fascination at the corporeal effect of death. Henry is obsessed with the "underground," with the bodies hacked up and hidden. Berryman offers one obvious autobiographical explanation for this:

in a modesty of death I join my father
who dares so long agone leave me.
A bullet on a concrete stoop
close by a smothering southern sea
spreadeagled on an island, by my knee.

Dream Song #76 is titled "Henry's Confession," but it is Berryman's own story. His father's suicide is the most concrete and terrible candidate for Henry's "irreversible loss," and it recurs throughout the Dream Songs, including the next-to-last poem in the sequence.

Whether this trauma caused Berryman's own suicidal tendencies is an unanswerable clinical question. Poetically, what matters is not etiology, but the desperate accuracy with which Berryman evokes Henry's death wish. Some of the most powerful Songs deal with his indifference to life and the world:

They blew out his loves, his interests. 'Underneath,'
(they called in iron voices) 'understand,
is nothing. So there.'

Characteristically, it is the childish taunt of "So there" that lifts the poem above mere confessional complaint. It signals to the

reader that Berryman is well aware of the element of self-pity in
Henry's laments, that the author has a wider perspective and
greater wisdom than his creation. When this sense disappears, in
Berryman's late work, his poetry suffers tremendously as a result.
In the Dream Songs, however, Berryman's authorial skepticism
grants the reader permission to luxuriate in Henry's immature
sense of grievance—which, he forces us to acknowledge, we also
share despite ourselves. A similar balancing act takes place in
Dream Song #74:

> *Henry hates the world. What the world to Henry*
> *did will not bear thought.*
> *Feeling no pain,*
> *Henry stabbed his arm and wrote a letter*
> *explaining how bad it had been*
> *in this world.*

Again there is Henry's unjust absolutism: his suffering is the
world's fault, and his suicide will punish the world. The reader
can't finally accept this as a justification for suicide, but Berryman's diction acknowledges our disapproval while still allowing
us to feel its dramatic truth. The brilliant phrase "stabbed his
arm" is an example of this strategy in miniature: it is childishly literal, but for that very reason it captures the violence of suicide
better than the nearly euphemistic "slit his wrist."

Faced with such a world, "unappeasable Henry" naturally
wants to complete his indictment by putting down the name of
the culprit, the world's creator. This is the third major theme of
the Dream Songs: theodicy, the attempt to reconcile God's existence with the evil of the world. At moments, Henry, in keeping
with his childish refusal of complexity, simply sees God as his per-

sonal tormentor: "God's Henry's enemy." But this is only one phase of Henry's constantly changing feelings about God. Berryman recognizes that it, too, is a form of infantile narcissism, that Henry's baby talk makes him seem merely petulant: "at odds wif de world & its god."

Yet the alternative, belief in a good and protective God, is unavailable to Henry. Only at rare moments does he remember the promise of Christian salvation, and then almost wistfully, wanting to believe rather than actually believing. In Dream Song #47, Berryman tells the legend of St. Mary of Egypt, a prostitute who ran out of church in the conviction that she was too sinful to be saved. She is a perfect patron saint for Henry: "We celebrate her feast with our caps on, / whom God has not visited." It is ironically appropriate that her saint's day (on the Greek Orthodox calendar) is "April Fool's Day," since Henry can't escape the suspicion that even hoping for salvation makes him a fool.

The earliest-written Dream Song to be included in the published work, #20, is only slightly more hopeful:

> *Hurl, God who found*
> *us in this, down*
> *something . . . We hear the more*
> *sin has increast, the more*
> *grace has been caused to abound.*

The reference is to Romans 5:20, where Paul declares that the sin of Adam is redeemed by the sacrifice of Christ, and the law of the Old Testament replaced by the love of the New Testament: "For just as by the one man's disobedience the many were made sin-

ners, so by the one man's obedience the many will be made right-
eous. But law came in, with the result that the trespass multiplied;
but where sin increased, grace abounded all the more. . . ." This
is the central promise of Christianity, but for Henry it remains
only a rumor, something "we hear." What's more, Henry sees
grace as at best a kind of lifeline hurled down to man by God,
who didn't create the world but merely "found / us in" it. And if
that is the case, then the world must be the work of another god
than God: the evil God, the tempter, Satan.

The religion Henry really believes in, then, is Manichean; he
sees God and the Devil as contesting deities, with the Devil holding the advantage. Dream Song #17, one of the most moving
Songs, shows the Devil tempting Henry to give in to despair:
"And Lucifer:—I smell you for my own, / by smug." Lucifer can
tell that Henry is a likely candidate for sin and damnation. But
while Lucifer's voice is heard, God's is conspicuously silent:
Henry prays to God that his "madnesses have cease," but no
answer comes. Like Job, Henry seems to have been handed over
by God to Satan, to be tortured for no reason.

In God's absence, however, Henry finds consolation and protection in the great theologians of all faiths: "Brother Martin, / St
Simeon the Lesser Theologian, / Bodhidharma, and the Baal
Shem Tov." Theology, for him, is less important as a statement of
truths about God than as an achievement of the human spirit,
like literature and art. Henry finds the same sort of spiritual sus-
tenance in the medieval carvings of Wells Cathedral:

> *while Keats sweat'*
> *for hopeless inextricable lust, Henry's fate, . . .*
> . . . .

> *while Abelard was whole,*
> *these grapes of stone were being proffered, friend.*

This is a secular alternative to religion: not personal salvation but an escape from death through the immortality of art. Art, not faith, provides the rare moments of calm and wholeness in the Dream Songs.

But these are only moments, which come and go; the logic of the poem does not allow anything like a final affirmation. Indeed, no piety, not even about art itself, is safe for long from Henry's satire. Dream Song #14—"Life, friends, is boring"—contains one of the best statements of that mood, which visits every reader, when the very idea of literature seems oppressive:

> *Peoples bore me,*
> *literature bores me, especially great literature,*
> *Henry bores me, with his plights & gripes*
> *as bad as achilles,*
>
> *who loves people & valiant art, which bores me.*

The pronouns are significantly slippery. Now it is Henry who has faith in "valiant art," while Berryman's own voice seems to declare that "literature bores me." Berryman seems to have traded places with his creation, claiming for himself the immaturity that we have come to associate with Henry, and making Henry, for the moment, nobler than his author. Moments like this make it impossible ever to define the relationship between Berryman and Henry, just as it is useless to try to hold Henry to just one of his contradictory moods or statements. "If something happened to

Henry," Berryman told an interviewer in 1969, "Henry thought of it as lasting forever." It is up to Berryman—and the reader—to see Henry whole, to judge him, and to pity him.

BY THE TIME *77 Dream Songs* was published, Berryman had been writing Songs for nine years. He was confident that this was the best work he had done: sending the first batch of poems to his editor, he wrote, "I sh[ould]n't be surprised if some of them proved more or less immortal." Yet he also knew that the book represented an enormous risk. He had long been immersed in Henry's world, but he was springing it on his readers fully formed; so much difficult, strange, indecorous poetry would be hard to assimilate. The Songs, as he wrote to Robert Lowell, "are partly independent but only if . . . the reader is familiar with Henry's tone, personality, obsessions, friend, activities; otherwise, in small numbers, they seem simply crazy." In 1962, he had a dream in which Randall Jarrell, the most authoritative critic of their generation, told him "to stop writing these pseudo-poems . . . come back & write *real* ones."

The dream was prophetic, for while the book was acclaimed, it baffled some of the readers whose opinions Berryman most valued: Lowell, in his review of the book, complained of "the threat of mannerism, and worse, disintegration . . . the relentless indulgence." For the first time, Berryman was not trying to master an established style but creating his own, and thus implicitly challenging his peers and teachers. Tellingly, it was younger poets who first embraced the book, and wrote him to praise it. Before long, however, the dimensions of Berryman's achievement became clear, and in 1965 he was awarded the Pulitzer Prize, the first major distinction of his career. By 1966, even Lowell had come to believe that Berryman was "the boldest and most brilliant spokesman for our common profession," and his own subsequent *Notebook* clearly showed the influence of the Dream Songs.

Berryman always knew that he would eventually publish a second volume of Dream Songs. Even in 1964 there were hundreds of poems not included in *77 Dream Songs*, and as the years went on he continued to write them unstoppably. He even had to warn himself not to "Henrify" poems that didn't necessarily belong in the sequence. But the writing of Dream Songs had become second nature, and the scope of the planned sequel continued to expand. Initially he wanted it to include 84 songs, for a total of 161; by the time *His Toy, His Dream, His Rest* was published, in 1968, the total had climbed to 385.

The effect on the published poem is unmistakable. In *His Toy, His Dream, His Rest*, Berryman is no longer exploring but exploiting the form: Henry becomes practically a nickname for John Berryman, the thematic range does not significantly expand, and there are fewer wholly successful Songs. Ironically, this is partly because of the poem's own worldly success. The first book of Dream Songs had been a risky enterprise conducted in private, as Berryman wrote in #67:

> *I am obliged to perform in complete darkness*
> *operations of great delicacy*
> *on my self.*

Now, Berryman was not performing an operation so much as a role, the famous poet sought after by readers and audiences:

> *—I write with my stomach: Henry ruefully;*
> *and my stomach is improved, I write with my purse*

and long sums have come
from foreign places.

One result of this success was Berryman's growing willingness to put the events of his life directly into the poem, without transformation. As he approached the transparency of confession, he abandoned the mysterious ironies that made the early Songs so suggestive. Dream Song #1, for example, speaks of Henry's outrage that "they thought / they could *do* it"—but who "they" are, and what they are trying to do, is left powerfully vague. Only Berryman himself knew that the inspiration for this line was something as petty as academic politics: "the long interdepartmental war against Humanities" at the University of Minnesota, where he taught. The poem is much better for declining to expose this trivial root. But by the time he wrote Dream Song #278, addressed to some colleagues about to leave Minnesota, Berryman was completely explicit:

Fresh from the woodwork issued our blue foes
botanists & peasants of elementary german
drones, drones in the hive. . . .

It is impossible to forget that Berryman, not Henry, was the one squabbling with professors of botany and German. More and more, Berryman also uses the public forum of the Songs to pay private debts of gratitude. One Song thanks a friend for clearing up some trouble at Berryman's bank while he was out of the country; in another he declares his affection for the otherwise unknown "Maris & Valerie" and "Ellen." Sometimes Berryman seems to be putting into verse anything that happens, as it happens: one Song was written while proctoring an exam, and names the students who caught Berryman's eye as he wrote. At such moments Berryman fulfills his own description of Pound, taking as his subject "the life of the modern poet," and in the process proving that such a life can be just as uninteresting as any other.

Worse, by collapsing the distance between Henry and Berryman, *His Toy* puts the reader in the uncomfortable position of having to ascribe to the author some embarrassing sentiments:

> *Miss Dickinson—fancy in Amherst bedding hér.*
> *Fancy a lark with Sappho,*
> *A tumble in the bushes with Miss Moore,*
> *a spoon with Emily, while Charlotte glare.*
> *Miss Bishop's too noble-O.*

This is a different kind of indecorum than in *77 Dream Songs*, less like fearlessness than simple bad taste.

The best poems in *His Toy, His Dream, His Rest* are more discursive, less dramatic treatments of the themes that energized the first book. Henry's obsession with death is carried to an extreme in the series of fourteen Songs that opens the volume, "Opus Posthumous," which are spoken by Henry after his death. In truth, Henry dead does not sound very different from Henry living: as always, he has a morbidly literal imagination of what it is like to moulder in the grave. Yet he is also tempted by death, as an escape from responsibility ("no deadline . . . no typewriters") and, more movingly, from the temptation to sin. Henry longs to be "Not Guilty by reason of death":

> *I add that all the crimes since all the times he*
> *died will be due to the breath*

of unknown others, sweating in their guilt
while my client Henry's brow of stainless steel
rests free, as well it may,
of all such turbulence. . . .

Finally, Henry's guilt is so painful that he prefers death to life. In Dream Song #91, the last of the "Opus Posthumous" series, he is resurrected, but finds that he was happier in the grave:

A fortnight later, sense a single man
upon the trampled scene at 2 a.m.
insomnia-plagued, with a shovel
digging like mad, Lazarus with a plan
to get his own back. . . .

This ghoulish image looms in the background of the elegies that crowd *His Toy:* whenever Berryman mourns for a fellow writer, there is also a whisper of envy. And a series of deaths in the 1960s gave Berryman many opportunities for elegy: old masters like Wallace Stevens, Yvor Winters, and R. P. Blackmur—and more tragically, contemporaries like Delmore Schwartz, Randall Jarrell, and Sylvia Plath—all died as the Dream Songs were being written. Some of these deaths call forth a merely official mourning, as with Plath, whom Berryman did not know personally. Others are occasions for literary criticism. In Dream Song #219, titled "So Long? Stevens," Berryman uses the death of Wallace Stevens to summarize his complaint against the symbolizing imagination of the Modernists: "That metaphysics / he hefted up until we could not breathe / the physics." The movement of Berryman's own work, of course, was in just the opposite direction, discarding "metaphysics" in favor of the local and particular. Like all the best poets of his generation, he acknowledged the mastery of the Modernists, but insisted that his own way was also valid: Stevens may have been "better than us," Berryman writes, but he was "less wide."

But it was Schwartz whose death meant the most to Berryman. They met in the late 1930s and remained close friends for many years; one of Berryman's early poems pays homage to "Delmore" and his "marvellous faculties." By the time he died in 1966, however, Schwartz had declined into severe mental illness, and his talent had largely evaporated. His death occupies "Ten Songs, one solid block of agony," in which Berryman recounts their early friendship, Schwartz's gradual degeneration, and his sordid death in a Times Square flophouse, "fighting for air, tearing his sorry clothes / with his visions dying." These are some of the best poems in *His Toy*, though their texture is different from the earlier Dream Songs, more discursive and openly autobiographical. Still, they succeed in transforming Schwartz—as their mutual friend Saul Bellow was also to do in *Humboldt's Gift*—into the emblematic modern poet, at once blessed and doomed: "His mission was obscure. His mission was real, / but obscure."

The deaths of so many friends and colleagues is another grievance for Henry to hold against God: "I'm cross with god who has wrecked this generation." The more he suffers, the less inclined he is to believe in a benevolent God: "long experience of His works / has not taught me his love." In the earlier Songs, Henry speculated that Lucifer was at least as powerful as God; now he offers a still more pessimistic view, that God is himself evil. This is the blasphemous conclusion of Dream Song #238, "Henry's Programme for God":

Perhaps God resembles one of the last etchings of Goya
& not Velasquez, never Rembrandt no.
Something disturbed,
ill-pleased, & with a touch of paranoia
who calls for this thud of love from his creatures-O.
Perhaps God ought to be curbed.

Yet the passion of Henry's argument with God is not purely negative. His conviction of his own guilt sometimes leads him to see his suffering as a deserved punishment. Donne implored, "Batter my heart, three-personed God," and Berryman echoes him:

If all must hurt at once, let yet more hurt now,
so I'll be ready, Dr God. Push on me.
Give it to Henry harder.

The paradox of Henry's faith is that he can credit God's justice, but not His mercy. Henry's guilt runs so deep that he cannot see his torment as unjustified; he may rebel against it, but he also suspects that he is forcing God to hurt him, in order to save his wretched soul. What remains inconceivable is God's love. In other words, Berryman's Christianity includes the Passion but not the Nativity:

let's exchange blue-black kisses
for the fate of the Man who was not born today,
clashing our tinsel, by the terrible tree
whereon he really hung, for you & me.

Among many other things, then, the Dream Songs must be accounted a great poem of bewildered faith, in the tradition of the Book of Job. Berryman provided several epigrams for the Dream Songs, but perhaps the best one would have been Job 7:11: "Therefore I will not restrain my mouth; I will speak in the anguish of my spirit; I will complain in the bitterness of my soul." Or, as Berryman puts it, in the best summary of his daring masterpiece: "Naked the man came forth in his mask, to be."

THE MASK, BERRYMAN knew, was the key to the success of the Dream Songs. Thin as the disguise sometimes wore, Henry was an indispensable camouflage for Berryman, allowing him to blaspheme, fantasize, and despair without taking final responsibility for his words. Henry had the Shakespearean Fool's freedom to speak the unspeakable.

But after the second volume of Dream Songs appeared—and won the National Book Award, confirming Berryman's fame—a combination of pressures made it necessary for him to take off that mask. His artistic motives are not hard to understand. Berryman had exhausted the possibilities of the form, as the increasing threadbareness of the later Songs makes clear, and like Lowell he always believed that he could only retain his mastery by extending it. He had already radically remade his style three times, with the sonnets, *Bradstreet*, and the Dream Songs. If he was significantly to add to his achievement, he would need another style.

The direction of the change, however, was determined by other motives, not just artistic but personal and spiritual. The years of Berryman's greatest artistic achievement had also been a period of accelerating personal decline. His drinking had reached the point of acute alcoholism, sending him to the hospital on several occasions, and producing ominous physical and mental symptoms. His opportunities for womanizing were multiplied by fame; he had run through a brief second marriage, and was now beginning to jeopardize his third. And he suffered all his life from suicidal depression, which he feared was his father's legacy. By the end of 1969, Berryman had landed in the intensive care unit, and finally enrolled himself in Alcoholics Anonymous.

As part of the twelve step program, Berryman had to write out "a searching and fearless inventory" of his problems. The day after Christmas 1969, he described what this involved: "giving specific instances of selfishness, alibis, dishonest thinking, pride, resentment & anger, intolerance, impatience, envy, phonyness, procrastination, self pity, oversensitivity, fear, etc." It is impossible to miss the irony that these are precisely the themes of the Dream Songs; they are the sins in which Henry was conceived. And now that his survival depended on purging those sins, it became essential that Berryman separate himself from Henry once and for all.

So it was that, in early 1970, Berryman began to write a new kind of poem. Just as in earlier moments of artistic crisis, he wrote with compulsive haste: four poems on the first day, an entire book between February and June. The key to the poems which became *Love & Fame* was that, as Berryman said, "the poet speaks in his own person, they're not dramatic, they're lyric." Years earlier, he had claimed that "the speaker can never be the actual writer, who is a person with an address," but now he was trying to get the actual writer, address and all, down on the page:

International art: . . . I feel friendly to the idea
but skeptical.
I live at 33 Arthur Ave. S.E.
& mostly write from here.

Like Lowell's late poems in *Day by Day*, the poems of *Love &
Fame* approach the purely confessional: they try to leave as little
distance as possible between the man and the poet. After the
ambiguities of the Dream Songs, their loose, unrhymed quatrains
are practically transparent. In the first half of the book, Berryman
seems simply to be telling stories from his youth—"Impressions,
structures, tales, from Columbia in the Thirties / & the Michael-
mas term at Cambridge in '36." And while any writing involves
selection—"It's not my life. / That's occluded and lost," he
insists—*Love & Fame* gives the impression of omitting nothing.
Berryman tells us the names of his allies on the Columbia Student Council, and the scores of Columbia's football games against
Princeton and Brown.

Paradoxically, however, this documentary realism proves more
poetically hazardous than the contorted language and dark fantasies of Henry. In the Dream Songs, even when the substance
was obscure, the tone was expertly controlled; Berryman kept an
uneasy distance from his creation. But now, writing about his
own life, it is hard to tell if he retains any saving irony. It is no
longer clear whether artistic design or mere narcissism leads
Berryman to tell the reader, for instance, which of his college girl-
friends refused to sleep with him, or why he failed his course in
eighteenth-century literature.

Finally, however, Berryman does have a purpose in mind.
Throughout his life, he pursued both love and fame (the Romantic ideals of Keats's sonnet "When I have fears that I may cease to
be") with fanatical energy. Now that he has achieved them, however, he finds them powerless to save him. And so he sets out to
undermine the prestige of love and fame by showing their grubby
origins in a young man's lust and pride. True to his Freudian

inspiration, Berryman tries to reverse the sublimation that turns egoistic fantasies into the elevated concepts of art. In "Two Organs," he pointedly parallels his sexual ambition "to satisfy at once all Barnard & Smith / & have enough left over for Miss Gibbs's girls" with his artistic ambition to write "big fat fresh original & characteristic poems." In both arenas, he is vain, insecure, clumsy, grandiose.

Berryman evidently means for the reader to see the foolishness of his youthful ambition, especially when it comes to women: in "Freshman Blues," he longs for "the great red joy a pecker ought to be / to pump a woman ragged." Yet the loving detail with which he tells his stories, the enchantment with trivia, and the constant sentimentality about lost youth, all make the adult Berryman seem very indulgent to his younger self. It is here that his decision to move from the "dramatic" to the "lyric" exacts a toll. It is impossible for Berryman to bring the same rigor and irony to his own autobiography that he brought to Henry's follies. Because these are his own memories, he inevitably finds in them an inherent interest that the reader cannot share.

The real justification for the switch to autobiography does not come until the third section of *Love & Fame*, which moves from Berryman's youth to the present day. Now we can see the unspoken motive behind his reminiscences: to find out how the promising young poet became a mental patient on the verge of suicide. The first poem in the third section, "The Search," asks the painful question:

> *I wondered ever too what my fate would be,*
> *women & after-fame become quite unavailable,*
> *or at best unimportant.*

Ostensibly Berryman is referring to the time after death; but this "fate" is also the present, when love and fame have become "unavailable," ironically, because they have been achieved and exhausted. The reader knows, though Berryman skips over it, that the young aspiring poet did become famous, and did have many lovers. Yet now he finds himself in "Despair":

> *I said in a Song once: I am unusually tired.*
> *I repeat that & increase it.*
> *I'm vomiting. . . .*
> *. . . . .*
> *I certainly don't think I'll last much longer.*

Here is the pathos, and the problem, of these late poems. Berryman's suffering has already been unforgettably expressed in the Dream Songs; all that is left for him is simply to assert it once again. But this time the lament is uttered in his own voice, and it strains against the limits of art. Like Robert Lowell in *The Dolphin*, Berryman has not mastered the experience he writes about; he is right in the thick of it, fighting for his life. But contrary to the expectations of confessional poetry, this extremity does not result in better, more passionate and authentic verse. Instead, it creates a desperate instability, a confusion of tone and style, which is repellent and pitiful.

This dilemma is shown in its purest form in the last section of the book, the sequence "Eleven Addresses to the Lord." Having descended to the depths, Berryman now turns—in accordance with AA doctrine—to a higher power: "Under new management, Your Majesty: / Thine." But these addresses are born of urgent personal need, and they throw overboard all the irony, doubt, and grief that made the Dream Songs authentically religious poetry. Instead, there is a limp and almost wheedling tone, addressed to a childishly conceived Providence. Berryman begs: "Surprise me on some ordinary day / with a blessing gratuitous."

Berryman's urgent need of rescue cannot help making his new-found faith sound suspect. Why, after the blasphemy and nihilism of the Dream Songs, is he now able to write: "I believe as fixedly in the Resurrection-appearances to Peter & to Paul / as I believe I sit in this blue chair"? The only valid reason would be a genuine conversion, and Berryman does claim to have experienced this: "My double nature fused in that point of time / three weeks ago day before yesterday." Yet the very recent date of the conversion, and still more the absence of any reticence or introspection, make this experience hard to credit; while it may have been real, it does not become poetically convincing. Berryman writes that "I fell back in love with you, Father, for two reasons: / You were good to me, & a delicious author," but such flippancy does not seem to justify overturning a lifetime of meticulously expressed doubt.

Critics of *Love & Fame* expressed such skepticism, and in *Delusions, Etc.*—his last book, published after his death—Berryman lashed out at them in "Defensio in Extremis": "Tell them to leave me damned well alone with my insights." But Berryman could have found a precise diagnosis of his condition in a writer he knew well and greatly respected. In *Either/Or*, Kierkegaard insists on the need for each human being finally to take responsibility for his or her soul:

Do you not know that there comes a midnight hour when every one has to throw off his mask? Do you believe that life will always let itself be mocked? Do you think you can slip away a little before midnight in order to avoid this? Or are you not terrified by this? . . . he who cannot reveal himself cannot love, and he who cannot love is the most unhappy man of all.

This is exactly Berryman's reason for discarding the mask of Henry. At the most serious moment, he must reveal himself as himself. But since he is doing this in poetry, he is simultaneously concerned with his soul and his audience, God and the reader; and neither is satisfied. Kierkegaard also foresaw this danger for the writer:

> A religious poet is in a peculiar position. Such a poet will seek to establish a relation to the religious through the imagination; but for this very reason he succeeds only in establishing an aesthetic relationship to something aesthetic. . . . Religious pathos does not consist in singing and hymning and composing verses, but in existing. . . . [But] aesthetically it is the poetic productivity which is essential.

For Berryman, "poetic productivity" had always been "essential," the real justification for his life and everything in it. Now, for the purposes of salvation—which in his desperate condition was more than a metaphor—he had to consider himself simply as a soul. But Berryman had been so long accustomed to turning his soul into art that he was driven to make poetry even of his rejection of poetry. Berryman thought he was writing religiously, but essentially he remained aesthetic; he had become Kierkegaard's "most unhappy man of all."

The last year of Berryman's life was spent in and out of treatment, in painful resolutions and shattering failures of sobriety. He wrote the poems published posthumously as *Delusions, Etc.*, similar in style and subject to the second half of *Love & Fame*; there is even a reprise of "Eleven Addresses" in the sequence "Opus Dei." And he began a novel based closely on his experience in AA, published in its unfinished state as *Recovery*. But the most important work to come out of this final year was a single poem, "He Resigns":

> *I don't feel this will change.*
> *I don't want any thing*
> *or person, familiar or strange.*
> *I don't think I will sing*
>
> *any more just now;*
> *or ever. I must start*
> *to sit with a blind brow*
> *above an empty heart.*

This is far more moving than the loquacity of his other late poems, because it does not seem to be addressing anyone for effect—neither God nor the reader. Its very bareness seems a token of earnestness: stripped of detail and rhetoric, with a simple rhyme scheme, it is a kind of zero point in Berryman's work. Having spent decades among the bizarre and particular, he gives voice in this poem to something simple and universal; it is even reminiscent of the desolation of late Yeats, who Berryman had begun his career trying to imitate. On January 7, 1972, at the age of fifty-seven, John Berryman ended his life by jumping off the Washington Avenue Bridge in Minneapolis.

RANDALL JARRELL

Oh, bars of my own body, open, open!

In the spring of 1953, Randall Jarrell met T. S. Eliot for the first time. At a reception at the University of Illinois at Urbana, where Jarrell was teaching, Eliot greeted him warmly and insisted: "We must have a chat." But, as his wife Mary later recalled, Jarrell "was so overwhelmed by Eliot that he immediately left the circle around him and sought refuge among strangers in the furthest corner of the room." Though Eliot died just a few months before the much younger Jarrell, the two never met again.

This encounter, in which modesty is indistinguishable from

pride, captures the essence of Jarrell's relationship, not just to Eliot, but to Modernism itself. As the leading poet-critic of his generation, Jarrell had no choice but to confront the figure of Eliot, whose achievements in poetry and criticism made him a virtually papal figure. Yet unlike Lowell and Berryman, whose rebellion against the great Modernists could be seen in their radicalism of style and subject, Jarrell responded to this burden with respectful, self-protective evasion. In his poetry and in his criticism, he would advance not by attacking the old values, but by almost naively discovering and practicing new ones. As Delmore Schwartz wrote in a review of *Poetry and the Age*—Jarrell's first collection of essays, published in 1953—he "goes beyond the standards and discriminations of T. S. Eliot, which have dominated the criticism of poetry for the past twenty-five years"; but he manages to do this without "the characteristic rejection and exclusion that almost always marks and cripples new movements and new points of view in criticism."

In fact, naivete—reading that is joyful, spontaneous, untutored; writing that imitates ordinary ineloquent speech—would be the cornerstone of Jarrell's poetics. If Lowell allied himself in imagination with tyrants and warriors, Jarrell was instinctively drawn to children and women, whose weakness in conventional terms he recognized as a different kind of power. In politics as in literature, his sympathy was with the vulnerable—everything that was excluded from, and therefore implicitly resisted, the domain of aggressive, masculine reason. Yet such sympathy can all too easily slip into sentimentality, which is the besetting sin of Jarrell's poetry. In his style, too, Jarrell's desire to assume a plain, feeling voice comes at a price, often threatening to lead him into banality. If he was not as aggressively ambitious as some of his peers, neither was he as commanding an artist.

Like Lowell, Jarrell learned the tenets of New Criticism directly from the source: John Crowe Ransom was his mentor in college and graduate school. (Lowell and Jarrell were roommates for a time at Kenyon College, where Ransom taught.) But as early as 1940, when he was twenty-six years old, Jarrell demonstrated in his first major critical statement how he could honor the achievements of his teachers, while still politely evading them. The occasion was his first book publication as a poet, in the 1940 New Directions anthology *Five Young American Poets* (which also included John Berryman). Jarrell used his prose introduction—which he wrote reluctantly, at the insistence of the publisher—to lay out a brief but comprehensive sketch of modern poetic history. Though he never extended its compact arguments, it can be read as the foundation for Jarrell's later poetry and criticism, and indeed as a manifesto for his generation.

Jarrell's forensic strategy was to deny Modernism the very quality its name insists on. Rather than being essentially new, a definitive break with nineteenth-century Romanticism—as Eliot and Pound had declared—Jarrell argued that " 'Modern' poetry is, essentially, an extension of romanticism; it is what romantic poetry wishes or finds it necessary to become." The essay goes on to catalogue at length the continuities between Romantic and Modernist poetry: "very interesting language, a great emphasis on connotation, 'texture'; extreme intensity, forced emotion—violence; a good deal of obscurity . . . experimental or novel qualities of some sort," and many more. They can be reduced to a common denominator: both Romantic and Modernist poetry, Jarrell suggests, strive for ever more complex and difficult expression. In its language, emotion, and organization, Modernism exponentially multiplies the strangeness and difficulty of poets like Wordsworth and Shelley. But this is only a "big quantitative change," not a qualitative one. The Modernists were not revolutionaries, as they believed, but inheritors, and their poetry represents not a new beginning but "The End of the Line"—the title Jarrell gave the essay when he revised it for magazine publication.

By asserting that Modernism is not modern, Jarrell makes it possible to divide the history of poetry in a new way, awarding the privilege of the new beginning to his own generation. Jarrell does not take it upon himself to predict what this genuinely new poetry will look like, and he specifically denies that his own poems are meant to inaugurate it. But he is certain that it will not be simply a continuation of the trends of "modernist romanticism," which no longer exert any compelling force on the young poet: ideas and styles "which once were axiomatic, permitting neither disagreement nor understanding . . . are no longer determining."

Jarrell seems on the verge of coining a word that would, decades later, enjoy a great career in literary criticism: "postmodern." (He came still closer a few years later, when praising Lowell's poetry as "post- or anti-modernist"—surely one of the first uses of the term in a literary context.) Just as the word suggests, Jarrell defines himself and his generation by a negative; they are what comes after the titanic achievements of Modernism. This was a sign of remarkable confidence: it took a decade or more for most of his peers to turn their backs on the principles and practice of Modernism. But even Jarrell is still unable to give positive substance to this new identity: between "the end of the line" and the new beginning there is a disquieting lull, as "the marionette looks reluctantly for another hand." And with hindsight it is clear that Jarrell's impression was correct. In 1940, the strongest poets of his generation were still writing in inherited Modernist idioms;

with the exception of Delmore Schwartz, their mature individual work was still years away.

This was certainly true of Jarrell's own poetry. He later distanced himself from his first book, *Blood for a Stranger*, which appeared in 1942, writing that "About 2 / 3 are poems I wish my worst enemy had written, or anybody else, just not me." In fact, many of the poems seem to have been written by W. H. Auden, whose style and concerns imposed greatly on Jarrell. The influence of Auden can be heard in Jarrell's abstract nouns and strikingly ill-assorted adjectives, as well as in his panoramic view of current events, darkly tinted with Marxist pessimism. The volume contains poems about the Spanish Civil War, the Nazi takeover of Austria, and European refugees, all omens of a sinister future: "The future already stirs like a spore, / Erects to our incredulous stare / The unknown organ, the tentacles / That bend to us in their long caress." The borrowed tones and concerns mean that these poems remain apprentice work, and Jarrell excluded most of them from his 1955 *Selected Poems*.

But even before *Blood for a Stranger* was published, Jarrell was already using his critical intelligence to pry his poetry loose from Auden's influence. In 1941, he wrote his single most extensive piece of destructive criticism, "Changes of Attitude and Rhetoric in Auden's Poetry." In part, the essay exorcizes Auden's seductive influence simply by anatomizing his style, with a ruthless comprehensiveness. Jarrell's catalog of twenty-six stylistic features, from "unusual punctuation" to "the use of unusual or unusually abrupt appositions," leaves Auden's poetry lying on the dissecting table like a stripped cadaver.

But all these precise observations are put at the service of a larger critique of Auden's poetry, one that would later be echoed by poets from Delmore Schwartz to Philip Larkin. Jarrell finds, already by 1940, a drastic decline in the originality and power of Auden's poetry. His early work is "concrete, startling, and thoroughly realized," full of "tough magical effects"; but the later poems turn this spontaneous, almost irrational style into a collection of "devices," repeated and exploited to the point of banality. "Auden has been successful in making his poetry more accessible," Jarrell concedes, "but the success has been entirely too expensive." In avoiding the sin of "modernist romanticism," he commits the opposite sin of writing only with "the head, the top of the head." To chart a middle course, Jarrell unmistakably implies, will be the task of his own poetry: "I am not going to try to tell the reader what the solution should be, but I can tell him where to find it: in the work of the next first-rate poet."

Writing with just "the top of the head" was certainly a temptation for the highly intellectual, erudite Jarrell. The most original poems in *Blood for a Stranger* try to avoid that trap by writing plainly and emotionally, "from the heart"—a course that held its own set of dangers. In "The Memoirs of Glückel of Hameln," Jarrell writes his first poem about a figure that would later dominate his poetry: the average middle-aged woman. He does not yet inhabit this woman and speak in her voice, as he will do later; instead, he picks one such woman out of history and addresses her. Glückel was a seventeenth-century German Jewish housewife whose memoirs chronicle a thoroughly dull and domestic existence. It is this very lack of excitement that Jarrell makes the focus of his poem:

> *One marries, one has children whom one marries;*
> *One's husband dies; one mourns, re-marries.*

The reader reads, reads, and at last, grown weary
With hearing the amount of every dowry,
He mumbles, Better to burn than marry . . .

Here Jarrell's style mirrors the very monotony he describes, repeating words over and over again ("marry" or "marries" appears four times in five lines). This unemphatic repetition would become one of Jarrell's major verse techniques; if Modernism was distinguished by "very interesting language," his own postmodern poetry would become deliberately uninteresting, with its circlings, hesitations, and repetitions.

Yet as "Glückel" shows, Jarrell's unemphatic style is well suited to the unemphatic life he is writing about; and increasingly he will find such lives a morally and psychologically compelling subject for poetry. His escape from Modernist "strangeness" would not be an advance into easy intellectual discursiveness, which he thought condemned Auden's poetry to become mere rhetoric. Instead, it will be a retreat—better, a descent—into the emotional depths concealed by the ordinary. In "Glückel," Jarrell deliberately opposes his subject to the famous intellectual heroes of her period—the kind of figures Lowell or Schwartz would have chosen to write about—and finds her compelling despite her mediocrity:

Yet when I think of those progressive years,
Of Newton, Leibnitz, Mandeville, and Pope,
You lend a certain body to the thought;
I am perplexed with your fat tearful ghost.

Ordinary women like Glückel will become one of Jarrell's major avenues into strong, simple emotion, whose expression had been stifled by the abstract symbolic rhetoric of Modernism. A second and equally important avenue is the child, whose imaginative world Jarrell begins to explore in "Children Selecting Books in a Library." Here he already locates the two qualities of childhood that would be most important to his later work: its vulnerability and its imaginative freedom, which he often associates with the freedom of reading. Children are helpless against adults, which explains their fascination with the monsters in fairy tales:

> *Their tales are full of sorcerers and ogres*
> *Because their lives are: the capricious infinite*
> *That, like parents, no one has yet escaped*
> *Except by luck or magic. . . .*

But while this makes the child pathetic, what makes him tragic is that he is helpless against time, which inexorably turns the child himself into one of those ogres. Childhood is always a lost paradise, since by the time we are old enough to be conscious of it, and bring it to poetic expression, it is already over. Only the adult can see the child as "Moving in blind grace," since only the adult knows that the child is subject to "a doom as ecumenical as dawn": the universal fate of growing up.

The child, then, is doubly pitiable: he cannot contend against adults, and he cannot contend against adulthood. For this plight Jarrell finds no remedy, only a compensation in the imaginative escape offered by reading. He is insistent that such reading cannot really help the child, only momentarily occupy him: "Read meanwhile," the poem advises, "For a little while, forget." By telling ourselves stories, we can temporarily alleviate the pain of existence. Already we hear, in "Children Selecting Books in a Library," what will become the great and double-edged theme of Jarrell's work: pity, which can turn at any moment into self-pity. Jarrell's children, like his women, sponsor an unselfconscious luxuriance of emotion, which is often hard to distinguish from sentimentality.

Jarrell's flight from the aggressive, masculine world of the intellect is not only a poetic principle; it also has serious political implications. "The Winter's Tale," though not one of his better early poems, clearly lays out the worldview that would increasingly animate Jarrell's poetry. The ultimate source of the twentieth century's wars, the poem argues, is the hubris of scientific rationalism:

> *We who have possessed the world*
> *As efficiently as a new virus; who classified the races,*
> *Species, and cultures of the world as scrub*
> *To be cleared, stupidity to be liquidated, matter*
> *To be assimilated into the system of our destruction . . .*

Such reason, which possesses and classifies and liquidates, is a kind of aggression against nature, a form of sublimated violence always about to break out into actual violence. Against this abstract intellect, Jarrell poses a set of contrary emblems:

> *Yet, through our night, just as before,*
> *The discharged thief stumbles, nevertheless*
> *Weeps at its crystals, feels at the winter's*
> *Tale the familiar and powerful delight;*
> *The child owns the snow-man. . . .*

The thief and the child, night and tears, the delight of the tale: these are holdouts against what the poem goes on to call the "western hegemonies" of aggressive, warlike reason. Add women, and it is also a comprehensive list of Jarrell's favorite subjects. What they share, in his telling, are passivity and imagination and emotion, all traits despised by the ordinary adult world. By identifying himself with them, he counts the poet as another resister to the forces that have brought the world "the disintegrating bomber."

There is an equally important personal implication to this posture. By imaginatively allying himself with women and children, Jarrell allows himself to express the ambivalence about male sexuality that will increasingly fuel his poetry. Instead of the domineering, even predatory lust that is found everywhere in the poetry of Lowell and Berryman, Jarrell's erotic poetry is always drawn to passive roles and scenes of transgression. Not to ravish but to be ravished—as a child is by his awakening sexuality, or a fairy-tale princess by her rescuer, or even a man by the image of a beautiful boy—is his repeated wish, and produces some of his most powerful and mysterious poems.

THE NEXT DEVELOPMENT in Jarrell's poetry, however, was prompted by his immersion in a wholly masculine world. In October 1942, he enlisted in the Army Air Corps, where he would spend the next three and a half years as an instructor of bomber crews. Though he was never sent overseas, Jarrell's military experience gave him a much closer view of World War II than peers like Lowell, Berryman, and Schwartz, all of whom avoided service. Jarrell's next two books of poems, *Little Friend, Little Friend* (1945) and *Losses* (1948), are largely devoted to the war as he saw and imagined it.

Perhaps the most surprising thing about Jarrell's war poems is what they do not contain. For one thing, the poet himself is almost completely absent. As he wrote to Lowell in December 1945: "I've never written a poem about myself in the army or war; unless you're vain or silly you realize that you, except insofar as you're in exactly the same boat as the others, aren't the primary subject of any sensible writing about the war." Neither does he address the rights and wrongs of the war, or even its causes in any concrete sense. For Jarrell, the war is not a historical event but a state of being into which the soldier is violently thrown, and where he learns essential truths about human nature and the nature of modern society. In that sense, the war did not change but only deepened the themes of Jarrell's poetry. As he was to write in late 1945, "The real war poets are always war poets, peace or any time."

Collectively, soldiers are the instrument of obscene violence, yet individually, they are utterly weak and bewildered: that is the paradox at the root of Jarrell's best war poems. Not only does the soldier not control his own actions, Jarrell insists, he doesn't even understand them. He is a sleepwalker in a dream, as in "Siegfried":

> *in the gunner's skull,*
> *It is a dream: and he, the watcher, guiltily*
> *Watches the him, the actor, who is innocent.*
> It happens as it does because it does.

This dreamlike detachment seems to Jarrell the normal condition of the soldier—in part, no doubt, because he saw the war from the vantage of the bomber crew, who are literally far removed from the damage they cause. To the bombardier, his bombs are "death under glass," and his function is abstract and mechanical: "to enter / So many knots in a window, so many feet; / To switch on for an instant the steel that understands."

The bleak wit of that last line encapsulates Jarrell's view of the war: the soldier lays the responsibility for understanding on a machine, and sees himself as just another component of that machine. Disturbingly, Jarrell suggests that the psychology of the American pilot is as slavish and irresponsible as that of the Nazi war criminal: "Do as they said; as they said, there is always a reason." The point is driven home still more forcibly in "Eighth Air Force," a poem from *Losses*:

> *The other murderers troop in yawning;*
> *Three of them play Pitch, one sleeps, and one*
> *Lies counting missions, lies there sweating*
> *Till even his heart beats: One; One; One.*
> O murderers! . . . *Still, this is how it's done:*
>
> *This is a war. . . .*

These ordinary American soldiers on their bunks—frightened, sleepy, or playful—are the very same men who will annihilate German cities. By calling them "murderers" rather than soldiers, Jarrell shocks us into realizing how deeply war distorts our usual moral categories. When the poem concludes "I find no fault in this just man," the ironies are layered three deep: the man is not just, because he is a murderer; but he must be just, because he kills in a socially accepted cause; but again, he is neither just nor unjust, because he is not responsible or aware enough to be considered a moral agent. That these are also the words of Pilate, as he washes his hands of the death of Jesus, adds yet another irony, turning the American soldier into the archvillain of the Gospels, and his German and Japanese victims into sacrificial lambs.

Another type of poet might charge this abdication of responsibility against the pilot as a crime. Jarrell abstains from such judgment, largely because his own experience as a flight instructor gave him the chance to observe pilots close up, and to see that they were not much more than boys. This allows Jarrell to assign them to a category with which he sympathizes—the innocent child—and reserve the blame for the military as a whole, or even more broadly for the "State."

This is the idea behind some of Jarrell's best war poems, including "The Death of the Ball Turret Gunner," the five-line poem that is his best known work. "From my mother's sleep I fell into the State," the gunner tells us, eliding his whole prewar life and giving the impression that he was literally an infant when he became a soldier. This suggestion is prolonged in the next image, "And I hunched in its belly till my wet fur froze": the ball turret on the underside of the bomber shades into the "belly" of the pregnant mother, and the "wet fur" of the aviator's jacket seems like the slick down of a newborn animal. All this makes the poem's grotesque final image—"When I died they washed me out of the turret with a hose"—seem to describe an abortion; the soldier-fetus is evacuated before he can even be born.

Jarrell works a similar surprise in the famous lines from "Losses": "In bombers named for girls, we burned / The cities we had learned about in school. . . ." Here the shock lies in the word "burned," incongruously sitting between two banal high-school memories—the girls the pilots dated and the geography textbooks they studied. How could such boys, the lines implicitly

ask, know what it means to burn a city? By eliminating any suggestion of motive from the pilots' actions, Jarrell makes the child-
pilot appear a victim of the State, even as he produces victims for
the State. For this reason, there is no significant moral difference,
in Jarrell's eyes, between combat deaths and deaths in training,
which he would have witnessed at his Stateside airfield. In
"Losses," the only difference lies in the euphemism used for a soldier's death; if he dies on a bombing run, rather than a training
flight, "It was not an accident but a mistake." Here, again, there is
a bleak understated wit: Jarrell refuses to use the ennobling terms
we might expect, like "sacrifice" or even "casualty," and instead
refers to a combat death as a mere "mistake," virtually indistinguishable from "accident." Similarly, a poem about the crash of a
plane returning to base in bad weather is titled "A Front": for Jarrell, the front is not just where men kill, but anywhere they die.

To be a soldier, then, is to suffer personally the fate that Jarrell
foresaw, in "The Winter's Tale," overtaking the whole planet: a
human being becomes "matter / To be assimilated into the system
of our destruction." Reckoning by the million, the Army treats
the soldier's individual identity as an unaffordable luxury, as in
"Soldier [T.P.]":

> Yet it is not You the sergeants hoarsely
> Curse at. . . .
> . . . .
> That You may be, perhaps—as Justice
> May be, may be; this world's justice
> Is here, is now—as you too are, soldier.

But there are moments when the military loosens its grip, and
offers the soldier a fleeting internal freedom. Jarrell's poetry is

drawn to such moments of escape, when reason is exchanged for sleep or memory, and community for solitude. The soldier can be "Absent with Official Leave," in the ironic phrase of one title, only when dreaming:

> *He covers his ears with his pillow, and begins to drift*
> *(Like the plumes the barracks trail into the sky)*
> *Past the laughs, the quarrels, and the breath of others*
>
> *To the ignorant countries where civilians die*
> *Inefficiently, in their spare time, for nothing . . .*

Civilian life is hardly a paradise in Jarrell's telling; like the war, it is a scene of dying. The crucial difference is only that civilians die "inefficiently," free from war's rationalization and systemization of death. The soldier's assertion of individual freedom, in Jarrell's poetry, is always pathetically reduced, a symbolic escape where the real thing is impossible. In "Mail Call," the soldiers are content with just hints of the civilian life they have lost: "In letters and in dreams they see the world." The letter and the dream are immune to military discipline, since they are addressed not to the mass but to a single soldier: "The soldier simply wishes for his name." Again, in "O My Name It Is Sam Hall," three military prisoners "stop and grin" when their guard sings the army song of the title, which—as Jarrell's note explains—is a little chant of insubordination: "O my name it is Sam Hall / And I hate you one and all." The guard and the prisoners are united in this token rebellion. Indeed, in Jarrell's view, the guard is just another kind of prisoner, as he writes in "Prisoners": "The prisoners, the guards, the soldiers—they are all, in their way, being trained."

Jarrell was in uniform until February 1946, when he was given his discharge papers at a base in Austin, Texas. The occasion inspired a final look at the dehumanizing mathematics of the army. In "The Lines," Jarrell reviews the many literal and metaphorical lines into which the army arranges its units: "the basic line" of "waiting / For meals or mail"; the front lines, "Where the things die as though they were not things"; the hospital ward, with "rows / Of the white beds"; the cemetery full of "the crosses' lines"; and the comically futile lines where the soldier waits "To form a line to form a line to form a line." All of these lines, the poem suggests, have one goal in common, to convince the men that a line is their natural habitat: "the things have learned that they are things, / Used up as things are." But now, at last, they are released back into freedom, the constant goal and true theme of Jarrell's war poetry:

> *The lines break up, for good; and for a breath,*
> *The longest of their lives, the men are free.*

JARRELL'S EXPERIENCE OF constraint and freedom in the army not only cemented his poetry's commitment to those themes; it also helped to seal his break with the style and sensibility of Modernism. The connection between his ethical and his formal evolution can be seen in a significant letter Jarrell wrote to Allen Tate in April 1945. Tate was one of Jarrell's most important early mentors and sponsors, but the two men had already begun to fall out as Jarrell asserted his poetic independence. In 1943, Tate wrote a sardonic poem addressed to American airmen, "Ode to Our Young Pro-consuls of the Air." In brittle, mock-Elizabethan stanzas, Tate treated the war as an assault on culture, in particular on his own efforts "To balk or slay / These enemies of mind" and "To live the past again." He saw the American pilots, sarcastically elevated to Roman "pro-consuls," as crusaders against the spirit:

And spying far away

Upon the Tibetan plain
A limping caravan,
    Dive, and exterminate
    The Lama, late
Survival of old pain.
Go kill the dying swan.

Fundamentally, Tate's feeling about the war is not so different from Jarrell's; both poets see it as a catastrophic threat to humane values. But the poem irritated Jarrell, who had helped to train the pilots against whom Tate deployed his satire. In his letter, he annihilates Tate's rhetoric with a homely image: "If you met your proconsuls you'd find you couldn't differentiate them from a high school football team, except for the fact that half of them had gotten killed during the season."

With this rebuke, Jarrell participates in his generation's growing impatience with the Modernist sensibility, in particular its tendency to abstract life into symbol. Jarrell's war poetry had made exactly the opposite movement, sympathizing always with the ordinary individual against the abstractions that tried to consume him. In the coming years, he would move still further in this direction, developing a style so ordinary that it risks banality, and so hospitable to simple emotion that it risks sentimentality.

At the same time, Jarrell used his criticism to undo the expectations and remake the canon of Modernism. In the late 1940s and early 1950s, he wrote the major essays collected in *Poetry and the Age*, his first and most important book of criticism. Significantly, the book contains almost no destructive criticism of the kind that Eliot and Pound had employed in their battle against their Victorian precursors. For those Modernist pioneers, the poetry they wanted to write could only be understood and valued if established poetic models—Swinburne, Arnold, Shelley, even Milton—were discredited. But Jarrell almost never conducted a frontal attack on the Modernists themselves. (The legendary venom of his poetry reviews was directed against insignificant minor poets, such as Oscar Williams, whose work, Jarrell said, seemed to be "written on a typewriter by a typewriter.") Instead, he chose to counter the influence of the New Critics, whose taste for ambiguity and impersonality was a legacy of the high Modernism of Eliot and Pound, by proposing different poets of the Modernist generation as role models.

The major essays in *Poetry and the Age* present themselves as acts of rehabilitation, pointing out the virtues in poets whom other critics have denigrated or ignored—especially Walt Whitman, Robert Frost, and William Carlos Williams. These are poets who do not lend themselves to the New Critical style of close reading, designed to squeeze the last drop of meaning from a poem. As a result, Jarrell complains, they are the objects of condescension from critics used to the dense, compacted style of Metaphysical and Modernist verse: "baby critics who have barely learned to complain of the lack of ambiguity in *Peter Rabbit* can tell you all that is wrong with *Leaves of Grass*." Comparing Jarrell's own plain, emotionally exposed monologues with the symbols of early Lowell, or the conceits of early Bishop, one can understand why he was so hostile to those "baby critics."

Jarrell's own criticism suggests a different way to read and evaluate poetry. Of course, Jarrell was a brilliant close reader when he wanted to be: his essay on Frost's "Home Burial" is exquisitely sensitive to its emotional and linguistic nuances. But usually he does not try to explain or analyze individual poems. Instead, he aims to infect the reader with his own enthusiasm, through long quotations and eloquent, witty praise. His critical creed can be summarized in his declaration, "I *like* liking poetry." Indeed, a characteristic gesture of Jarrell's criticism is to fall dramatically mute, as though nothing he can say would do justice to his subject. About Whitman: "the critic points at his qualities in despair and wonder, all method failing, and simply calls them by their names." About Frost: "such an article as this is not relatively but absolutely inadequate to a body of poetry as great as Frost's, both in quality and in quantity—can be, at best, only a kind of breathless signboard." About Marianne Moore: "It might be better to say . . . 'Words fail me, my lords,' and to go through [Moore's poetry] pointing."

As a result, even Jarrell's major essays don't engage with individual poems with the precision and depth that the New Critics achieved. In a sense Jarrell's essays are not criticism at all, if criticism means an attempt to explain and evaluate a work of art. Instead, they are urgent recommendations, promises of the pleasure the poet holds in store: of Frost, for instance, Jarrell writes that "the least crevice of the good poems is saturated with imagination," which sounds more like advertising than criticism. And the object of Jarrell's encomia is usually not the poem itself, a work with certain beauties of construction; it is the poet whose personality is expressed in the work. Jarrell urges us to make the acquaintance of the poet for his qualities of mind and feeling: Frost's "humor and sadness and composure," Williams's "moral and human attractiveness."

One effect of such criticism is greatly to democratize the reading and discussion of poetry. To appreciate a poet does not require specialized skills or training, such as the New Critics taught; the critic is just a marriage broker who brings poet and reader together, and then gets out of the way. Jarrell made this point explicitly in one of his most important essays, "The Age of Criticism," which constitutes a plea for what might be called amateur reading. Thanks to the influence of the New Critics and their quarterly journals, Jarrell argued, American literary culture had become obsessed with professional, technical criticism, to the point that criticism seemed more important than poetry or fiction: "look at the literary quarterlies, listen to the conversation of literary people: how much of it is criticism of criticism, talk about talk about books!"

In such a literary climate, readers must be reminded that criticism is purely instrumental, not an end in itself: "Criticism *does* exist, doesn't it, for the sake of the plays and stories and poems it criticizes?" And to write this kind of subservient criticism, Jarrell argues, requires "a terrible nakedness," a willingness to admit that the critic is nothing more than an articulate reader: "We do not become good critics by reading criticism and, secondarily, the 'data' or 'raw material' of criticism: that is, poems and stories. We become good critics by reading poems and stories and by living; it is criticism which is secondary. . . ." Jarrell advises his contemporaries to read with the enthusiastic openness he displays in his own work: "read more widely, more independently, and more joyfully." Or, as he puts it still more succinctly in another essay: *"Read at whim! read at whim!"* It is no wonder that, in later essays like "A Sad Heart at the Supermarket" and "The Taste of the Age," Jarrell became less a critic than a propagandist for literature.

This evasion of the technical and intellectual, in favor of the spontaneous and emotional, sheds a good deal of light on Jarrell's ambitions for his own verse. Throughout *Poetry and the Age*, he is more interested in the poet than the poem, more concerned with personality and emotion than with verbal structure. Of course, with great poets like Frost, the two are finally inseparable; and Jarrell is finely sensitive to the nuances of poems even when he does not choose to discuss them at length. But the same hierarchy of values carries over, more crudely and problematically, into his evaluations of lesser poets: in one review, for instance, Jarrell writes that "it is a pleasure to read a new poet who understands and cares for people and the world, instead of language and rhetoric and allusions." Conversely, he rebukes the young Richard Wilbur by saying that "after thirty or forty pages . . . [the reader] would pay dollars for one dramatic monologue, some blessed graceless human voice that has not yet learned to express itself so composedly as poets do."

Finally Jarrell came to believe, as he wrote to Elizabeth Bishop in 1957, that "life beats art, so to speak, and sense beats eccentricity, and the way things really are beats the most beautiful unreal visions, half-truths, one can fix up by leaving out and indulging oneself." All the major poets of his generation would eventually come to a similar conclusion. But for Jarrell, whose gift for language was smaller than that of Bishop or Lowell or Berryman, this evolution exacted a higher cost. By endorsing such an opposition between life and art, "the world" and "language,"

Jarrell's poetry suffers aesthetically, even as it strives for emotional and psychological truth.

IN HIS WAR poetry, Jarrell wrote in praise of the hidden and the private, everything that eludes the rational and aggressive daylight. But while this commitment was deepened and confirmed by the war, it was not merely a reaction to war; it can be seen in his work as early as *Blood for a Stranger*, and would continue in his postwar poems. For, as "The Lines" implies, the soldier is not really emancipated when he is discharged: he is free only "for a breath," before he is consumed once more by the rigid geometries of civilian life. In fact, Jarrell already begins in *Losses* to broaden his idea of freedom, from a social and political concept to a psychological and mythical one.

This is the theme of "The Märchen," which returns to the subject of "Children Selecting Books in a Library" and anticipates many future poems about childhood imagination. The title is the German word for "tales," like those told by the Brothers Grimm, and indicates Jarrell's increasing tendency to associate the German language with his other magical subjects:

> *Listening, listening; it is never still.*
> *This is the forest: long ago the lives*
> *Edged armed into its tides. . . .*
> . . . .
> *We felled our islands there, at last, with iron.*
> *The sunlight fell to them, according to our wish,*
> *And we believed, till nightfall, in that wish;*
> *And we believed, till nightfall, in our lives.*

Like Frost, whose dramatic monologues he greatly admired, Jarrell offers one half of a metaphor and requires the reader to unearth the other half, a procedure that makes his images seem mysteriously charged. The clearing in the forest is Jarrell's emblem for human consciousness, where the "sunlight" of reason falls. But this clearing can exist only thanks to the painful, even violent struggle to cut back the surrounding darkness with "iron"—that double-edged substance which, like reason itself, is both tool and weapon. The "clearing" of consciousness was made "long ago," echoing the fairy-tale formula of "once upon a time," and Jarrell leaves it nicely ambiguous whether this was long ago in an individual life—that is, in childhood—or long ago in the history of humanity. It is a poetic version of the biologist's maxim that "ontogeny recapitulates phylogeny": as the primitive is to the modern, so the child is to the adult. But these clearings of reason are merely "islands" in a surrounding forest, and while we dwell in the daylight, the noises of the forest are "never still." In a classically Freudian sense, that is, the realm of unreason is barely repressed by the rational ego. And we can regain that access to that buried world in childhood, in dream, and in story—Jarrell's numinous trinity.

"The Märchen" goes on to relate, in rapid and often confusing shorthand, stories out of Grimm. But it begins and ends with Hänsel, a fairy-tale figure who, like the poet, ventures into the forest and subjects himself to its dark powers. Jarrell ends with an address to "poor Hänsel" that condenses his tale, and every tale, to a motto:

Had you not learned—have we not learned, from tales
Neither of beasts nor kingdoms nor their Lord,

But of our own hearts, the realm of death—
Neither to rule nor die? to change, to change!

The fairy tale, Jarrell at last says openly, is not really about strange beasts or enchanted kingdoms, but about "our own hearts," which body themselves forth in such symbols. And the forest, which is the "realm of death" and night and dream, cannot be shut outside of us, as though it were simply territory to conquer. That would be the solution of the technologist and the rationalist—those villains of "The Winter's Tale," "who classified the races, / Species, and cultures of the world as scrub / To be cleared." Instead, Jarrell's last line proposes a compromise between opposites: neither to rule by reason, nor to die by submitting wholly to unreason, but to acknowledge the boundary where these opposites meet, the imagination. "To change!" is the goal and motto of the fairy tale, where the irrational is accepted and lifted up into the consciousness of art. All through Jarrell's later poetry, he will seek symbols of this fruitful union.

Other poems in *Losses*, however, show the perils to which Jarrell was exposed by these themes. There is a fine line between artistic interest in children and death, and sentimental effusion about them. It is a line Jarrell crosses in "Lady Bates," a maudlin poem addressed to a dead child:

"Try to open your eyes;
Try to reach to one, to the nearest,
Reach, move your hand a little, try to move—
You can't move, can you?
You can't move. . . .
You're fast asleep, you're fast asleep."

Jarrell is tugging at the heartstrings with the same shameless enthusiasm as Charles Dickens, whose Little Nell is a direct ancestress of Lady Bates. In this connection, it is interesting to note Jarrell's reaction when he was told that, when one of his poems was read aloud to an audience, "they'd practically cried." He was frankly delighted: "I feel like the Dickens *de nos jours,* a very lovely feeling."

But the lachrymose effect of "Lady Bates" comes entirely from the situation, not from the language, which is banal and repetitive. In fact, the poem sounds like a script, needing a human voice to supply the pathos and the pacing that the text lacks. As Jarrell wrote about one of his earlier tear-jerking monologues, "The Christmas Roses," the poem "is supposed to be *said* (like a speech from a play) with expression, emotion, and long pauses." In this it is very different from the monologues of Frost, which create their own strict verbal music, rather than handing off that responsibility to a performer.

In *The Seven-League Crutches,* Jarrell's next collection, published in 1951, "The Face" reveals Jarrell's continuing susceptibility to this sentimental style. If "The Christmas Roses" was supposed to be said, "The Face" announces in its epigraph that it is really meant to be sung. The epigraph is a quotation from *Der Rosenkavalier,* in which a beautiful and still-young woman imagines how she will one day be described as "The old woman! The old Field Marshal's wife!" Jarrell's poem is an attempt to re-create or borrow the lush nostalgia of Strauss's music, simply by reiterating the basic situation:

Not good any more, not beautiful—
Not even young.

This isn't mine.
Where is the old one, the old ones?
Those were mine.

But as always happens in Jarrell's most sentimental poems, the emotion is not actually created by the language and the rhythm; intention takes the place of performance. As a result, when "The Face" reaches for an elevated dramatic conclusion, it reads like the worst kind of melodramatic self-pity: "It is terrible to be alive."

Even when Jarrell does not succeed in communicating his own emotion to the reader, however, it is interesting to see what subjects he finds moving. In "The Face," it is a woman suffering from getting older. In "A Sick Child," it is a child suffering the trivial indignity of a wounded ego: "I want a ship from some near star / To land in the yard, and beings to come out / And think to me: 'So this is where you are!' " In "The Truth," it is another child suffering the serious trauma of a bombing raid: "it was Mother crying— / She coughed so hard she cried. / She kept shaking Sister, / She shook her and shook her."

The people who evoke Jarrell's sentimentality, in other words, are all those excluded from the active, rational, male world—but only when they are considered under the aspect of weakness and passivity. The women and children in Jarrell's weakest poems are victims, and the poet simply luxuriates in his sympathy with them. But these very same figures are the focus of Jarrell's successful poems, too, when they are considered in their secret strength. Then they do not evoke pity but awe, since they accomplish the artist's and child's dream of "The Märchen": "to change, to change!"

That is the difference between the woman who speaks in

"The Face" and the woman who speaks in "*Seele im Raum*." This strange poem has its own flaws, chiefly that it is built around a very labored bilingual pun. The speaker says that she has suffered her whole life from visions of an eland—"the largest sort of African antelope," as Jarrell's note explains. It is clear that the beast must be metaphorical, yet Jarrell insists awkwardly on its literal presence, imagining it sitting at the dinner table "between my husband and my children." But when its meaning is revealed, it comes down to "a joke," as the woman herself acknowledges: for "eland" is a homonym of the German word *elend*, meaning "wretched." The animal is an arbitrary symbol of the woman's suffering and depression, chosen, as it seems, simply for its name.

Yet this poem has a power that "The Face" lacks. It comes from Jarrell's ambiguous attitude toward the eland, which is not—like aging in "The Face"—simply a curse on womankind. It is also a kind of blessing, since it grants the woman access to "a different size / And order of being," a realm that is painful but significant, and therefore obscurely gratifying: "One could not wish for anything more strange— / For anything more," she says. And "*Seele im Raum*" rises to an effective peroration, in which the woman's wretchedness is affirmed as a proof of her hidden life:

> Is my voice the voice
> Of that skin of being—of what owns, is owned
> In honor or dishonor, that is borne and bears—
> Or of that raw thing, the being inside it
> That has neither a wife, a husband, nor a child
> But goes at last as naked from this world
> As it was born into it—

This is the incongruity between "soul" and "space," the two German terms of the title. The eland, like the dark forest in "The Märchen," stands on the side of the soul—it is strange, irrational, but essentially more real than what we agree to call reality. "Shall I make sense or shall I tell the truth?" the poem asks; "sense" is the pale daylight reflection of the truth that we learn in suffering and in dreams.

Those forms of knowledge come together in "A Quilt-Pattern," which narrates a young boy's darkly symbolic dream. This dream is "the oldest tale of all," a Freudian parable in which the child ventures into another Hänsel-and-Gretel-like forest. The poem arrives at a fraught moment, which makes no more logical sense than the eland, when the boy breaks off a "finger" from a house made of bread and eats it:

> He sucks at the finger; and the house of bread
> Calls to him in its slow singing voice:
> "Feed, feed! Are you fat now?
> Hold out your finger."
> . . . .
> The taste of the house
> Is the taste of his—
>   "I don't know,"
> Thinks the boy. "No, I don't know!"

But Jarrell counts on us, dwellers in a Freudian age, to recognize that this refusal to know is the best evidence that the boy does know. He has run up against some taboo that forces him to repress his knowledge, a taboo that is obscurely yet definitely sexual. The phallic "finger" that he puts in his mouth, the maternally nourishing "house" that he eats—these are ciphers for infantile sexual desires that the conscious mind cannot accept. In "A Quilt-

Pattern," sex is added to the list of "raw things" that bring us closer to essential, forbidden truth.

In fact, Jarrell's poems are at their most powerful when their subject is sex, precisely because his treatment of sex is never explicit, always hedged around with guilt and taboo. Here biography becomes a tempting, if dangerous, resource. The common thread running through all his friends' descriptions of Jarrell is that he was not fully adult or fully masculine. Hannah Arendt, for instance, said that "he was, down to the details of physical appearance, like a figure from fairyland." Robert Lowell thought his mind "boyish, disembodied, and brittle," his body "a little ghostly in its immunity to soil." Robert Watson observed that Jarrell "identified with children and the cozy world of the child," and remembered, "When we asked callers what they would have to drink, he was the only guest who would call for 'milk and cookies.' " Even the loving recollections of his second wife, Mary, strike the same note: "Sometimes we were brother and sister 'like Wordsworth and Dorothy' and other times we were twins, Randall pretended."

All this is fascinatingly consonant with the sexuality that informs Jarrell's best poems: nervously chaste, childishly constrained. In *The Seven-League Crutches* there are no fewer than three poems that make use of the legend of Sleeping Beauty, where sex—in the fairy-tale symbol of a kiss on the lips—is at once a violation to be dreaded and an eagerly awaited liberation. In "The Sleeping Beauty: Variation of the Prince," Jarrell takes on the voice of the Prince, who makes his way through the castle frozen in time to the "center of all the webs," where the maiden lies. Highly alert, once again, to the Freudian textures of the fairy tale, Jarrell first has his Prince symbolically deflower the Sleeping Beauty:

> *the drop of blood*
> *Is there still, under the dust of your finger:*
> *I force it, slowly, down from your finger*
> *And it falls and rolls away, as it should.*

The bloody breaking of the maidenhead is an approved, socially necessary violation—it is what "should" be between man and woman. Yet Jarrell's Prince does not seek to wake his lady with a kiss, as the legend has it. Instead, he yearns to join her in sleep: "Then I stretch myself beside you, lay / Between us, there in the dust, His sword." The capitalized "His" belongs to "the hunter, Death": Death uses his sword, as in the legend of Tristan and Isolde, to enforce the lovers' chastity. It is this cold eternity that the Prince desires, and not the Beauty's return to life and fertility: " 'For hundreds of thousands of years I have slept / Beside you,' " he goes on to declare. The slightest hint of the erotic, it seems in this poem, must be expiated by an eternity of sleep and death.

In "Hohensalzburg: Fantastic Variations on a Theme of Romantic Character," Jarrell writes this episode again, with a still starker and more frustrated eroticism. After a long introduction, the poem brings its speaker once more into Sleeping Beauty's castle:

> I shall come to you there asleep,
> I shall take you and . . .
> > *Tell me.*
> No, no, I shall never.
> > *Tell me.*
> You must not know.
> > *Tell me.*

I—I shall kiss your throat.

My throat?

There, it is only a dream.
I shall not so—I shall never so.

It is an extraordinary seduction, in which the lover is so ashamed of his desire that he must be coaxed three times (the standard magic number of fairy tales) before he reveals it. When he does, it is only to "kiss your throat," another censored and displaced desire. And immediately the Prince retracts it, promising the Sleeping Beauty—and also himself—that "it is only a dream." His nervous warning, "You must not know," echoes the boy's panicked denial in "A Quilt-Pattern": here, again, sex is a taboo so powerful that the speaker cannot admit to knowing what he knows, wanting what he wants.

Next to this dark erotic power, even some of Jarrell's most famous poems can seem too fluent and complacent. One of the best known, "A Girl in a Library"—which Jarrell liked well enough to put it first in his *Selected Poems*—suffers from such cleverness. It is not just the quotations and allusions—to Kipling, Pushkin, Goethe, Chekhov—that make the poem a self-conscious intellectual performance. Still more, it is the condescension Jarrell shows toward the girl of the title, an all-American coed used as an emblem of animal stupidity. Unlike the child of "Children Selecting Books in a Library," she cannot enter into the imaginative world of the books that surround her: "So many dreams! And not one troubles / Your sleep of life?" But while Jarrell makes a show of pitying affection for the girl ("I love you—

and yet—and yet—I love you"), she does not really exist except as a target for his acid wit. Her drawling accent where each sound "Murders its own father, marries its own mother"; her "calf's brown eyes" and "brows like an orangoutang"; her "bachelor's degree / In Home Ec.": these do not create a character, but only a caricature that the reader is invited to mock. In this respect, the poem resembles Jarrell's only work of fiction, *Pictures from an Institution*, which is less a novel than an occasion for the author's jokes at the expense of his characters. "A Girl in a Library" shows how much trouble Jarrell has sympathizing with a satisfied and worldly woman. It is only women in distress, like Sleeping Beauty, or the speakers of "The Face" and "*Seele im Raum*," who earn his pitying identification.

JARRELL THE POET was prolific in the 1940s—he published four collections between 1942 and 1951—but the 1950s brought a much slower pace, as he spent more time writing criticism and fiction, translating from German, and working as a teacher and as Poetry Consultant to the Library of Congress. In the early 1950s Jarrell published *Pictures from an Institution* and *Poetry and the Age*, and in 1955 he drew on his first four books to assemble his *Selected Poems*. This volume was organized not chronologically but thematically, with his war poems in one section, grouped by subject ("Bombers," "Prisoners," "Camps and Fields," and so on) and his "civilian" poems in another, with their own broad rubrics ("Dream-Work," "The Wide Prospect"). By omitting a large number of poems from *Blood for a Stranger*—including most of his immature, Auden-influenced work—Jarrell sought to emphasize the continuity in his style and subjects. The *Selected Poems* shows that he had found his poetic voice early—the loose casual style, the fondness for dramatic monologue, and the interest in women, children, and fairy tales. Perhaps he also recognized that this absence of development, especially in comparison to the fierce evolution of poets like Lowell and Berryman, was a sign of weakness as well as strength.

All the same elements returned again in Jarrell's next collection, *The Woman at the Washington Zoo*, published in 1960. In fact, the title poem—another monologue spoken by a middle-aged woman—fits into the series that includes "The Face" and "*Seele im Raum*." Its Washington setting is a product of Jarrell's time at the Library of Congress, from 1956 to 1958. But while the Zoo and the foreign embassies are new in his poetry, the woman's sentiment is not; once again Jarrell assumes the voice of ordinary, suffering womanhood. The speaker is aging and neglected: "The world goes by my cage and never sees me," she complains, since her "serviceable / Body that no sunlight dyes" is as drab as the "dull null / Navy I wear to work." This is a richer, more detailed version of the aging woman in "The Face," and Jarrell finds in the zoo animals a more appropriate symbol than the eland in "*Seele im Raum*":

> *these beings trapped*
> *As I am trapped but not, themselves, the trap,*
> *Aging, but without knowledge of their age,*
> *Kept safe here, knowing not of death, for death—*
> *Oh, bars of my own body, open, open!*

This is the kind of internalized, psychological imprisonment that Jarrell has always found most burdensome: the woman is "trapped" in her body rather as the soldier was in his lines. And just as the soldier could be "absent with official leave" only in dream, so the woman's only escape is into the realm of imagination. She envisions an animal spirit, a "wild brother" in the form of a vulture, who could grant her wish:

You know what I was,
You see what I am: change me, change me!

The power of the image is heightened by its whisper of sexual violence. When the woman begs the vulture to "step to me as man," there is another echo of the Sleeping Beauty, who can be brought to life only by a violation she desires and dreads. Myth and sex are the electric currents in Jarrell's poetry; when they are introduced the poem jolts to life, when they are absent it remains motionless.

It follows that the most vital poems in *The Woman at the Washington Zoo* are those that return, with confused intensity, to the subject of sex. The heroine of "The End of the Rainbow" is another ordinary woman, a painter from Massachusetts who is living out her old age in Southern California. This time, however, the woman's sense of thwartedness and lost possibility is not spoken in the first person, but revealed gradually in a complex third-person narrative. Jarrell's technique is to introduce without explanation symbols and allusions that are familiar to his heroine, but which the reader must decipher as they recur throughout the poem.

For instance, when the woman, who is never named, goes to a mail a letter, Jarrell writes that "The Frog-Prince, Marsh-King / Goggles at her from the bottom of the mail-slot" and seems to speak to her: " 'Say. / Say. Say now. Say again.' " Not until later can the reader deduce that the Frog-Prince is her private, fairy-tale nickname for her former fiancé, whom she discarded many years before. The connection is made when she recalls a conversation with a female friend, who comments: " 'A *strange* man. . . . But all men are, aren't they? / A man is like a merman.' " The merman leads, by a chain of associations, to the image of the seal or silkie, and thus to the legend of the Frog-Prince—a series of emblems of the heroine's fascinated mistrust of men:

> *The Great Silkie,*
> *His muzzle wide in love, holds out to her*
> *His maimed flippers, and an uncontrollable*
> *Shudder runs through her flesh. . . .*

That ambiguous shudder, full of revulsion as well as desire, is the characteristic sensation of Jarrell's erotic poetry.

The narrative in "The End of the Rainbow" is elaborately detailed, filled with wry observations about California culture—at one point, the heroine lunches on "a date milkshake and an avocadoburger"—and disordered memories of her earlier life. But the poem returns again and again to the forsaken lover, mirroring the heroine's own ill-concealed obsession. Ostensibly, she broke her engagement out of simple caution—she thought of her fiancé as "a risk / Uncalculated, incalculable"—and she congratulates herself that she is not "saddled with" him. Yet the durability of her regret, and the recurrent imagery of the "silkie" and "merman," make clear that her timidity was related, at bottom, to sex and the fear of sex. The poem's climax comes in a dream encounter, very much like that in "Hohensalzburg," where the woman can act out in imagination the desire she represses in waking life:

> *He pulls his feet with a slow sucking sound*
> *From the floor where he is stuck, like a horse in concrete,*

And, reaching to her, whispers patiently
—Whispers, or the wind whispers, water whispers: "Say.
Say. Say now. Say again."

Those enigmatic words from the beginning of the poem—"Say.
Say now"—are now revealed as a sexual proposition. And in the
dream she can admit what must be denied by daylight, that the
prospect excites her: "A slow / Delicious shudder runs along her
spine." Yet at the crucial moment, the heroine hesitates even in
her dream, warding off the advance with a threat: " 'If you come
any closer I'll call Father.' " At that her suitor melts away, leaving
her alone—just as she is alone in real life, an old maid with only
a dog for company.

"The End of the Rainbow" is the richest of Jarrell's long
poems, in its wealth of detail, its sophisticated narrative technique, and its subtle invocation of his most deeply felt themes. It
also marks a distinct change in Jarrell's attitude toward sex. In his
earlier lyrics, he always embraced or enacted the repression of sexual desire: the young boy in "A Quilt-Pattern" and the Prince in
"Hohensalzburg" both break off, in shame and fear, just as they
are about to declare their lust. Indeed, it is by envisioning sex as
a transgression that Jarrell endows it with such poetic allure. But
in "The End of the Rainbow," having escaped from the intimacy
of dramatic monologue to the critical distance of the third-person
narrative, Jarrell offers an opposing view. Taboo, he suggests now,
is not the secret to erotic pleasure, but pleasure's enemy. Because
the poem's heroine accepts the childish view of sex as a violation,
she condemns herself to neurotic loneliness. Trusting the "slow /
Delicious shudder" of desire might have saved her life.

Jarrell opens his poetry to that shudder, with all its lawlessness and ambiguity, in "The Bronze David of Donatello," one of the strangest and most compelling poems he ever wrote. Like his earlier poem "The Knight, Death, and the Devil," which reflects on an etching by Dürer, "The Bronze David" is a close description of a work of art. But the energy of the poem comes from the way Jarrell uses the statue as a focus for erotic meditation. Above all, it is the statue's nudity that provokes the poet, who returns to it three times: "He is naked. Shod and naked. Hatted and naked." Of course, David is male, but the poem insists on describing his hat and hair in conventionally feminine terms, dwelling on their "frills," "curls," and "tassels." This androgyny quickly becomes the heart of the poem, and the source of the statue's sexual power:

> *The rib-case, navel, nipples are the features*
> *Of a face that holds us like the whore Medusa's—*
> *Of a face that, like the genitals, is sexless.*
> *What sex has victory?*

The poet finds this "sexless" sexuality both alluring and threatening, like the Medusa who turned men to stone with a glance. And since Jarrell is the half-willing victim of the statue's beauty, he goes on to identify himself with David's legendary victim Goliath, on whose head the statue's foot is planted in "victory":

> *death came to it like a girl,*
> *Came to it, through the soft air, like a bird—*
> *So that the boy is like a girl . . .*

Now the boy has gone from being sexless to being girlish, and he conquers Goliath almost flirtatiously: "The boy stands at ease, his hand upon his hip." This David resembles no one so much as Tadzio, the beautiful boy who thoughtlessly seduces Aschenbach in Thomas Mann's *Death in Venice*. And the poem concludes with an extremely Mann-like peroration, in which sexual rapture is equated with defeat and death: "Blessed are those brought low, / Blessed is defeat, sleep blessed, blessed death." It is impossible not to see in this death the orgasmic pun of Elizabethan poetry, and at the same time a Wagnerian *Liebestod*. And it is hard to resist the conclusion that the homo-erotic love-death of "The Bronze David" is the consummation toward which so many earlier poems have been striving, from "Hohensalzburg" to "The End of the Rainbow." By permitting both partners in this erotic surrender to be men, Donatello's statue assists Jarrell's poetry to a greater intensity than ever before.

BY 1965, WHEN Jarrell published *The Lost World*, his last col-lection of poems, the sort of guarded, metaphorical revelation made in "The Bronze David of Donatello" had been far outstripped by the audacious self-exposures of Lowell's *Life Studies*, which appeared in 1959, and Berryman's *77 Dream Songs*, published in 1964. It is tempting, therefore, to see in the autobiographical title sequence of *The Lost World* Jarrell's hesitant steps in the same direction. The fact that Jarrell died later the same year adds to this sense of a confessional road not taken. (So, perhaps, does the manner of Jarrell's death: he was hit by a car in circumstances that could be interpreted as suicide, thus allowing him to be counted in the ranks of suicidal poets like Berryman and Sylvia Plath.) But on closer examination, "The Lost World," which recounts mem-ories of Jarrell's childhood, does not seem like a fundamental departure from his earlier work; and the other poems in the book are absolutely continuous with Jarrell's earlier styles and subjects.

The three sections of "The Lost World" return in memory to the childhood year Jarrell spent living with his grandparents in Los Angeles. The absence of his mother and father is indicated only obliquely, as it becomes clear that the people Jarrell calls "Mama" and "Pop" are in fact his grandparents; but the reason for this temporary abandonment can only be guessed, and if there is a trauma in the background Jarrell keeps it thoroughly hidden. Unlike in Bishop's "Sestina," however, this metaphorical orphanhood is not a source of grief but an occasion for adventure. From the very first lines, Jarrell takes advantage of his Hollywood setting to imagine childhood as a marvelous movie set, where nothing is threateningly real: the title of the poem is borrowed from a film, where even the dinosaurs have "immense pale / Papier-mâché smiles."

If there is melancholy in "The Lost World," it is a product not of childhood suffering—as in *Life Studies*—but of adult distance. As Jarrell had lamented ever since "Children Selecting Books in a Library," the magic of childhood is necessarily nostalgic, since it can only be appreciated when it is over. His poem about childhood, he writes, merely "sets upright, in the sands / Of age in which nothing grows, where all our friends are old, / A few dried leaves marked THIS IS THE GREENWOOD." The poet's grief is simply that he can no longer enter that magically benign precinct where "Happiness / Is a quiet presence, breathless and familiar." The final image of the first section of "The Lost World" emphasizes this sense of childhood as a secure, womblike enclosure, as the child Jarrell rides in a neighbor's car: "The glass encloses / As glass does, a womanish and childish / And doggish universe."

The tragedy of "The Lost World," if it rises to the level of tragedy, is simply that old "doom as ecumenical as dawn," growing up. The poem's third section shows the child Jarrell beginning to leave his Garden of Eden, afflicted by the dawning knowledge of death. This comes in a homely form, as "Mama" kills a chicken for dinner: "lunging, reeling, it begins to run / Away from Something, to fly away from Something / In great flopping circles." The child draws the obvious, terrible conclusion that this "Something" is lying in wait, not just for the chicken, but for his pet rabbit, and—unthinkably—for himself. Inspired by a science-fiction magazine, he even wonders if the whole world could be destroyed; but his grandfather reassures him that this is impossible, "just make-believe." Jarrell doesn't need to underscore the irony that even this horror is now possible; the lost world is also the preatomic age, when human life on Earth seemed indestructible. The opposing forces in "The Lost World," then, are just the same as in "The Winter's Tale," written a quarter-century earlier. The adult, rational, scientific world, with its capacity for terrifying violence, is the greatest enemy of childhood safety and innocence. And this continuity in Jarrell's understanding of childhood, linking his first book to his last, is proof of how little "The Lost World" represents a new departure.

Indeed, most of the poems in *The Lost World* are in Jarrell's usual vein. "Next Day" is another aging-woman monologue, the last in a line from "The Face" through "The Woman at the Washington Zoo." This time we meet the speaker in a supermarket, giving Jarrell the chance for a celebrated pun: "Moving from Cheer to Joy, from Joy to All . . ." By reducing these primary emotions to the names of detergents, the poem enacts in a single line the argument of Jarrell's essay "A Sad Heart at the Supermarket":

"The act of buying something is at the root of our world; if anyone wishes to paint the genesis of things in our society, he will paint a picture of God holding out to Adam a check-book or credit card. . . ."

But of course, this sort of consumption does not answer the woman's real needs: "as I buy All from these shelves . . . What I've become / Troubles me even if I shut my eyes." What she has become, like Jarrell's earlier heroines, is old and unattractive. In this poem, however, the sexual element of her complaint is more vivid:

> For so many years
> I was good enough to eat: the world looked at me
> And its mouth watered. How often they have undressed me,
> The eyes of strangers!

Here Jarrell carries his identification with women to a new extreme, imagining himself—like the Sleeping Beauty in "Hohensalzburg" and Goliath in "The Bronze David of Donatello"—as the victim of male sexuality. He even assumes the woman's view of intercourse: "holding their flesh within my flesh." From this point, however, the poem returns to Jarrell's familiar sentimentality, ending in an ineloquent rush: "I stand beside my grave / Confused with my life, that is commonplace and solitary." As in the last line of "The Face"—"It is terrible to be alive"—Jarrell's attempt at large statement comes across as sententious and rhetorical.

Grieving women dominate three other poems in *The Lost World*. "The Lost Children" is another dramatic monologue, in which a middle-aged mother regrets the death of one daughter and the growing up of another. Again Jarrell imagines the physicality of women's existence, this time in giving birth: "It is strange / To carry inside you someone else's body." Yet this poem has a still more palpable design on the reader's heartstrings, brewing a thick soup of grief, loneliness, and nostalgia:

> *the fair one carrying*
> *The tin lunch box with the half-pint thermos bottle*
> *Or training her pet duck to go down the slide*
> *Is lost just as the dark one, who is dead, is lost.*

Like "Lady Bates," this is Jarrell in Dickensian mode, squeezing every drop from a sentimental subject.

More sentiment is exactly what the reader might expect from a Jarrell poem titled "Woman," which seems to promise a major statement on one of his major subjects. In the event, however, "Woman" is an oddly boisterous and uncomfortable poem, which lays bare the questionable assumptions of many of Jarrell's studies of women. Essentially, the poem is a catalog of sexist clichés, recited in a tone of condescending affection that means to make them sound inoffensive. Women, the poem declares, are indulgently maternal, pure and redemptive, disposed to mercy rather than justice. But as is usually the case, these pleasantries go hand in hand with amused contempt. For women are also catty, ethically primitive, and mercenary. When it comes to sex, women are appealing only for a brief period in youth, after which they become "stale," "sagging," and frigid, "murmur[ing] with averted breasts: 'Not now.' " Even at their best they are inadequate to man's real desire, "The Good Whore who reminds him of his mother." And yet, despite all this, women belong on a pedestal, since they are actually too good for men: "The boy grew up and got to love a woman, / The girl grew up and had to love a man." Indeed, they are "the last human power," "a dark source / That brims over" with the life force.

It is hard to say which is more irritating, the sexism or the sentimentality. "Woman" is such a dismal performance, from a poet who has written so feelingly about women, that some explanation seems necessary. Perhaps the reason is simply that, in "Woman," Jarrell is writing very self-consciously as a man; indeed, the poem is a compendium of the attitudes men conventionally adopt toward women. In his best monologues, by contrast, Jarrell inhabits a woman's mind and voice, leaving the expectations of conventional masculinity behind. In one of his sprightliest poems about women—"Cinderella," from *The Woman at the Washington Zoo*—it is the very absence of men that constitutes a sort of paradise:

> *The Heaven to whose gold-gauzed door there comes*
> *A little dark old woman, the God's Mother,*
> *And cries, "Come in, come in! My son's out now,*
> *Out now, will be back soon, may be back never,*
> *Who knows, eh? We know what they are—men, men!"*

Here it may be relevant to consider Mary Jarrell's opinion: "Randall was in thrall to the feminine mystique, and life gave him a habitat rich with a mother, grandmother, and great-grandmother; an aunt and aunt-figures; two wives, two mothers-in-law, and two stepdaughters. Furthermore, as Freud had said, 'There *are* no accidents,' and it was no accident that Randall taught at what was formerly the *Woman's* College of the University of North

Carolina, now coed." Nor does it seem accidental that, in poems like "Hohensalzburg" and "The End of the Rainbow," male sexuality is nearly strangled by guilt over its violation of women, while in "The Bronze David of Donatello" sexuality is deliriously "blessed" only when it assumes a conventionally feminine, passive role.

The poems where these conflicts are expressed and enacted are Jarrell's best. And they show that, while *The Lost World* did not break much new ground for Jarrell's poetry, he had no need of autobiographical explicitness to treat his most intimate and charged subjects. In fact, well before his last book appeared, Jarrell had already accomplished many of the goals that confessionalism served for his peers. He had abandoned Modernist obscurity, creating a flexible and colloquial style; he had dissociated himself from Modernist impersonality, treating basic emotions with intense sincerity. He may even have succeeded too well on both scores, since the poised and deliberate informality of his peers often seems, with him, like mere relaxation. No less important, as a critic he had serenely moved past the orthodoxies of New Criticism, demonstrating in his style, no less than his judgments, a more intimate and democratic way of reading poetry. In all of Jarrell's work, what lives most intensely are those poems where his kingdoms of freedom—childhood and story, dream and sex—are explored with deep respect for their mysterious power. As he wrote in his last book, in "Field and Forest":

> *When you take off everything what's left? A wish,*
> *A blind wish; and yet the wish isn't blind,*
> *What the wish wants to see, it sees.*

DELMORE SCHWARTZ

Pain is creative more than Pleasure is

In 1943, Delmore Schwartz published *Genesis*, the long poem that he regarded as his major work. He had been writing it for years, alternating between dicouragement and the most exalted confidence: "it is so good that no one will believe that I, mere I, am author, but rather a team of inspired poets," he wrote jokingly to his publisher. A few months before the book appeared, he made a more serious claim: "In days to come—mark you!—this poetic style will be seen as the beginning of Post-Symbolism."

By the time *Genesis* appeared, Schwartz had already been the leading poet of his generation for five years. While contemporaries like Robert Lowell and Elizabeth Bishop had published only a few poems in magazines, the twenty-five-year-old Schwartz caused a sensation with *In Dreams Begin Responsibilities*, his 1938 volume of poems and stories. Allen Tate anointed him as the future of modern poetry, "the only genuine innovation we've had since Pound and Eliot."

But Schwartz's claim to be the "beginning of Post-Symbolism" has been almost forgotten. *Genesis*, in spite of its flaws, was indeed Schwartz's best work; but the poem was badly received, disappointing his high expectations, and he soon began to succumb to mental illness and alcoholism. In the next twenty years, he wrote nothing to rival his early work. By the time he died, a paranoid recluse, in a Times Square hotel in 1966, Schwartz seemed less significant as a writer than as literary material for his surviving contemporaries. In John Berryman's Dream Songs he is mourned as the chief victim of a "wrecked" generation, his "young male beauty" and "beautiful & fresh poems" giving way to sordid failure. As told by Saul Bellow, in the novel *Humboldt's Gift*, his life is a cautionary tale about the fate of the artist in commercial America.

Today, even Schwartz's legend is losing its potency. Some of his poems and stories are still found in anthologies, but his complete body of work is almost unknown. In particular, *Genesis*, the poem in which he placed so much hope, went out of print immediately and has never been republished. Yet if the achievement of Schwartz's generation of poets was to relax the chaste restrictions of Modernism, to expand poetry's diction, tone, and range of reference, to turn from myth and history to the private life, then Schwartz was certainly his generation's pioneer. Above all, it was

Schwartz who first demonstrated that the most intimate experiences, especially the griefs of childhood, could be made the basis of a dignified and complex poetry. In his explicit determination not just to record but to master his personal suffering through art, Schwartz set the course that Robert Lowell, John Berryman, and Elizabeth Bishop would follow. Already in the late 1930s, he enacted the transition from Modernist to post-Modernist that was to take his peers another twenty years.

One reason for Schwartz's precocity was that, unlike his peers, he did not undergo a long period of discipleship. Bishop, Lowell, and Berryman each chose poets of the Modernist generation as their models and teachers. They spent years or decades demonstrating mastery of the established poetic idiom before they had the ability, or the confidence, to assert themselves in their own style and subject. Schwartz, on the other hand, immediately sought and proudly accepted a place among the leading poets of his time. It is remarkable to read the letters he exchanged, while still a very young man, with poets like Ezra Pound and Wallace Stevens: always appropriately modest, he is never intimidated. Perhaps he knew that, in his early twenties, he was already doing his best work.

But Schwartz paid a price for his confidence. Though his mastery came early, he was also the only important poet of his generation whose work declined, rather than improved, with the years. And while this may have been the inevitable result of his serious mental illness, the fact remains that even in his prime, Schwartz did not write anything to rival the best of Lowell or Bishop. In fact, though being a poet was at the center of his identity, in a sense Schwartz never really attempted to write great lyric poetry. His generation's common rebellion against Modernism took the form, with him, of an evasion of the lyric: his best work was done in verse drama, pseudo-epic, or prose fiction. A relatively small group of lyrics, in his first book, is his only substantial achievement in the genre.

Schwartz's work took this form in part because of the nature of his talent, but also because of his principled discontent with the idea of lyric poetry that he inherited. This disaffection grew out of profound appreciation: Schwartz revered French Symbolist poetry—he published a translation of Rimbaud's *A Season in Hell*—and the English Modernist poetry that was influenced by it. Indeed, he saw Baudelaire as "the first or the typical modern poet," above all in his belief that poetry stands apart from, and opposed to, society and its values: in the nineteenth century, for the first time, the poet "is a stranger, an alien, an outsider." Because the modern world does not make a place for the poet, Schwartz argued, he has no choice but to cultivate the inner world of his own sensibility. This internal exile is what gives modern lyric poetry its extreme sophistication, its resources of nuance and suggestion: "Because this private life of sensibility is the chief subject available to [the poet], it becomes increasingly necessary to have recourse to new and special uses of language." Like an exotic species in the Galápagos, the modern poet's lack of communication with the outside world has led to a fantastic, wayward evolution.

Schwartz readily acknowledged that any modern poet, writing after Baudelaire and Rimbaud, Eliot and Pound, was "bound to be drawn toward an emulation of the marvelous refinements in the uses and powers of language" these poets achieved. Yet the title of his best essay, "The Isolation of Modern Poetry," already suggests Schwartz's ambivalence toward Modernism: to call the poet isolated is to imply that he would be better off on the mainland. And Schwartz sees modern poetry's contraction to the lyric as a symptom of its isolation. For a modern reader, a poem is by definition a relatively short lyric, never an essay in verse, a drama, an epistle, or an epic. Yet Schwartz recognizes this for the anomaly that, historically considered, it is: "Nothing could be more peculiar than the fact that modern poetry is lyric poetry." Lyric, he suggests, is the genre of isolation, the last resort of poets for whom "the lives of other men" can no longer be grasped in poetry.

If modern poetry stands in hostile opposition to life, Schwartz's work attempts a reconciliation, using both negative and positive methods. The negative is his renunciation of the rich, obscure, musically perfect language of Symbolist poetry. Like Randall Jarrell, Schwartz deliberately sought a looser, more prosaic style than the mandarins of Modernism had cultivated. Less charitably, one might say that Schwartz was simply not capable of writing such poetry. But Schwartz insisted that his sometimes awkward and prolix style was a deliberate choice, a sacrifice that he made in order to achieve a greater range of tone and subject. In the introduction to *Genesis*, he defiantly acknowledged that his style was not musical but "pedestrian"; but he linked this quality with his desire to "regain for Poetry the width of reference of prose." He was especially irritated when the critic R. P. Blackmur wrote that his poems seemed spontaneously written, that is, casual and unformed: "The artifice of spontaneity does exist in the book . . . as a dramatic means," he objected, "but the *artifice* of spontaneity is the opposite of spontaneity."

Still, it is easy to see how the mistake might be made. One group of poems in *In Dreams Begin Responsibilities* is labeled

"Poems in Imitation of the Fugue," but in fact they substitute for the fugue's mathematical rigor a swirling vagueness, as in "Abraham and Orpheus, Be With Me Now":

Love love exhausts and time goes round and round,
Time circles in its idiot defeat,
And which circles falls, falls endlessly,
Falls endlessly, no music shapes the air
Which did, can, shall restore the end of care,
For love exhausts itself and time goes round. . . .

The vices of this style—uncontrolled repetition, vacant abstraction—would become disastrous in Schwartz's late work, and even here he seems to dignify them by implying that they are deliberate elements of the "fugue." Yet the loosening of his language—especially after the extreme richness and compression of American Modernist poets like Wallace Stevens and Hart Crane—was part of a necessary process, and anticipates the similar relaxation of Lowell and Berryman in their mature work. As Schwartz wrote to a critic in 1939, his deliberately casual verse "enables me to mention things usually kept out of recent verse and thus to write narrative poetry"; or again, "to refer, with the least strain and the quickest transition, to anything from the purely personal to the international."

This phrase points to the positive means of reconciliation in Schwartz's work: his attempt to bring into poetry the ways of thinking that he associated with Marx and Freud. Schwartz's poetry is by no means doctrinaire, or even especially precise, in its use of Marxist and Freudian ideas. Rather, for Schwartz, Marx represents the "international," the sense that individual lives are affected in the most intimate ways by vast historical forces; and Freud is the "personal," the complementary sense that character is determined by uncontrollable inner drives and traumatic early experiences. Together, these inner and outer compulsions leave little room for the free will of the individual. And Schwartz sees this double pessimism as the essential twentieth-century world-view: "the development of the historical sense and the awareness of experience which originates in psychoanalysis are two aspects of the view of experience which is natural to a modern human being."

Schwartz's best work is an unsparing demonstration of the limits of freedom, above all in his own life. By taking himself as a case study—much as his hero Freud did when pioneering the techniques of psychoanalysis—Schwartz was compelled to much greater revelations of personal experience, and a much more realistic understanding of contemporary history, than was thought desirable by the canons of Modernist taste. In particular, Schwartz's candor violated the principle, laid down by T. S. Eliot in "Tradition and the Individual Talent," that poetry "is not the expression of personality, but an escape from personality"; that "it is not in his personal emotions, the emotions provoked by particular events in his life, that the poet is in any way remarkable or interesting." For Schwartz, by contrast, the poet's life is his best subject, perhaps his only possible subject—not because he believes, narcissistically, that he is unusually interesting, but because nowhere else can he so vividly witness the forces that define the "modern human being."

From his earliest poems, Schwartz demonstrates the power of his double perspective. "The Ballad of the Children of the Czar," written when he was just twenty-four years old, juxtaposes his own childhood in a Jewish immigrant household with that of the children of Czar Nicholas II, doomed to be executed in the Bolshevik Revolution. In swift, unrhymed couplets, Schwartz introduces the royal children, playing with a bouncing ball "In the May morning, in the Czar's garden," and then himself, "aged two, irrational," eating a baked potato in Brooklyn. Nothing seems to connect the two childhoods but Schwartz's wide-angled vision, which automatically situates his own life against the background of world history. But the lack of connection points to what is essentially modern in Schwartz's historical consciousness: he cannot forget the fact that his own experience, seemingly independent and self-sufficient, is in fact being affected by political events thousands of miles away.

The poem goes on to suggest a still more intimate connection, by switching from the perspective of "Marx" to that of "Freud," from the political to the psychological. From this point of view, what unites the infant Schwartz with the Russian princes is their childish egotism; though placed in vastly different stations, they are identical in their Freudian drives. When the two-year-old Schwartz drops his baked potato—"my buttered world," as he sees it with the child's total egotism—"I begin to howl," outraged that things do not immediately conform to his needs. Exactly the same thing happens to the children of the czar, who lose their ball "under / The iron gate which is locked," and have the same childish reaction: "Sister is screaming, brother is howling."

These trivial examples of loss and outrage are, for Schwartz, revelations of essential human nature, which is always selfish: "The heart of man is known: / It is a cactus bloom." And in a pivot back to the "international" perspective, Schwartz suggests that, when the child grows up, its reaction to historical tragedy will be the same selfish howl. When the poem evokes "February and October," the months of the Russian Revolution that would end up taking the lives of the children of the czar, it compares that world-historical cataclysm to the loss of the ball: for the individual, history is just another instance of life's resistance to his will. If "Even a bouncing ball / Is uncontrollable," how much more so the world itself:

> *The ground on which the ball bounces*
> *Is another bouncing ball. . . .*

> *A pitiless, purposeless Thing,*
> *Arbitrary and unspent,*

> *Made for no play, for no children,*
> *But chasing only itself.*

With this brilliant image, Schwartz deftly unites the two forms of consciousness, the personal and the historical, in a profound pessimism. The individual will, he declares, is depraved and selfish, while the will of history is arbitrary and ruthless. There seems to be no way for the individual, caught in the middle, to take control of his destiny. Freedom is ground to dust in the clash of determinisms.

The best lyrics from *In Dreams Begin Responsibilities* return again and again to this harsh knowledge. For Schwartz, the ego is irrevocably corrupt, always at bottom the child howling for its buttered world. But Schwartz does not want his poetry simply to amplify this howl in verse, in the way that would later be called confessional. Rather, he insists, the poet writes in order to understand, and thus gain control over, the outer and inner forces that would otherwise dominate him. If Schwartz's youth is evident anywhere in these poems, written in his late teens and early twenties, it is in the grim satisfaction he takes in reminding himself of that responsibility. In "Tired and Unhappy, You Think of Houses," for instance, the poet interrupts his reverie of aristocratic ease—"The servants bring the coffee, the children retire"—with a furious wake-up call:

> *It is time to shake yourself! And break this*
> *Banal dream, and turn your head . . .*
> *. . . . .*
> *Where close in the subway rush, anonymous*
> *In the audience, well-dressed or mean,*
> *So many surround you, ringing your fate,*
> *Caught in an anger exact as a machine!*

Once again, Schwartz cleverly connects Marxist and Freudian notions of guilt. The dream of wealth and leisure is idle escapism, when faced with the reality of Depression life as seen in the New York subway. But it is equally an escape from accurate self-knowledge, and the subway serves Schwartz as a metaphor for the subconscious, whose buried appetites determine the ego's "fate."

Indeed, in these early poems, Schwartz tends to view any form of pleasure as a lying distraction from unpleasant truths. In "Far Rockaway," he both envies and despises the holiday crowds at the beach, who relish "Fun, foam, and freedom." He combats their "lolling," "drunken" pleasure with a renewed commitment to consciousness, identifying himself with the figure of "the novelist," who observes the beach scene but does not participate. The duty of the writer is to be "that nervous conscience among the concessions," a fine piece of wordplay: the concessions are the stands that sell food and drink on the beach, but they are also the concessions to his animal nature that the average man happily makes.

Schwartz offers his most striking image of the selfish, appetitive ego in "The Heavy Bear Who Goes With Me." It suffers less than his other "fugue" poems from its drumming rhythm and repetitions, perhaps because these seem appropriate to the image of the "lumbering" bear:

> *The heavy bear who goes with me,*
> *A manifold honey to smear his face,*
> *Clumsy and lumbering here and there,*
> *The central ton of every place,*
> *The hungry beating brutish one*
> *In love with candy, anger, and sleep. . . .*

The bear is the ego Schwartz castigated in "The Ballad of the Children of the Czar," but now fully grown, its appetite undiminished and its strength increased. Ridiculous, like a circus animal, it is also powerful and potentially violent. And if it yearns childishly for "candy," or a baked potato, it also has other lusts:

> *Stretches to embrace the very dear*
> *With whom I would walk without him near,*
> *Touches her grossly, though a word*
> *Would bare my heart and make me clear,*
> *Stumbles, flounders, and strives to be fed—*
> *Dragging me with him. . . .*

Sex, in this vision, is just another brute demand of the "heavy bear," interfering with the genuine communion the soul desires.

Indeed, in several poems, Schwartz proposes a chaste and spiritu-
alized love as a possible escape from the gross ego. In "In the
Slight Ripple, The Mind Perceives the Heart," he warns that
"night comes soon . . . unless Love build its city"; in "Concern-
ing the Synthetic Unity of Apperception," he refuses to "sit in the
sun," like the bathers in "Far Rockaway," and demands instead:
"What is love?" In each case, love is presented as the opposite of
pleasure, a strenuous selflessness.

This is love as charity, not romantic passion, and it seems an
intellectual ideal rather than a lived experience. The actual frailty
of such love is revealed in "Prothalamion," a troubled poem written on the occasion of Schwartz's first marriage. He proposes that
marriage will be a final self-surrender, the transcendence of ego
and appetite in love:

> *"For fifty-six or for a thousand years,*
> *I will live with you and be your friend,*
> *And what your body and what your spirit bears*
> *I will like my own body cure and tend."*

Yet the whole tenor of "Prothalamion" suggests that the poet is
not, in fact, capable of this kind of love. Starting with the first
line—"Now I must betray myself"—Schwartz sees marriage as a
test that he is by no means sure he can pass. His declarations that
he is ready to love—"I will / Forget myself before your unknown
heart"—are notably less convincing than his hesitations, which
recall the "heaviness" of the bear:

> *"But you are heavy and my body's weight*
> *Is great and heavy: when I carry you*

I lift upon my back time like a fate
Near as my heart, dark when I marry you."

The poem is finally not a celebration, but a plea for forgiveness, offered in advance of failure. (And in fact Schwartz's marriage did end in divorce, after five years.) Perhaps Schwartz's whole dilemma is captured in the poem's final apostrophe to his wife-to-be as "my only sister": he can conceive of a generous love between siblings, or a selfish transaction between brutes, but not the synthesis of the two a successful marriage allows.

Schwartz is more convincing when he imagines a different, purely intellectual transcendence of the ego, involving not the satisfaction of appetite, but an escape from appetite. In "Socrates' Ghost Must Haunt Me Now," he associates this transcendence with Socrates, who according to Plato taught the existence of a timeless, unchanging realm of Ideas, beyond the temporal world we inhabit. Schwartz invokes the philosopher as a guide to this realm:

All is not blind, obscene, and poor.
Socrates stands by me stockstill,
Teaching hope to my flickering will,
Pointing to the sky's inexorable blue
—Old Noumenon, come true, come true!

The last line risks overkill by introducing a technical term from yet another philosopher, Kant: the noumenon is the thing-in-itself, the unattainable essence, as opposed to the mere appearance that we know with our senses. But Schwartz's pomposity, here as often in his poetry, is made pardonable by its guilelessness.

He is not trying to impress the reader with his philosophical vocabulary; this is the genuine language of his emotional life. For him, Plato's Ideas and Kant's Noumenon are real objects of desire, the only possible refuge from the "obscene and poor" everyday world. Socrates points to the sky to indicate the world beyond, where the soul escapes from bondage to the body and moves freely among the Ideas that are its genuine home. Schwartz echoes the poetic longing with which Plato himself describes this escape, in the *Phaedo*:

> But when [the soul] examines by herself, she goes away yonder to the pure and everlasting and immortal and unchanging; and being akin to that, she abides ever with it, whenever it becomes possible for her to abide by herself. And there she rests from her wanderings, and while she is amongst those things she is herself unchanging because what she takes hold of is unchanging; and this state of the soul has the name of wisdom. . . .

By asking that this ideal "come true," like a child's wish, Schwartz acknowledges that he does not actually believe it is true; the poem's pathos lies precisely in this gap between belief and desire.

In fact, the theme of Schwartz's best work is not escape from the ego but confrontation with the ego. The self and its complaints, in Schwartz's poetry, are always interrogated, never indulged; when he scrutinizes his own experience, it is not out of narcissism, but as part of a principled search for the truth about the human predicament. And the truth Schwartz finds is determinedly dark. Though couched in psychoanalytic language, his understanding of human nature goes beyond Freud to an almost Augustinian belief in original sin—with the crucial difference that, in this secular version, the soul cannot be redeemed through grace. All that remains is a painful watchfulness, which Schwartz captures in "By Circumstances Fed":

> *The gaze which is a tower towers*
> *Day and night, hour by hour,*
> *Critical of all and of one,*
> *Dissatisfied with every flower,*
> *With all that's been done and undone . . .*
> *. . . . .*
> *Beyond all disappointment,*
> *My own face in the mirror.*

AFTER *IN DREAMS Begin Responsibilities*, Schwartz would not publish a collection of lyrics for another twelve years. Instead, he would concentrate on verse drama and the autobiographical epic *Genesis*, in which the bleak psychology of the early poems is given a much deeper and more novel expression. His way forward was pointed by the longest and most adventurous poem in *In Dreams*, the nearly uncategorizable "Coriolanus and His Mother," which is best described as a fantasia on Shakespeare's *Coriolanus*.

Shakespeare's play tells the story of Caius Marcius, a fantastically proud Roman general who singlehandedly conquers the enemy city of Corioli and wins the new name Coriolanus as a reward. But when he is nominated to be consul of Rome, he cannot humble himself to ask for the approval of the common people, ordinarily a mere formality. His arrogance is so offensive to the plebeians that he is exiled from Rome, whereupon he offers his services to the enemy general Aufidius to take revenge on his ungrateful city. Just as he is about to put Rome to the torch, however, Coriolanus's revenge is averted by the intercession of his mother, who has an irresistible and strangely intimate power over him. This last-minute change of heart leads to his own death at the hands of Aufidius.

Schwartz grasped that the play was a perfect vehicle for his own double pessimism, lending itself to both Freudian and Marxist interpretations. It is hard to miss the Oedipal cast of Coriolanus's relationship with his all-powerful mother Volumnia, who goes so far as to speculate: "If my son were my husband, I should freelier rejoice in that absence wherein he won honor than in the embracements of his bed where he would show most love." And the class conflict in the play is even more pronounced. From the first scene, Shakespeare shows that the common people believe that the nobility are deliberately starving them. Coriolanus's contempt is just a match to the fuel of this economic grievance.

Out of these Shakespearean materials, Schwartz built his own genre-defying work. "Coriolanus and His Mother" is a narrative poem in blank verse, in which the poet watches the performance of a play about Coriolanus that both is and is not Shakespeare's play: the plot is the same, but the language is Schwartz's. Schwartz reports both what is said on stage and the reactions of the four presences in the audience with him, who turn out to be the ghosts of Marx, Freud, Beethoven, and Aristotle. In between each act, the poet himself takes the stage and delivers a long speech, in prose, commenting on Coriolanus's story.

Schwartz is not unaware that there is something preposterous about all this, especially the literal presence of the ghosts of great thinkers: "Absurd and precarious my presence there," he writes. There would always be something of the precocious immigrant child about Schwartz, eagerly consuming the products of high culture, which then turn up undigested in his own work. As he once wrote in a humorous autobiographical sketch, "By 1938, I had read so many books that I wrote one."

In fact, in "Coriolanus and His Mother" the actual presence of the ghosts of Marx and Freud risks undermining Schwartz's genuine Marxist and Freudian insights into the play, which come out clearly in his own retelling of the story. Volumnia's speech "If my son were my husband" is made more explicitly sexual:

> *"Were he my husband as he is my son,*
> *This would delight me O much more than when*
> *In the ecstasy of the darkness I conceived,*
> *Moved by the thrusting self-delighting spoon*
> *Which made my son, my spear."*

Similarly, the rabble-rousing tribunes employ a 1930s rhetoric of class warfare:

> *"To live in Rome, to live*
> *In this great city is to be used and slain*
> *In the murderous war warred to increase*
> *The rich man's riches."*

What Schwartz is doing is obvious enough that the ghostly Freud's remarks on "the identity of mother and bride," or Marx's references to Hegel and "the ruling class," seem superfluous. Still, even Schwartz's subtlest invocations of Freud and Marx remain more analytic and critical than genuinely poetic; there hovers over the whole poem the air of an intellectual exercise. "Coriolanus and His Mother" is most important as a laboratory for the forms and ideas that would find fuller expression in Schwartz's later writing, especially *Genesis*.

Where "Coriolanus and His Mother" comes to life is in the prose interludes, when the poet himself takes the stage and comments on the play. These speeches are often naively pretentious ("I have been thinking about justice"), but they are also where Schwartz raises the question that concerns him most intimately: Can Coriolanus's pride be overcome by his own conscious determination, or does it have the inevitability of fate? After all, if the ghosts of Freud and Marx are right, Coriolanus's history—both personal and political—has ordained his future. As Freud is made to declare, "The past is always present, present as past, / It grasps us like Athena by the hair!" But if this is true, then Coriolanus does not have free will, and cannot be morally at fault for his own actions. If the past is all-powerful, then individual human beings are reduced to automatons.

It is here that Schwartz's choice of Coriolanus as a hero proves especially fruitful. After all, Coriolanus's pride is based on a conviction of his own total freedom: his constant refrain is that he is solely responsible for himself. Indeed, he claims a blasphemous autonomy, wanting to be his own God:

> "O I will stand as stiff and staunch as stone,
> As if a man were author of himself,
> I will be author of myself alone!"

Schwartz has taken over this idea from Shakespeare ("As if a man were author of himself / And knew no other kin"), but in the new context it seems less a boast than a metaphysical paradox. If Coriolanus is right, and he is free from all outside influences, then he should be able to repudiate his own pride, which was bred in him by his class and his overweening mother. Yet it is that very pride that makes him claim that he is free from outside influences.

Finally, of course, Schwartz cannot provide a solution to the ancient problem of freedom and determinism. Instead, he offers a resolution, an act of faith. In the final prose interlude, titled "He Is a Person," Schwartz lists all the factors that shape an individual's character, both the "personal" and the "international":

> What is he? He is his father and mother . . . He is his childhood . . . He is his adolescence . . . He is his fatherland . . . His past holds him and he must move forward in time, dragging every fear and every beauty of every year with him. They will never release him!

In other words, the ghosts of Freud and Marx are right: everything about Coriolanus, or any human being, can be explained with a sufficient knowledge of his inner and outer history. Yet if this is true, it seems there is no chance of ever escaping the conditioned for the unconditioned. The ego is corrupted by its circumstances, and there is no other power in the human soul able to resist its depraved will. Schwartz looks on this state of affairs with such horror that he cannot help yearning for an alternative, even if logic seems to allow no way out. Finally, he simply asserts that, while the past is unalterable, the future is free:

> The repetition of yesterday and the day before will never suffice, but he must create again and again from what has been the unheard-of future. The future of time which is nothing cannot be grasped by the repetition of what has been. . . . The necessity of the future intrudes and he must choose, although as most often he merely chooses what has already existed.

Schwartz cleverly places this speech just before the last act of the play, in which Coriolanus in fact "chooses what has already existed"—obedience to his mother, whose Oedipal stranglehold is unbreakable—and thus ensures his own destruction. But by insisting that this failure is a choice, rather than a fate, Schwartz at least maintains the possibility of a different and better choice: we are free to choose right, even if the pressure to choose wrong is nearly irresistible. By the end of "Coriolanus and His Mother," it has become clear that the true, vital subject of Schwartz's poetry is human freedom: freedom from world history, from psychological compulsions, from the ego itself. In his next two works, Schwartz would pursue the question of freedom to its most intimate ground: his own childhood.

SHENANDOAH, THE VERSE play Schwartz published in 1941, was written in the mid-1930s, at the same time as most of *In Dreams Begin Responsibilities*. Like "Coriolanus and His Mother," *Shenandoah* uses the device of introducing the author into his own poem to comment on the action. In this case, however, that action is not borrowed from literature, but imitated from life: Schwartz himself, thinly disguised as "Shenandoah Fish," looks on as his parents and relatives choose his preposterous name.

Schwartz was always bemused by his name—the unidiomatic "Delmore," an immigrant's idea of WASP elegance, clashing with the inescapably Jewish "Schwartz." Shenandoah Fish is an analogous mismatch; as Schwartz readily acknowledged, the premise of the play is "obviously personal in a painful way." *Shenandoah* takes place on the eighth day of its hero's life, when Jewish boys are traditionally named and circumcised. Elsie Fish, the child's mother, plans to name him Jacob, after her dead father. But as the play begins, her husband's father, also called Jacob, demands that she choose another name, since, according to Jewish custom, it is bad luck to name a child after a living relative—"it will be my death warrant!" he insists.

Jacob uses flattery to convince Elsie to change the name, and she consults the newspaper society page for other ideas. But of course, the names of the "glamorous ruling class"—Julian, Llewellyn, Bertram, and so on—are entirely inappropriate for a boy named Fish. (Schwartz winks at the autobiographical element by inserting his own name, and his brother Kenneth's, in the list.) Finally, egged on by a social-climbing neighbor, Elsie Fish decides to name the boy after the Shenandoah Valley, where one of the society swells has an "estate." The baby immediately starts to wail, with comic foreboding, but Elsie loves the name. So does her husband Walter, a crude, bullying businessman closely modeled on Schwartz's own father, who likes the very pretentiousness that makes the name ridiculous: "My son has a right to a pretentious name," he insists. Only the boy's uncle Nathan realizes that the name is a mistake, and tries to argue the parents out of it: "It is foolish in every way. . . . The boy will be handicapped as if he had a clubfoot." But they refuse to listen, and the play concludes with the ceremony of circumcision, as the child's fate is sealed.

With slight modifications, Schwartz could easily have turned *Shenandoah* into a short story, like those collected in his 1948 volume *The World Is a Wedding*. The best of Schwartz's stories—small classics like "In Dreams Begin Responsibilities," "The Child Is the Meaning of This Life," and "America! America!"—are intimate observations of his childhood milieu: the striving immigrant fathers, the proud, self-sacrificing mothers, and the

children, already more American than Jewish, dismayingly alienated from their parents. Many stories simply recount things that
happened to Schwartz's relatives, neighbors, and friends; the Fish
marriage in *Shenandoah* is clearly based on his own parents' disastrous marriage, also portrayed in "In Dreams Begin Responsibilities."

But the most important similarity is that in his play, as in his
fiction, Schwartz is fatally alienated from his family, condemned
to observe and criticize their mistakes. What the narrator of
"America! America!" (again named Shenandoah Fish) thinks
about his family applies equally well to the Shenandoah of the
play: "He reflected upon his separation from these people, and he
felt that in every sense he was removed from them by thousands
of miles, or by a generation, or by the Atlantic Ocean. . . . The
lower middle-class of the generation of Shenandoah's parents had
engendered perversions of its own nature, children full of contempt for every thing important to their parents."

The play *Shenandoah* makes this separation tangible. While
the action proceeds, the adult Shenandoah stands on the stage,
moving unseen among his relatives, unable to communicate with
them. At one point he tries to take his uncle Nathan's hand, but
cannot: "I am divorced from those I love, my peers!" he exclaims.
It is a metaphor for the intellectual son's alienation from his family, as well as for the gulf dividing present and past. Still more
important, it is a way for Schwartz to represent his own self-
division: he is both the writer trying to make sense of his experiences, and the suffering ego condemned to live them. For here,
unlike in "Coriolanus," the tragicomedy taking place on stage
does not allow the poet to be a mere spectator or critic: this is his
own story, the beginning of his life. By doubling himself into

actor and observer, Schwartz expresses his sense that such self-consciousness, such compulsive analysis of one's own experience, is an essential part of modern life. As he once wrote, "this story-succeeded-by-commentary is one of the profoundest most deeply-rooted and most accepted experiences in modern life: The newspaper story-editorial, the play-and-review-of-the-play . . . are all primordial examples of what is going to be an inevitable literary form (inevitable because the life we live forces it upon us)."

From the very beginning of *Shenandoah*, Schwartz steps outside his own life in order to see it, as always, in both a Freudian and a Marxist perspective. As in "The Ballad of the Children of the Czar," he situates his birth against the background of European history:

> *In January 1914 a choice was made*
> *Which in my life has played a part as endless*
> *As the world-famous apple, eaten in Eden,*
> *Which made original sin and the life of man*
> *—Or as the trigger finger with a bitten nail*
> *Which Prinzip's mind was soon to press*
> *In Sarajevo, firing at Verdun. . . .*

The assassination of the Austrian Archduke in Sarajevo, by the Serbian nationalist Gavrilo Prinzip, precipitated World War I; later, Shenandoah comments that just as in other cultures a child is named after "the event / Which happened near his birth," so he should have been named "The First World War." Here we see the same historical consciousness that led Schwartz to connect his own childhood with the children of the czar.

Still more important is the Jewish history that affects his fate, in ways both trivial and terrifying. It is a religious superstition that leads his grandfather Jacob to insist that the boy's name be changed: "It is written again and again in various commentaries and interpretations of the Law. It has been believed for thousands of years." More ominously, at the moment of circumcision, Shenandoah warns his infant self of what the twentieth century has in store for the Jews:

> *with a wound*
> *—What better sign exists—the child is made*
> *A Jew forever! quickly taught the life*
> *That he must lead, an heir to lasting pain:*
> *Do I exaggerate, do I with hindsight see*
> *The rise of Hitler?*

At the same time, Shenandoah also observes the psychological and familial influences that will determine his future. Each member of his family acts out of the blind, selfish will that Schwartz sees as humanity's original sin. Elsie Fish's narcissism allows her father-in-law to win her over with naked flattery, calling her "so intelligent, so good-looking, so kind and refined." As the adult Shenandoah observes, the ego's most basic desire is to think well of itself:

> *Do not suppose this flattery too gross:*
> *If it were smiled at any one of you*
> *You would not mind!*
> . . . .
> *Each ego hides a half-belief the best is true.*

Likewise, Walter Fish's ambition makes him approve the grandiose name "Shenandoah"—"It sounds fine to me, very impressive." And his touchy vanity makes him insist on the name simply because Nathan opposes him: "Just because you are a doctor does not mean you are better than us in every respect." In this tangle of egos, no one thinks about whether the name will actually injure the child—no one but Nathan, who is drowned out by the voices of unreason. In the most intimate and concrete way, his family's egotism ruins Shenandoah's life.

Like Coriolanus, then, Shenandoah Fish is trapped by fate, both the domestic fate of his family and the international fate of world history. In his earlier work, Schwartz had struggled to find some means of escape from this trap, but without much success: the lyrics of *In Dreams* placed a shaky hope in love and mystical experience, while "Coriolanus" could only assert the individual's freedom without conviction. Only now, in *Shenandoah*, does Schwartz articulate a durable response, which is made possible by the splitting of the main character into suffering actor and observing narrator. Shenandoah Fish is not immune to history— that was the error of Coriolanus, with his insane pride—but thanks to his ironic self-consciousness, he is able to understand history, and express his understanding in poetry. He is redeemed from the determinism of life by the freedom of art.

Unfortunately, this crucial insight is expressed in one of Schwartz's most pretentious passages, in which he reels off a list of his writer heroes—Joyce, Pound, Rilke, Kafka—and mentions where they were at the time he was born. But this awkwardness should not obscure the real, and moving, insight that Shenandoah achieves:

This child will learn of life from these great men,
He will participate in their solitude,
And maybe in the end, on such a night
As this, return to the starting-point, his name. . . .

It is in writing itself, the artist's vocation of distance, observation, and representation, that Shenandoah, and his creator, can attain freedom. Like all the best poets of his generation, Schwartz would not simply confess the chaos and pain of his experience, but rather strive to master it through deliberate artistry. That ambition would provide both the impetus and the theme for Schwartz's best, least-known poem, his flawed epic, *Genesis*.

SCHWARTZ WAS AT work on a long verse autobiography as early as 1931, when he made notes for a poem to be called "Having Snow." The work was close to its final form by 1940, when he mentioned it in a letter to his publisher, James Laughlin of New Directions: "about my long poem, which I have almost decided to name *Genesis* . . . I want to be sure that it is as good as I can make it, not be haunted with remorse at what I might have done and did not. Nothing is more ridiculous than an ambitious *fiasco*. Not only that, my impression endures, mistaken though it may turn out, that it might be popular as well as good."

Schwartz's ambivalence was only to grow as the poem took shape. His letters chronicle his extremes of confidence and self-doubt, tracking the manic-depressive cycle that eventually destroyed his sanity. At times Schwartz declares that "I was never so sure before" of writing well; then "disillusion and disappointment" return, and "the whole poem looks blank or foolish." This lack of confidence prompted some unseemly, Machiavellian plotting for good reviews; he felt that his early reputation would be either secured or lost with *Genesis*.

In fact, he had good reason to be uncertain of the poem's reception. For *Genesis* broke decisively with the accepted standards of Modernist poetic taste, and judged by those standards it was bound to appear a monstrosity. Writing to John Berryman in 1940, Schwartz declared: "Every time I read or see the long poem as a whole, my hair stands on end at my own daring or shamelessness or whatever quality of character moves me to do what I am doing."

What he was doing was to take his own childhood as his subject, at great length and in great detail. In a period when T. S. Eliot's theory of impersonality was at the height of its influence, this meant risking ridicule. Eliot had proclaimed that, in a poem, the "man who suffers" must be kept separate from the "mind which creates." But the insight of *Shenandoah* was that the man who suffers can only escape his suffering by turning his creative mind upon it, giving it objective form in art. And in *Genesis*, Schwartz's goal was to show exactly how the creative mind is the product, and in a sense the cure, of the suffering man.

For this reason, *Genesis* deserves to be remembered as the first in the great sequence of self-revelatory poems that Schwartz's generation produced, the predecessor of *Life Studies* and *The Dream Songs*. It is painfully ironic that, twenty years before Berryman published his masterpiece, Schwartz should have written anxiously to him about his own "shamelessness." For Schwartz's poem, though it received some good notices, was widely seen as a failure, and began the long eclipse of his reputation; while Berryman's far more shameless work won the Pulitzer Prize and secured his fame. In 1943, the taste and critical vocabulary for poetry like *Genesis* had not yet been created, so that, as his friend William Barrett wrote, Schwartz could only seem "hypnotized by the personal subject matter . . . trapped in his narcissism." In a very concrete sense, Schwartz came before his time.

Genesis extends the technique that Schwartz experimented with in "Coriolanus": it is a narrative interrupted by commentary from a chorus of ghosts. And like *Shenandoah*, it deals with Schwartz's own childhood, under another transparent pseudonym, "Hershey Green." But here the scale is vastly increased: Schwartz spends more than two hundred pages recounting his family's history, beginning with his grandparents, and his significant childhood experiences up to the age of seven. The narrative, in prosy free verse, is interrupted by the observations of ghosts— anonymous, this time—who converse with the adult Hershey in blank verse. By the end, we have a pretty comprehensive picture of Schwartz's own childhood. But far more important, we have his most searching and moving treatment of his great theme: the redemption from history through art.

As Schwartz envisions it, such redemption is not therapeutic, since his aim is not the Freudian one of relieving suffering by identifying its causes. If the goal were simply to feel better, Schwartz believes, ignorance would be preferable to introspection; after all, the "heavy bear" was in love with sleep. In *Genesis*, too, Schwartz sees "sleep as essential sin," and it tempts Hershey: "When will / I sleep? when will I be allowed to close / My mind, and look no more at my long life?"

It is the ghosts who refuse to allow this "desperate abandonment" of self-scrutiny. As the poem begins, they visit Hershey in his bedroom at night, literally depriving him of sleep, and ask to be told his story: "Many a night you told yourself your life, / Tell it to us, we have no more to do." In return, they promise to release him from its obsessive sway: "This is the way to freedom and to power, / This is the way to knowledge and to hope."

As Hershey's saga unfolds, it becomes clear that Schwartz has found the consummate expression of his double pessimism, the view of history that animated his best poems ever since "The Ballad of the Children of the Czar." In *Genesis*, the intertwining of personal and international influences can be demonstrated concretely; that is why Hershey does not begin his tale with his own birth, but with his grandfather, Noah Green, "a young man in Czarist Russia." Noah Green, a soldier in the Russo-Turkish War of 1877–78, deserts from the czar's army with the intention of abandoning his home and his unloved wife. He makes his way to another town and falls genuinely in love with a young girl, whom he plans to marry. Yet this most personal of desires is thwarted by geopolitcs: the war suddenly ends, after Great Britain intervenes to settle it, and a fellow soldier returning to Noah's hometown informs his wife of his whereabouts. She reclaims him, and his hope for a new life is destroyed. Noah's fate—and by implication Hershey's—is thus determined by the large motions of history:

> *England destroys this fugitive's romance!*
> *All these long range effects are marvellous!*
> *And I have seen the moonlight rule the bay!*

Hershey's birth is due to another such "long range effect." After describing how his paternal and maternal grandparents came to America, he tells of his parents' miserable marriage, clearly the same one portrayed in *Shenandoah* and "In Dreams Begin Responsibilities." Hershey's mother, Eva, desperately wants a child, hoping it will stop her husband Jack's philandering, but she cannot afford the operation she needs in order to get pregnant. Only when her uncle, back in Poland, sends her a French war bond as a gift can she afford to pay the doctor. International finance is, in this sense, Hershey's real father: "The prosperity of Eastern European capitalism sent the French bond west. It went through Paris, the capital of Western culture, / And entered her marriage and entered her womb."

Once again, the interplay of the personal—Jack Green's womanizing, Eva Green's jealousy—and the international—the Polish investor, the French bond—creates the individual's fate. As the ghosts observe of Hershey's father:

> *I see now how Jack Green's life by his will*
> *Was made, yet, of necessity,*
> *By the great causes made essentially:*
> *Europe, America, Capitalismus,*
> *Stupid deities in each other's arms. . . .*

If the forces of history are "stupid," so too are Hershey's relatives—for two generations back, he can find nothing but blind egotism and willfulness. Hershey's maternal grandfather comes to America as an act of revenge against his brother-in-law; Hershey's parents get married out of mutual aggression, "on the edge of their tempers, each convinced that the other was outrageously self-willed."

The second half of *Genesis*, chronicling Hershey's own childhood, is less stormily dramatic. Schwartz now turns his Freudian pessimism on himself, relating significant episodes to show how he developed his own imperious ego. Psychological growth, in

Schwartz's view, is a product of failure to "be justed with the external world"—that is, of the refusal of the external world to meet the child's wholly egotistical demands. When Hershey's mother gives birth to his younger brother, and he is excluded from her bedroom for the first time, the shock and insult provoke him to invent a scheme to sneak in: "faced with this problem, difficulty, and pain, the small mind became creative." Already, the imagination is seen as a tool for asserting power over pain—just as it would become in Schwartz's adult poetry.

Genesis continues through Hershey's childhood, dwelling on the episodes of lust, jealousy, pride, and fear that will determine his character: "fearful, cowardly, fugitive, the nice boy seduced in his weakness." The culminating scandal comes at the end of the poem. After his parents have separated, his mother, with Hershey in tow, comes across his father at a restaurant with another woman. Eva denounces him in front of the boy and the crowd of strangers:

> *Her passionate righteous anger, inspired and shouting phrases she*
> *had read in the Hearst papers about divorce cases,*
> *Pointed to Hershey, his hand still clutched in hers, his joy at see-*
> *ing his father destroyed at that moment,*
> *Shouted to the diners on the mezzanine floor that her husband*
> *had left her and her children to dine with a whore!*

The episode is a summation of all the cruelty and blind will that has brought Hershey to this pass, and his mother's speech is like a curse on Hershey's future. It is the kind of traumatic episode that a later confessional poet would expose with gleeful self-pity. But Schwartz's purpose in *Genesis* is the opposite of self-pity.

The poem is not simply an occasion to display his wounds; rather, it is a forum for the ghosts to observe, explain, and judge Hershey's story. As in *Shenandoah*, Schwartz splits himself into the suffering, passive actor and the coldly objective observer. The ghosts warn Hershey, at the very beginning of the poem, that they are not there to excuse his failings:

> *we will not*
> *Deny (as you expect!) the worst self-fears*
> *You bring against yourself. . . .*

Hershey's life and character may be beyond his control, but he cannot console himself with the thought that he is just a victim. In truth, he is as guilty as the ancestors who victimize him, since he shares their fatal egotism. In "Coriolanus and His Mother," Schwartz had made a plea for the possibility of human freedom, which allows individuals to choose a future different from the past. The ghosts of *Genesis*, however, are freed by death from such hopeful illusions. They see the chain of causality as absolute, in a passage that gives the poem its title:

> *Like Oedipus,*
> *No one can go away from genesis,*
> *From parents, early crime, and character,*
> *Guilty or innocent!*

This is the essence of their ghostly wisdom, and it is repeated in many forms throughout the poem. Indeed, if *Genesis* is dull at times, it is not because Schwartz is narcissistically absorbed in his own story—the family history is always dramatic and interesting—but because the ghosts' response to each episode is essentially the same. In this story about immigrants—and Schwartz saw himself as the poet of "the Atlantic migration, which made America"—the ghosts deny the possibility of any genuine new start: "And since one cannot have a childhood twice, / No one begins again, nothing is lost!"

If the ghosts condemn Hershey to "lie in the coffin of your character," then why do they so eagerly undertake his instruction? The answer reveals the extreme, even shocking darkness of *Genesis's* moral vision. The overwhelming burden of the poem is that understanding the past does not allow us to escape it—and that we must try to understand it anyway. Self-knowledge is necessary for its own sake, but because this knowledge does not bring power, it has a deathlike bitterness. That is why Hershey's instructors must be ghosts: only the dead have the detachment necessary to understand life completely, since only they are beyond hope of changing it. Their credo, repeated like a refrain throughout the poem, is a line from Virgil: *Felix qui potuit rerum cognoscere causas*, "Happy the man who can understand the causes of things." But this is a reduced, self-lacerating kind of happiness, since it does not lead to redemption:

> *"I only meant that knowledge was a joy,*
> *A painful joy perhaps, and yet what else?*
> *Nothing but knowledge through eternity!"*

Why, then, should Hershey seek this "painful joy"? Why try to understand his past, if the only conclusion he can draw is that "everyone is wrong and everywhere / At all times"? The answer comes in a line that could be the motto of Schwartz's best poetry:

"Pain is creative more than Pleasure is." Only the writer can triumph over history, not by escaping it, but knowing it and expressing his knowledge in art:

> *"None can long live free of the worst despair,*
> *Anxiety, boredom, and the worst despair . . .*
> *. . . . .*
> *But it brings doubt, doubt is intelligence,*
> *—Brings criticism and serenity,*
> *Calm gayety and careful conscious*
> *Contemptuous indifference to all Life,*
> *Inseparable from utmost seriousness. . . ."*

Through art, the living poet can approach the ironic freedom of the dead; and in *Genesis*, his most complete act of self-understanding, Schwartz attains the "utmost seriousness" of this freedom. Once again, Schwartz shows himself to be a profound Platonist, for his idea of art parallels Plato's definition of philosophy: "The fact is, those who tackle philosophy aright are simply and solely practicing dying, practicing death, all the time." Or as Schwartz has it, in the terrible last lines of *Genesis*:

> O what a metaphysical victory
> The first morning and night of death must be!

WHEN *GENESIS* APPEARED in 1943, it carried the subtitle "Book One," and Schwartz's preface described it as "the first book of a work which is almost finished." There is no intrinsic reason why Hershey's story couldn't be extended; indeed, it would have been a thematically appropriate symmetry to have the poem end with the beginning of its own composition. But the generally poor reception of *Genesis* discouraged Schwartz, who was always dangerously sensitive to fluctuations in his literary standing. Complaining to his publisher, he compared himself self-pityingly to another unappreciated writer: "Melville went to the grave thinking that *Moby-Dick* was a failure because the stupid reviewers of the day said that it was. Stupid reviewers so inhibited him that he could not write any more."

Schwartz did not stop writing, or even stop writing *Genesis*— fragments of the second "book" were published after his death. But the poem joined a long list of projects, in verse and prose, that he was never able to complete. The reason was not only discouragement, but increasing mental illness, which took a disastrous toll on his powers. Schwartz's creative flourishing came to an end only five years after his triumphant debut. The two books of poetry still to come showed a drastic decline in thought and expression.

Vaudeville for a Princess, published in 1950, mixes serious poems with parodies and prose sketches. As the title of the book suggests, it is intended to be comic, at least in parts; but the tone of the humorous pieces is uncertain and self-conscious. In the proliferation of literary trivia, there is a painful sense that Schwartz is no longer able to master his knowledge, but has been reduced to cataloguing it:

> *Emily Brontë gazed awestruck to see*
> *Passion consume her brother on the moor.*
> *Emily Dickinson went to Washington,*
> *Falling in love like flowers to the floor.*

Schwartz's versification in *Vaudeville* is considerably more regular than in his early work, where the blank verse can seem slovenly.

Yet this only proves that Schwartz was right to believe that a loose meter was better suited to the tone and movement of his thought; for now, writing regular sonnets and quatrains, he is far less substantive. A group of love poems hide the experience that inspired them behind stilted Elizabethan rhetoric, a disappointment after his early "shamelessness." And a series of political poems, each beginning "Dear Citizens," is very far from adequate to the World War that provoked them; Schwartz is alternately defensive about not serving in the military (he was deferred as a college instructor) and condescending to an America obsessed with "television and Broadway, / Victrolas, coca-colas, powerful cars."

The best poems in *Vaudeville* are those that return to Schwartz's earliest themes: guilt, memory, and freedom. Any reader of *Genesis* would recognize the exhortations "To look long at the crime, to know it well," "to praise unmasking and unmaskers." But as these lines suggest, Schwartz is now referring to his ideas, not employing or extending them. He has abstracted the morality of *Genesis* into maxims, or exhortations to himself.

And where Schwartz does put a new spin on his old ideas, it seems like a retreat rather than an advance. In "All Guilt and Innocence Turned Upside Down," he returns to his proclamation in *Genesis* that "Orestes is the name of every son, / Bearing the guilt his forebears have begun," and specifically repudiates it:

He named each child Orestes, hunted down.
Two years are lived and now he sees more truth,
The furies turned to mercies. . . .

This is the way, to halt, turn, and go back
To look long at the crime, to know it well . . .

—Then, then, denouement done, like a May sun
Forgiveness frees and blesses everyone.

In *Genesis*, Schwartz had been stern in his insistence that knowing the past does not absolve one from it: the only lesson of history was that "everyone is wrong." Now, however, he hopes for a universal amnesty.

But it is hard to say whether Schwartz intended this as a major revision of his earlier artistic beliefs, or was even fully aware of the contradiction. Only a few brief poems in *Vaudeville* address the themes that had dominated *Genesis* and virtually all of his earlier work. It is only in his last collection of poetry that we can see clearly how Schwartz's thought had been developing. *Summer Knowledge* appeared in 1959, as a new group of poems in a *Selected Poems* that also included the lyrics from *In Dreams*. The juxtaposition is unintentionally tragic, since it shows how radically Schwartz had declined in twenty years. The new poems are in rambling free verse, and combine jingling rhymes with windy abstraction, as in "The First Morning of the Second World":

> *The measure of pleasure, heart of joy, the light and the heart of*
> *   the light*
> *Which makes all pleasure, love and joy come to be*
> *As light alone gives all colors being, the measure and the treasure*
> *Of the light which unites and distinguishes the bondage and*
> *   freedom in unity and distinction*
> *Which is love . . .*

Still more troubling than the style of these poems is their leading idea, reiterated again and again. This is a complete reversal of

Schwartz's earlier ethic, which prized difficult self-knowledge as the only escape from the bondage of history and the appetites of the "heavy bear." For the young Schwartz, pleasure was always the opposite of knowledge. But now, a banally empty "pleasure"— along with other clichés, "love," "joy," "treasure," "light"—has become Schwartz's lodestar. No longer a poet of knowledge, he has become a poet of ecstatic amnesia:

> *this*
> *Is supreme consciousness,*
> *The self-forgetting in the self possessed and mastered*
> *In the elation of being open to all relation*
> *No longer watchful, wakeful, guarded, wary, no longer striving*
> *and climbing. . . .*

To Schwartz himself, of course, this did not seem like a decline. In arranging his *Selected Poems*, Schwartz put his early poems first, under the rubric "The Dream of Knowledge," followed by his new work under the title "The Fulfillment." This has a grim irony for anyone familiar with Schwartz's life, which by 1959 had been ruined by alcoholism and full-blown paranoia. But no biographical knowledge is needed to see that these late poems are the opposite of a "fulfillment" of youthful promise. To hear the voice of the essential and enduring Schwartz, one must go back to his earliest days, when he summarized his poetic credo in a few lines written in a friend's copy of *In Dreams Begin Responsibilities*: all human beings, he declared, "Hide private parts which I disclose / To those who know what a poem knows."

SYLVIA PLATH

I am the magician's girl who does not flinch

In 1953, when she was twenty years old, Sylvia Plath won a competition to spend the summer working for the magazine *Mademoiselle*. Plath's eagerness to join this literary demi-monde is typical of her often confused relation to her own poetic calling. It is hard to think of a writer of comparable gifts who would say, as Plath did in her journal at the age of twenty-four, that an idea for a story could be made "either Kafka lit-mag serious or SATEVEPOST [*Saturday Evening Post*] aim high," as though these were both "high" options.

Yet even as she longed for success in this conventional, middle-realm, Plath was accumulating her contempt for it. Nowhere is that contempt stronger than in a scene from *The Bell Jar*, Plath's autobiographical novel, where Esther Greenwood, her surrogate and narrator, is asked to pose for a photograph holding an emblem of her ambition:

> I said I wanted to be a poet.
> Then they scouted about for something for me to hold.
> Jay Cee suggested a book of poems, but the photographer said no, that was too obvious. It should be something that showed what inspired the poems. Finally Jay Cee unclipped the single, long-stemmed paper rose from her latest hat.
> The photographer fiddled with his hot white lights. "Show us how happy it makes you to write a poem."

The irony is so enormous that Plath does not need to make it explicit. For in her great poems, almost all written in the last year of her life, the characteristic properties are not inanely feminine roses but concentration camps and aborted fetuses, the surreal detritus of a mind in agony. The famous lines from "Lady Lazarus" could be taken as a direct response to the photographer's question: "I do it so it feels like hell. / I do it so it feels real."

A chasm separates the smiling all-American girl of such photographs from the ferocious blasphemer of Plath's best poems; and countless attempts have been made to bridge it with legend, gossip, and speculation. Her life, her marriage to the poet Ted Hughes, and her suicide at the age of thirty have been dramatized in novels, plays, and films; the stream of biographies and memoirs about her shows no sign of abating. Like Byron in his time, Plath has become something more and less than an artist: she is an icon, onto whom our culture's fears and fantasies can be projected.

But to treat Plath only as an icon, or the heroine of a melodrama, is to obscure her actual achievement. Plath's poems grew out of her life, of course, but they are never merely documents of that life; the better they are, the more thoroughly they transmute it into something like a myth. In particular, the great poems Plath wrote in her last months—most of them published posthumously in *Ariel* (1965)—gain their uncanny power from her ability to transform the most intimate experience almost beyond recognition. The techniques and themes of Plath's best poems were not simply given to her, but evolved over years of immensely disciplined writing. To understand Plath's explosive late work, it is crucial to understand the dialectic that drove her art from the beginning: her ongoing debate with herself over the proper limits of the poetic imagination.

Plath's writing life was so brief that it lacks the usual milestones. She published one book, *The Colossus*, in 1960, but her best work came later and remained unpublished until after her death. Most of her lasting poems were written in an incredibly short period of time—roughly the five months before her suicide in February 1963, to which they inevitably seem connected. As a result, her artistic growth seems to take place not in stages, as with most poets, but in a few violent convulsions.

If Plath had continued to live and write, it is likely that many of the poems now in her *Collected Poems* would never have been published. Certainly the fifty poems gathered under the heading "Juvenilia" are just that: the kind of practice in writing that all young poets need, but few would expose to the light of day. Even the first poems presented in *Collected Poems* as her mature work—written in 1956, when she was only twenty-three—show Plath still far from achieving a distinctive style.

The juvenilia proper is of interest mainly for what it reveals about Plath's reading. "Aquatic Nocturne" imitates the precise vision and contorted stanzas of Marianne Moore, "Lament: A Villanelle" the impassioned rhetoric of Dylan Thomas, and "A Sorcerer Bids Farewell to Seem" the themes and dandyish extravagance of Wallace Stevens. But the most common presence is W. H. Auden, whose coy abstractions can be heard in "Song for a Revolutionary Love," "Metamorphoses of the Moon," and "Love Is a Parallax." Stevens and Auden, in particular, remain strong influences on Plath's poetry into the late 1950s.

What stands out in Plath's early work are the occasional, rudimentary approaches to her mature themes. "Female Author," for instance, begins to address the conflict, which would provoke some of Plath's best writing, between the self-sacrifice conventionally demanded of women and the selfish demands of art. Here, however, Plath's treatment remains on the level of clichéd social protest: the "female author" is condemned for being hedonistic, with her "chocolate fancies in rose-papered rooms," and ignoring her responsibility to the "gray child faces crying in the streets." In Plath's later work, both roles, artist and mother, would be much more ambiguous, each offering a threat and a promise.

Other early poems address the failure of love affairs, usually in a semi-comic vein. In "Jilted," for instance, Plath seems less cast down than stood up: "I wear the wry-faced pucker of / The sour lemon moon." More intriguing are the poems in which Plath is the one doing the jilting, where her guilt and desire seem to drive her to exaggerate her lover's power. In "To a Jilted Lover," the man in question becomes "incandescent as a god," while in

"Bluebeard" he is compared to the legendary wife-killer: "in his eye's darkroom I can see / my X-rayed heart, dissected body." In these exaggerations there is a foretaste of Plath's heedless transformation, at the end of her life, of her husband and neighbors into figures of evil; more and more in her poetry, other people will appear not as they are, but as they seem in her fears or nightmares. Similarly, in "Lament," Plath's father, Otto, who died when she was a child, is turned into a demigod: "O ransack the four winds and find another / man who can mangle the grin of kings." The same violent father-god will dominate some of her most famous poems, from "The Colossus" to "Daddy."

A few of Plath's early poems also experiment with the metaphorical technique that she would later perfect: the transformation of living things into inanimate objects. In "Sonnet: To Eva," however, Plath keeps this unsettling notion at arm's length with careful diction and proficient rhymes:

This was a woman: her loves and stratagems
Betrayed in mute geometry of broken
Cogs and disks, inane mechanic whims,
And idle coils of jargon yet unspoken.

Still other early poems draw on fairy tales, always for Plath a realm of specifically feminine menace: "Admonitions" warns "The magic golden apples all look good / although the wicked witch has poisoned one." And "The Princess and the Goblins" features a princess who is ordered by her fairy godmother to rescue a young boy held captive by goblins.

But the denouement of "The Princess and the Goblins" shows that Plath had not yet discovered the crucial role that such magical figures were to play in her work. Instead, the poem turns into a straightforward fable about the importance of growing up. When the boy scoffs at the fairy who has contrived his rescue, the "indignant godmother / vanishes," leaving behind a disenchanted world, a "desolate tableau / of clockwork." The boy's disbelief marks his passage into adulthood, the triumph of reason over childhood imagination. To become an adult and a mature poet, Plath suggests, means to set aside the "gilded fable," no matter how painful the loss.

Of all the paths hinted at in her juvenilia, this is the one that Plath initially followed. In the mid-1950s, her poetry returns again and again to the notion that she must reconcile herself to a disenchanted world. Not until several years had passed did Plath discover that, in fact, her true gifts lay in the opposite direction: not objective description of the world, but an overpowering subjectivity that turns the entire world into a myth. Not until she embraced the recklessness of her imagination would she become a great poet.

FROM 1956 TO 1959, Plath's poems record a perpetual struggle between the claims of truth and the desires of imagination. These opposite ways of experiencing life, and of writing poetry, are often symbolized by two different ways of seeing. With an uneasy conscience, Plath urges on herself the secular mode of vision she describes in "Black Rook in Rainy Weather":

I do not expect a miracle
Or an accident

To set the sight on fire

In my eye, nor seek
Any more in the desultory weather some design. . . .

This is the principled objectivity of what might be called Plath's poetic superego, and the poems it inspires are conscientious exhortations, addressed not so much to the reader as to the poet herself. In "Tale of a Tub," she tells herself that while "Twenty years ago, the familiar tub / bred an ample batch of omens," now those imaginary monsters are "definitely gone." In "The Ghost's Leavetaking," she contrasts the "ambrosial revelation" of dreams, the "lost otherworld" where "Chair and bureau are the hiero-glyphs / Of some godly utterance," with the "meat-and-potato thoughts" of waking consciousness.

But Plath clearly experiences this disenchantment as a painful loss; if it weren't so difficult to accept, she wouldn't need to remind herself of it in poem after poem. As a result, she is com-pelled to find some other source of pleasure and significance, both in her life and in her writing, which will not depend on the childish visions she has abandoned. Her only hope, Plath pro-poses, is to submit to reality, but with an awareness so heightened that the ordinary becomes strange. This is the hopeful realism imagined by Wallace Stevens in "Sunday Morning":

Shall our blood fail? Or shall it come to be
The blood of paradise? And shall the earth
Seem all of paradise that we shall know?
The sky will be much friendlier then than now. . . .

Plath dutifully endorses this prospect in "Poems, Potatoes," using Stevens's own style (and a very Stevensian title) to repeat his praise for the actual: "Unpoemed, unpictured, the potato / Bunches its knobby browns on a vastly / Superior page. . . ."

Plath sums up both parts of this dialectic, her disappointment and her resolution, in two companion poems of 1957. "On the Difficulty of Conjuring Up a Dryad" takes the mythological tree nymph as a metaphor for the kind of supernatural vision Plath will no longer permit herself. "The honest earth," she writes,

> Spurns such fiction
> As nymphs; cold vision
> Will have no counterfeit
> Palmed off on it.

Her Stevensian remedy, offered in "On the Plethora of Dryads," is to redefine enchantment in strictly naturalistic terms. "No visionary lightnings / Pierced my dense lid," she acknowledges when looking at a tree; but she now insists that the tree itself can be seen as a kind of dryad. The "miraculous art," both in seeing and in poetry, is not to embellish what the earth offers us, but to receive the earth in all its sensual plenitude:

> Instead, a wanton fit
> Dragged each dazzled sense apart
> Surfeiting eye, ear, taste, touch, smell;
> Now, snared by this miraculous art,
> I read earth's burning carrousel. . . .

If Plath were genuinely content with this way of seeing, she might have become a very different kind of poet, a precise recorder of surfaces like Moore or Bishop. But in fact, the self-conscious, argumentative cleverness of the "Dryad" poems shows that Plath is working against her own gift. Nothing in her writing suggests that she is poetically satisfied with evoking sensory experience in rich detail. The very fact that she must urge herself to such strict observation implies that it does not come naturally to her. If she is in fact obligated to cast a cold eye on the world, she can do so only with the ironic regret of "The Times Are Tidy":

> *The last crone got burnt up*
> *More than eight decades back*
> *With the love-hot herb, the talking cat,*
> *But the children are better for it,*
> *The cow milks cream an inch thick.*

Yet even as she was writing these poems in praise of disenchantment, other subjects compelled Plath to use the very magics she was swearing off. In the mid-1950s, it is sexual passion that calls forth her most charged fantasies. Plath's journals from the early 1950s record a moving protest against the conventional sexual role that American society seemed to force upon her. She is troubled by her strong sexual desires, but finds her actual suitors impossible to imagine as partners, since she recognizes that she could never be satisfied in the kind of marriage they expect. She even feels forced, by the humiliating hypocrisy of sexism, to apologize for her own strength: "I need a strong mate: I do not want to accidentally crush and subdue him like a steamroller." Only a man she perceives as stronger than herself could allow her to exert all her strength, and to express the lust she usually feels she must conceal.

Plath's most vivid poems of the mid-1950s dramatize this complex of desires and anxieties. And she finds herself driven, by her most powerful expressive needs, to perform the reckless imaginative transformations that her poetic superego had so often denounced. The male figure that compels her imagination is violent and insatiable, a fantasy version of the "strong mate" she could not yet find in real life. In "Pursuit," she turns him into a panther, around whom "Charred and ravened women lie, / Become his starving body's bait." In "The Queen's Complaint," he becomes a "giant" with "hands like derricks, / Looks fierce and black as rooks," who ravages a queen's "dainty acres." And in "The Glutton" he is a "hunger-stung" devourer, "With heat such as no man could have / And yet keep kind." All of these poems, far from "spurn[ing] such fiction / as nymphs," find that only fictions can convey the truth of feeling.

A different kind of mythmaking takes place when Plath turns from this overmastering lover to herself, the woman who expresses such guilty desires. On the one hand, Plath writes contemptuously of any woman who withdraws from the sexual arena altogether. In "Two Sisters of Persephone," she prefers the fertile sister, who "grows quick with seed" and "bears a king," to the spinster sister who, "wry virgin to the last, / Goes graveward with flesh laid waste, / Worm-husbanded, yet no woman." In this poem, as in "Spinster" and "Virgin in a Tree," Plath writes in vindication of women's sexuality.

But as her journals make bitterly clear, she also felt intense shame over her sexual appetite, which she expressed in poems like "Strumpet Song":

After a lean day's work
Time comes round for that foul slut:

Mere bruit of her takes our street
Until every man,
Red, pale or dark,
Veers to her slouch.

When Plath writes of "that mouth / Made to do violence on," the violence of the fantasy lover in "The Queen's Complaint" takes on a disturbing new dimension. To be victimized, it seems, is the deserved punishment for a woman who makes herself sexually available. Yet at the same time, such violation is also a woman's only opportunity to express her shameful appetite: her humiliation expiates the sin of her desire. This seems to be the hidden motivation behind the fantasies of Plath's journals: "What is more wonderful than to be a virgin, clean and sound and young, on such a night? . . . (being raped.)"

Like so many women of her time and place, Plath suffered greatly on account of these frustrated, self-canceling desires. Her writing—the journals more than the poems—is a valuable document of the injustice that feminism set out to redress, just around the time Plath died. But while Plath's historical and political circumstances certainly affected what she wrote, her work is more than simply a document of or complaint about those circumstances. She is significant not as a sociological case study—millions of other women could serve that purpose just as well—but as an artist; not for what she suffered but for what she did. Her sexual predicament is important, from this point of view, because it helped to propel the imaginative daring of her best poems.

For whenever she writes about love and desire, Plath finds that she must violate her self-imposed ban on fictions. When the subjects closest to her must be treated in poetry, she turns, not to the objective vision praised in "On the Plethora of Dryads," but in the vocabulary of fairy tale and myth: queen and giant, panther and Persephone. And these fictions are, paradoxically, more true to Plath's actual experience than the naturalism she attempts in descriptive poems like "Mussel Hunter at Rock Harbor." Truth, Plath discovers, is not the same as fact.

But she also recognizes that there is a moral risk in approaching truth by way of fiction: a poet's symbols can willfully distort the outer world into a mere shadow of her inner life. Plath signals her awareness of this danger in "Soliloquy of the Solipsist":

> *my look's leash*
> *Dangles the puppet-people*
> *Who, unaware how they dwindle,*
> *Laugh, kiss, get drunk,*
> *Nor guess that if I choose to blink*
> *They die.*

In fact, Plath's best poems will exercise this artist's solipsism to the utmost, flagrantly exalting the power of her words over the people and situations she writes about. This is exactly why her poetry cannot be described as confessional; instead of simply reciting her history, Plath ferociously transforms it into surreal parables. For the same reason, it is exceptionally dangerous to try to reduce Plath's poems to evidence about her life, as so many interpreters have done. To insist on the distinction between art and life is simply to honor Plath's own contemptuous judgment, recorded in her journal in 1958, on what would later be called confessional poetry: "As if poetry were some kind of therapeutic public purge or excretion."

. . .

IN 1957, PLATH began to mark out the territory that would become distinctively hers. Just at the same time that she was lamenting her inability to "beguile sight" in "On the Difficulty of Conjuring Up a Dryad," she did exactly that in "The Thin People":

> *Wrapped in flea-ridden donkey skins,*
>
> *Empty of complaint, forever*
> *Drinking vinegar from tin cups . . .*
> . . . .
> *They persist in the sunlit room: the wallpaper*
>
> *Frieze of cabbage-roses and cornflowers pales*
> *Under their thin-lipped smiles,*
>
> *Their withering kingship.*
> *How they prop each other up!*

The figures in this poem are not quite ghosts. Plath grounds them in actual images of starving refugees, as seen "in a war making evil headlines," and thus leaves open the possibility that the "thin people" are simply thin people, who haunt the well-fed in the manner of a bad conscience. But by the end of the poem, they seem to have forgotten their origin, and take on the unaccountability of nightmares. This ambiguity is echoed in the verse, which pays deference to a more conventional rhyme scheme— each stanza is a half-rhymed couplet—while tugging toward the untrammeled speed of free verse, which would become the medium of some of Plath's best late poems. The poem also features two of the rhetorical techniques that would characterize Plath's mature work: exaggerated assonance, as in "withering kingship," and exclamations like "How they prop each other up!" in which polite observation shades into dread.

But it would take several years for Plath to exploit such effects fully. For the time being, her verse remained elaborate and wordy, even as her subjects became more potent and individual. In "The Lady and the Earthenware Head," Plath regards a sculpture of her head as a totem, linked to her by sympathetic magic; she imagines a "sly nerve" that "knits to each original its coarse copy," and fears that damage to the sculpture might harm her as well. It is a first crude step toward what will become a common technique in her poetry, and a major source of its uncanniness: the blurring of the boundary between animate and inanimate.

The poems where this blurring is most successful, however, do not speculate about magic in a merely whimsical or self-conscious way, like "The Lady and the Earthenware Head." Instead, they allow magic—in the form of curses, witches, and gods—to become a definite emotional reality, while leaving open the possibility that it is simply being used as a literary metaphor. This uncertainty deliberately leaves the reader at a loss, unable to decide whether the poet is using her fictions or being used by them.

That is the technique of "The Disquieting Muses," one of Plath's best early poems. Inspired by the painting of the same name by de Chirico, Plath turns its dressmaker-dummy "muses" into characters in her own personal legend. As in the story of Sleeping Beauty, Plath imagines that an offended relative,

"Unasked to my christening," "Sent these ladies in her stead / With heads like darning-eggs" to put a curse on her. Significantly, this curse takes the form of excluding her from the world of conventional femininity, the cheerful and optimistic domain presided over by her mother. In her mother's bedtime stories, Plath writes, the "witches always, always / Got baked into gingerbread"; later, her mother sent her to dances and piano lessons, the normal pursuits of young girls. But the poet, under the control of real witches "with stitched bald head," cannot sing or dance, and cannot finally join her mother's pretty dreamworld, with its "million / Flowers and bluebirds that never were / Never, never, found anywhere." Instead, she acknowledges at the poem's conclusion, she is doomed to spend her life in the company of the muses, with their ambiguous blank faces and ominous shadows.

"The Disquieting Muses" can be read as a simple allegory, with the curse representing the child's intelligence, or unfeminine ambition, or poetic sensitivity. But in later poems on the same theme, Plath deepens and darkens her personal myth, imagining herself marked out by fate in a more dangerous sense. And if her mother represents the conventional world from which she is exiled, she will turn her father into the tutelary deity of that uncanny realm where she belongs. Because Plath's actual father died (of untreated diabetes) when she was still a child, she was free—in a series of poems culminating in "Daddy"—to transform the man she barely knew into a pure fantasy, one of the malign presences of her enchanted world.

This process can be seen at work as early as "Lament," but it begins to take shape in Plath's mature poetry around 1958. In "Full Fathom Five," Plath finds a father figure in Neptune, the "Old man" who is the god of the sea. Watching the tide, the poet allows herself to see with the mythic vision she has so often abjured, discerning in the sea foam the god's "white beard" and "spread hair." On one level, then, "Full Fathom Five" seems to be continuing her poetic debate about ways of looking at nature, as in the "Dryad" poems. But Plath's title establishes a more intimate connection between the poet and the sea god. It is a phrase from Ariel's famous song in *The Tempest*:

> *Full fathom five thy father lies;*
> *Of his bones are coral made:*
> *Those are pearls that were his eyes:*
> *Nothing of him that doth fade,*
> *But doth suffer a sea-change*
> *Into something rich and strange.*

Just as the ocean transforms a dead body into precious gems, so Plath's art remakes her father—actually a quite ordinary man, an entomologist who wrote a textbook on bees—into a beckoning, menacing god. She underscored the connection in her journals, when she considered making "Full Fathom Five" the title poem of her first book:

> Another title for my book: *Full Fathom Five.* . . . It relates more richly to my life and imagery than anything else I've dreamed up: has the background of *The Tempest*, the association of the sea, which is a central metaphor for my childhood, my poems and the artist's subconscious, to the father image . . . and the pearls and coral highly-wrought to art: pearls sea-changed from the ubiquitous grit of sorrow and dull routine.

By embracing the notion of poetry as a "sea change," Plath takes a decisive step away from life and nature, toward art and symbol. This is the crucial evolution that separates Plath's pedestrian poetry of the mid-1950s from the mythic intensity of her late work. Yet it exacts a double price, on the poet and on the things and people she writes about. Once Plath's actual father is turned into Neptune, the feelings inspired by the god can no longer be attributed to the man: things can be said about and to the "father image" that would be shockingly unjust to the father.

At the same time, as Plath's myths and symbols move to the center of her poetry, they lose the consciously hypothetical quality of metaphor. Instead of comparisons, Plath begins to deal in transformations. As a result, she increasingly seems to inhabit a surreal and violent parody of reality, in which every thing and person takes its shape only from her own emotions and desires. This is why Plath's late work often seems like the whirlwind that carries away the sorcerer's apprentice: her imagination is magnetized by self-destruction, to the point that something completely private and irrational seems to determine what she sees and feels. She can be seen practicing this dangerous spell at the end of "Full Fathom Five," when she follows her metaphor to its logical, fatal conclusion:

> *I walk dry on your kingdom's border*
> *Exiled to no good.*
>
> *Your shelled bed I remember.*
> *Father, this thick air is murderous.*
> *I would breathe water.*

The fantasy of drowning also appears in two other poems from this period. In "Lorelei," the "ice-hearted calling" of the legendary creature tempts the poet to the "Drunkenness of the great depths"; "Suicide off Egg Rock" takes a realistic, psychological approach to the same situation, imagining the last moments of a man tempted to drown himself by "the forgetful surf." In all of these suicidal drownings, there seems to be an echo of Virginia Woolf's death, which Plath invoked in her journal: "But her [Woolf's] suicide, I felt I was reduplicating in that black summer of 1953 [when Plath made her first suicide attempt]. Only I couldn't drown." But even more, they are like a dare Plath issues to herself, a challenge to follow her imagination past the bounds of self-preservation.

Two poems written in 1959 further elaborate on Plath's father myth, and in doing so reveal its genuine dangers. In "Electra on Azalea Path," as in "Full Fathom Five," she turns to Greek legend, imagining herself as Electra, the princess who loved her father and killed her mother. Plath acknowledges, with a certain irony, that this parallel inflates her own father's death beyond its proper dimensions: "I borrow the stilts of an old tragedy," she admits. This sounds like an attempt to recognize and repudiate her own mythologizing impulse. Remembering her childhood fantasies about her dead father, she acknowledges that even then she wildly exaggerated his stature: "Small as a doll in my dress of innocence / I lay dreaming your epic, image by image." Now, by finding his actual grave in the cemetery, Plath implies, she can "awaken" from those dreams to reality: "The day I woke, I woke on Churchyard Hill." In all this, "Electra on Azalea Path" is a deliberately Freudian poem, setting reason to undo the work of fantasy.

But in the last stanza, Plath seems to lose her grip on this dawning realism. She knows intellectually that her father's death was not a magical event or a punishment for something she did, but the result of a simple disease: "It was the gangrene ate you to

the bone / My mother said; you died like any man." Yet by ascrib-
ing this truth to her mother, Plath disclaims her own share in it.
As in "The Disquieting Muses," the mother represents a state of
healthy adjustment that the daughter cannot achieve: "How shall
I age into that state of mind?" she wonders hopelessly. Instead,
"Electra on Azalea Path" (whose title puns on the name of the
poet's mother, Aurelia Plath) concludes by falling back into the
neurotic illusion that Plath's father died as punishment for her
own excessive, forbidden love: "It was my love that did us both to
death." Strangely and ominously, Plath reclaims her identity as
Electra, even though, on good Freudian principles, naming her
"Electra complex" should have put it within her power. It is as
though, in "Electra on Azalea Path," Plath considers a psychological interpretation of her life and world—one based on reasoned
insight and the conquest of illusion—and deliberately rejects it,
in favor of the intoxication of myth.

"The Colossus" provides a stark image of this myth and its
consequences. The poem is built on a simple, even primitive kind
of surrealism, which operates by making the figurative literal—a
technique Plath will greatly refine in later poems. Here, she indicates that her father has assumed enormous psychic dimensions
by giving him the physical dimensions of a huge broken statue:

Scaling little ladders with gluepots and pails of Lysol
I crawl like an ant in mourning
Over the weedy acres of your brow
To mend the immense skull-plates and clear
The bald, white tumuli of your eyes.

This image is the core of "The Colossus," and once it is established in the third stanza the rest of the poem simply expands on

it; Plath creates a static emblem, not a dramatic situation. To put her myths into action, to inhabit them instead of just proposing them, would be the decisive next step in Plath's work, marking the beginning of her major poetry. But it would also mean surrendering her art to the fantasies it had so far consciously weighed and manipulated. She made the surrender reluctantly, writing in her journal that she wanted to move her poetry in exactly the opposite direction: "My main thing now is to start with real things: real emotions, and leave out the baby gods, the old men of the sea, the thin people, the knights, the moon-mothers, the mad maudlins, the lorelei, the hermits, and get into . . . [t]he real world." But her artistic instinct was surer than her rationalizations; these weird presences were, in fact, her "real things." And she seems to prophesy the actual future of her poetry in "The Manor Garden":

The small birds converge, converge
With their gifts to a difficult borning.

THE FIRST STAGE in the "difficult borning" of Plath's mature style came, appropriately enough, in "Poem for a Birthday." A suite of seven short poems written around the time of her twenty-seventh birthday, in 1959, at first it seems nearly as derivative as her juvenilia. Plath's model now is not Auden or Stevens but Theodore Roethke, whose poetry attempted to give voice to the unconscious life of plants and animals with a vaguely menacing baby talk:

It's dark in this wood, soft mocker.
. . . .

It's a great day for the mice.
Prickle-me, tickle-me, close stems.
Bumpkin, he can dance alone.
Ooh, ooh, I'm a duke of eels.

Clearly Plath is echoing lines like these, from Roethke's "Praise to the End!", in the second section of "Poem for a Birthday":

This is a dark house, very big. . . .
. . . .
It has so many cellars,
Such eelish delvings! . . .
. . . .
These marrowy tunnels!
Moley-handed, I eat my way.

The first five sections of Plath's poem experiment with this voice of preconsciousness, creating a world disconcertingly free of distinctions and boundaries. In the first part, "Who," the speaker seems to be now a plant, now a woman in a madhouse; in "Dark House," she is a burrowing mole. The fourth section, "The Beast," is full of presences like "the little invisibles" and "the blue sisters," "Mumblepaws" and "Fido Littlesoul," halfway between animals and imps.

The sequence comes into sharp focus only with the sixth poem, "Witch Burning," where Plath's style and imagination break free of Roethke's. Witches were already familiar presences in Plath's poetry; but instead of treating them as figures in a consciously designed allegory, as in "The Disquieting Muses," Plath now tries on the role of witch herself. The uncertain gabbling of

the earlier parts of "Poem for a Birthday" is given a definite setting, and becomes an ideal vehicle for the frantic exclamations of
a madwoman:

A black-sharded lady keeps me in a parrot cage.
What large eyes the dead have!
I am intimate with a hairy spirit.

Plath's witch sounds not like a fairy-tale figure but like a real
woman accused of witchcraft in the Middle Ages. She even
accepts the logic behind her own burning: "Only the devil can eat
the devil out." And by the end of the poem, she seems to welcome the flames that consume her, as "Brightness ascends my
thighs." In its imagination of madness and torture, it is a rehearsal
for Plath's late poems, where the explicit narrative frame of "Witch
Burning" is discarded, and we are left with the disturbing impression that the poet herself, not one of her characters, is speaking.

Indeed, the last section of "Poem for a Birthday," "The
Stones," is already a major advance in this direction. Instead of
the borrowed voices of the first poems, and the historical setting
of "Witch Burning," "The Stones" offers a situation completely
original to Plath, a surreal embodiment of her own deepest concerns. Even before her suicide attempt in 1953, Plath had used
the mythic language of death and rebirth to express her feelings
of depression and recovery: "You are twenty. You are not dead,
although you were dead. The girl who died. And was resurrected.
Children. Witches. Magic. Symbols." In "The Stones," she imagines a soul in the interval between death and resurrection. But
what begins as a moist Roethkean idyll soon becomes a hellish
factory floor:

The grafters are cheerful,

Heating the pincers, hoisting the delicate hammers.
A current agitates the wires
Volt upon volt. Catgut stitches my fissures.

Rebirth is no longer a supernatural or even a natural process, but a completely mechanical one, like the repair of an engine. The human body has become an inanimate machine—and not in a deliberate allegory, as in "The Colossus," but as it were spontaneously, without the poet's intention or consent.

Between "Poem for a Birthday" in early November 1959 and "In Plaster" in March 1961, Plath wrote only twenty-one poems, making it, for her, an unusually fallow period. In various ways, however, these poems experiment with the technique of "The Stones," dissolving the boundary between life and matter. Sometimes Plath achieves this effect with a single adjective: in "Candles," the candles are "nun-souled"; in "Morning Song," even an affectionate lullaby turns faintly unpleasant, as a baby is compared to "a fat gold watch." In "You're," a poem addressed to her unborn child, Plath does the same thing in a riddling spirit: "Vague as fog and looked for like mail. / Farther off than Australia. / Bent-backed Atlas, our traveled prawn." The riddle, which depends on the estrangement of a familiar object, would become a favorite technique of Plath's late poetry.

More often, however, the air of menace is explicit, as in "Stillborn," where her own failed poems are compared to dead fetuses:

They sit so nicely in the pickling fluid!
They smile and smile and smile and smile at me.

And still the lungs won't fill and the heart won't start.

They are not pigs, they are not even fish,
Though they have a piggy and a fishy air. . . .

It is the very fact that the fetuses are halfway between animal and human, with "a piggy and a fishy air," that makes them uncanny: they are a reminder of the origins of human life in the inhuman. Plath knows that simply to describe a pickled fetus is a violation of taboo. Yet she heightens the reader's discomfort with her mock-politeness, which refuses to acknowledge that she is mentioning something abhorrent. Such a mismatch between tone and subject will become another important tool of her late work.

"In Plaster" is the first poem in which Plath successfully fuses all of these developing strains. At first it seems to be another riddle, with only the title as a clue: "I shall never get out of this! There are two of me now: / This new absolutely white person and the old yellow one." Not until halfway through the poem does it become certain that the "white person" is, in fact, a plaster cast, "Holding my bones in place so they would mend properly." But Plath's language endows the cast with a life of its own: it is "she," at once alter ego and parasite. And by deliberately refusing to assign the "white person" a single identity or allegorical meaning, Plath achieves an unsettling richness of suggestion. The cast could be the poet's corpse; it could be her living body, which imprisons her mind; it could even be the constricting feminine role against which she rebels. But finally, and most characteristically for Plath, the cast is a vampire, an inanimate object with a malicious will of its own:

And secretly she began to hope I'd die.
Then she could cover my mouth and eyes, cover me entirely,
And wear my painted face. . . .

Because the title of "In Plaster" hints in advance that the poem is about a cast, Plath's transformations of the threatening "she" can keep the air of a riddle, a demonstration of ingenuity. This is what keeps the poem, finally, in the realm of black comedy, rather than outright horror. In "Tulips," however, Plath begins to cross that boundary. Here, as in her most powerful late poems, it is no longer so obvious that the poet is in control of her imagination; using the art that conceals art, Plath creates the impression that she could be slipping away into paranoid fantasy.

At first, however, "Tulips" is slyly self-conscious, making sure to say nothing that cannot be read as basically rational. When the poet, lying in a hospital bed, announces that "I have given my name and my day-clothes up to the nurses / And my history to the anesthetist and my body to surgeons," the logical surface meaning is clear. But the reader cannot miss the suggestion that, by "given," Plath really means "given away." For it seems that the poet has literally dismantled herself, leaving nothing but a pure consciousness, "Like an eye between two white lids that will not shut."

This is the consummation of the narcissism that Plath began to explore as early as "Soliloquy of the Solipsist." For this bodiless mind, the external world exists only as the screen on which its desires are projected; and its deepest desire is for extinction, the calm of death. The tulips shatter this deathliness with their vitality, just as they break the hospital white with their "vivid" color:

Then the tulips filled it up like a loud noise.
Now the air snags and eddies round them the way a river
Snags and eddies round a sunken rust-red engine.
They concentrate my attention, that was happy
Playing and resting without committing itself.

The tulips call the poet back to a life she was glad to leave behind. The poem's brilliant last line, one of a whole crop of unforgettable phrases in Plath's late poetry, captures this ambivalence: the tulips speak of "a country far away as health," but though the poet is in the hospital to convalesce, it is not a country to which she wants to return. A death wish, it begins to seem, is the price of Plath's self-enclosed imagination—or, to put it another way, the curse of the solipsist. If the entire world, including other people, exists only as a mirror of the poet's own consciousness, then there can be no escape from the self except in the unconsciousness of death.

And Plath seems willing to accept this fatal bargain. That is the bleak affirmation of "The Moon and the Yew Tree," her last major poem of 1961. On the surface, it is a description of the grounds of her house in Devon, England, which happened to be situated near a graveyard. But symbolically it lays out the terrain where her poetry would dwell in her final months. It is a stark, dead landscape, "cold and planetary," over which the poet presides "as if I were God"—the achieved dream of the solipsist. Its ruling symbols are the lifeless moon and the yew tree, traditionally associated with graves:

The yew tree points up. It has a Gothic shape.
The eyes lift after it and find the moon.
The moon is my mother. She is not sweet like Mary.

In these lines, Plath endorses the decision made as early as "The Disquieting Muses" and "Electra on Azalea Path": she will align herself not with pious, maternal Mary, but with the weird and violent femininity of Diana, the huntress.

Acknowledging that the territory of her art is "blackness—blackness and silence," Plath will no longer just explore that blackness; she will allow it to speak through her, becoming its impresario and its victim. This is evident already in "Elm," written in early 1962, several months before the great eruption of Plath's poetry in the fall. The elm tree is another one of Plath's inanimate objects; but this time, unlike the tulips, it does not stand outside the poet and address her. Instead, Plath inhabits it, having become the dryad she once failed to conjure:

> *I know the bottom, she says. I know it with my great tap root:*
> *It is what you fear.*
> *I do not fear it: I have been there.*

"I HAVE BEEN THERE": Plath's late poems, especially the *Ariel* poems written at white heat in her last months, insist on their source in personal experience. That is why Plath's life continues to be such an inexhaustible source of interest: every reader must wonder what "actually" happened to her to provoke poetry of such incomparable suffering and anger. But if one follows the evolution of her work, from the "Dryad" poems onward, it becomes clear that Plath's poetry never transcribes events in the real world, or even reacts directly to them. Instead, she creates a world in her own image, with only the most tenuous and contingent relationship to reality. Even more than with most poets, with Plath what matters is the inner experience a poem embodies, not the outward event it may or may not encode. This is particularly important to remember in the case of a poet whose myths, especially about her father and husband, have often been accepted by readers as true bills of indictment.

Plath found an appropriately strange image for the relationship of her art to her life when she copied out in her journals a passage from Daniel Defoe's *A Journal of the Plague Year*: "it was the opinion of others that [the plague] might be distinguished by the party's breathing upon a piece of glass, where, the breath's condensing, there might living creatures be seen by a microscope, of strange, monstrous & frightful shapes, such as dragons, snakes, serpents & devils, horrible to behold." The application to her own "monstrous and frightful" poems was clear to Plath: "The chaemeras [sic] of the sick mind also," she added. This is not to imply that her late poems are symptoms of mental illness; rather, it suggests the effect that Plath's artistry was deliberately striving to achieve. The bizarre "shapes" in her poems are not meant as faithful portraits, but as objective correlatives or exhalations of her inner experience.

The distinction can be seen in a slight poem that Plath wrote in July 1962, "Words heard, by accident, over the phone." Like "You're" and "In Plaster," the poem begins as a riddle, deliberately withholding the true name of the thing being described: "O mud, mud, how fluid!— / Thick as foreign coffee, and with a sluggy pulse." Only the title reveals that this substance is not an actual liquid but a voice; with the logic of surrealism, Plath has made a metaphor literal, imagining the filthy, repulsive words as mud "pressing out of the many-holed earpiece." She even recognizes the comedy of this transformation: there is something childishly delighted in her repetition of the near-obscenity "Muck funnel, muck funnel," whose sound and meaning are equally expressive.

Yet whose words are being overheard, and why they should provoke such loathing, Plath is not at all concerned to reveal. Biographers may record that "Words heard" was written after Plath
jealously eavesdropped on her husband's phone conversation with
another woman; but to locate this little horror in a narrative, to
provide it with motivation and history, is entirely contrary to
Plath's intention.

The refusal of psychology is, in fact, the key to the unaccountable terror of Plath's late poems. As in a dream, things and people are transformed for no reason; or else, as in a fairy tale, they
are compelled to reveal their true, loathsome natures, which are
ordinarily hidden under a facade of normality. In "The Detec-
tive," Plath casts herself as Sherlock Holmes, trying to uncover a
hidden crime even though, on the surface, nothing seems amiss:
"This is a case without a body. / The body does not come into it
at all." Yet because the poet is the only one who seems to believe
that a crime has taken place, the reader is forced to wonder
whether she is not, in fact, simply paranoid. This is again the case
in "Berck-Plage," where Plath looks at bathers on a French beach
and demands, "Why is it so quiet, what are they hiding?"; and in
"A Secret," when she imagines "an illegitimate baby" hidden away
in a "bureau drawer." Using a venerable literary technique—the
unreliable narrator—Plath creates the illusion that she is
employing no technique at all, that the poem is somehow out of
her control.

In "The Bee Meeting," Plath erects this paranoia into a dread
that rivals Edgar Allan Poe. The poem begins with another nervous interrogation: "Who are these people at the bridge to meet
me?" But while Plath goes on to give a perfectly rational answer
to the question—"the rector, the midwife, the sexton"—the very

fact that she needs to ask it suggests that something is deeply amiss. In the same spirit, the mild hobby for which these English villagers are gathered is transformed into an obscene ritual, made horrible by the very fact that the poet cannot name it: "Is it some operation that is taking place?" In their protective gear, "nodding a square black head," the villagers lose their individuality, becoming more of the semi-inanimate presences that have populated Plath's world ever since "The Disquieting Muses."

All this foreboding works the poet's nerves, and the reader's, up to a painful pitch; Plath compares herself to the knife thrower's assistant, "the magician's girl who does not flinch." But the conclusion of the poem brilliantly withholds any relief, offering only a shiver: "The villagers are untying their disguises, they are shaking hands. / Whose is that long white box in the grove, what have they accomplished, why am I cold." The deadened tone of voice, signaled by Plath's omission of the final question mark, is a compound of fear and guilt—she has been both victim and participant in this nameless crime.

But for such poems to succeed, it is crucial that the reader not wonder too urgently about the facts behind Plath's myth. That is the lesson of "Burning the Letters," in which an actual episode—Plath's vengeful burning of Ted Hughes's papers in the summer of 1962—can be all too easily discerned. Plath herself seems to acknowledge her failure of art: "I am not subtle, / Love, love, and well, I was tired. . . ." There is still a movement toward magical thinking in this poem—with the husband's letters gone, Plath writes, "at least it will be a good place now, the attic," as though by burning them she had performed an exorcism. But the underlying motives of revenge and jealousy seem all too human, leaving the poem finally just a record of sordid domestic sabotage.

What's more, because we learn of Plath's action but not the reasons for it, we are left to wonder if it is justified—if there is not something peculiarly reprehensible in a writer setting fire to another writer's words. In this way, "Burning the Letters"—like Lowell's *The Dolphin*, or Berryman's *Love & Fame*—demonstrates that, when the question of the ethics of confession arises in a poem, there has already been an aesthetic failure. It is because Plath has not raised the poem to the realm of art that it is open to censure from the canons of life.

This distinction is especially important when it comes to appreciating the splendid aggression of Plath's late poems. Many biographical interpretations, dwelling on the collapse of Plath's marriage in 1962, try to reduce this ferocity to the mere vengefulness of a woman scorned. They are abetted in this effort by Plath's weakest and most personal poems, like "Burning the Letters." But when she is most successful as a poet, Plath does not seem to be writing out of a personal grievance against an individual. Men and women, intimates, neighbors, and society are all attacked, with delightful recklessness. What these poems are really about, in their blend of anger and comedy, is the intoxicating power of the completely unrestrained imagination. From the beginning, Plath has desired and dreaded the artist's solipsistic freedom to transform her world according to her own whim; now she embraces it, and relishes her own daring.

As "The Applicant" shows, one mode of Plath's aggression is feminist. Once again using her riddle technique, Plath does not come right out and say what is being applied for in this poem; but it quickly becomes clear that the applicant is a suitor, and the "thing" which he is being offered is a wife. The speaker of the poem, a kind of manic salesman, exaggerates the qualities of the conventional good wife to the point of savage satire. The wife—always referred to simply as "it"—is "willing / To bring teacups and roll away headaches"; "It can sew, it can cook, / It can talk, talk, talk." But the poem makes clear from the beginning that only a pathetically inadequate man would ever "apply" for such a wife: he has to have something "missing," to "wear / A glass eye, false teeth or a crutch," to be "empty." In this context, the poem's repeated refrain—"Will you marry it?"—becomes a taunt, directed at the man and the male society that would erect such a "living doll" into a feminine ideal.

Yet it would be a mistake to read Plath's late work as simply or consistently feminist. For one thing, the acid she directs against men is equally potent against women. The title of "Lesbos" is thoroughly ironic, for the poem speaks not of love between women but bitter hatred. Plath exposes the real feelings buried under a superficial friendship. She cruelly mocks her friend's marriage, children, taste in clothes, and delusions of grandeur; she addresses her as "vase of acid," "blood-loving bat," "sad hag." Yet the comically exaggerated music of the poem's first line— "Viciousness in the kitchen!"—establishes the gleeful tone of this abuse. As in "The Applicant," Plath delights in expressing a taboo rage; this, more than any feminist grievance, is the spur to her genius. "The blood jet is poetry," she declares in "Kindness"; "There is no stopping it."

Plath's most problematic late poems are those in which the force of that "blood jet" pushes her across the line separating self-dramatization from narcissism. "Daddy," probably her best-known poem, is also the worst casualty of this impulse. It opens by recalling the father myth of "Full Fathom Five," "Electra on Azalea Path," and especially "The Colossus"; here again the father is a "ghastly statue." But this time Plath invokes the image only to renounce it: "You do not do, you do not do / Any more," "Daddy" begins defiantly.

However, by turning her unreasonable reverence for her father into unreasonable hatred, Plath does not succeed in dispelling her self-created myth. Instead, she makes it a hundred times more potent, by forcing the reader to wonder what could justify the extremity of her attack. For in Plath's new myth, her father appears as a Nazi, a "swastika" and "Panzer-man" with an "Aryan eye." Correspondingly, she herself becomes "a bit of a Jew," and associates her own suffering with that of Jews killed at "Dachau, Auschwitz, Belsen."

This rhetorical strategy is a serious mistake, and not just on grounds of taste or morality. Plath writes as though the Holocaust belonged to the world of myth, and Nazis were an archetype like the witches of "The Disquieting Muses." But in fact the Holocaust belongs to history, and what the Nazis did is inescapably real. As a result, the reader has no choice but to wonder whether the injury that Plath claims to have suffered deserves the comparison, and the answer can only be negative. As in "Burning the Letters," but much more damagingly, Plath allows the ethical to intrude on the aesthetic, and the result is that her myth is punctured. Instead of allowing "Daddy" to be read as the objective correlative of an emotional experience, she forces the reader to treat it as a claim that must be judged true or false.

The beginning of "Lady Lazarus," a considerably better poem, is also damaged by Plath's Nazi imagery. Here she insists on making use of one of the most gruesome details of the Holocaust, comparing herself to a "Nazi lampshade" and a "fine / Jew linen"; and once again the narcissism of such a claim is revolting. But unlike in "Daddy," in "Lady Lazarus" Plath is willing to admit her narcissism, and indeed to turn her considerable irony against it: for she goes on to imagine herself as a circus freak, a performer of her own death and resurrection. The main target of her contempt is the "peanut-crunching crowd" that "shoves in" to witness her agony. Yet by figuring her own suicide as a kind of "strip tease," Plath acknowledges her own complicity with this crowd; after all, it is the very poem she is writing that allures them. The exaggerated, nearly camp seductiveness of her language carries an implicit critique of the performer's self-absorption:

> *Dying*
> *Is an art, like everything else.*
> *I do it exceptionally well.*
>
> *I do it so it feels like hell.*
> *I do it so it feels real.*
> *I guess you could say I've a call.*

Here the savage mockery of "The Applicant" is directed against the poet herself. It is this self-division that gives "Lady Lazarus" its "large charge," an unstable compound of hatred and self-hatred, grief and comedy, which threatens to explode at any moment in the reader's and the poet's face.

But if this instability is exciting, it is also terrifying, an accelerating recklessness that seems to have only one possible conclusion. "Ariel" shows Plath severing almost all connection with the external world, until the poet is alone with her violence. It is just possible to recognize in the poem the experience that provoked it—"The brown arc / Of the neck" belongs to the horse, named

Ariel, which ran away with Plath while she was riding. Yet she
strips the experience of almost all identifying details, turning it
into a sequence of abstract images: "Stasis in darkness. / Then the
substanceless blue / Pour of tor and distances." The tremendous
progress of Plath's art in her last year can be gauged by comparing these lines with Plath's awkwardly literal description of a similar occurrence in "Whiteness I Remember," a poem written in
1958: "the hard road / An anvil, hooves four hammers to jolt /
Me off into their space of beating." Then Plath was recording an
event; now she is creating a symbol. "Ariel" is no longer a horse,
but—in a return to the Shakespearean imagery of "Full Fathom
Five"—the spirit of poetry itself, whose abduction of Plath her
last poems seem to document.

> *White*
> *Godiva, I unpeel——*
> *Dead hands, dead stringencies.*
>
> *And now I*
> *Foam to wheat, a glitter of seas.*

Finally she is nothing but motion, "at one with the drive" that
cannot be reined in or guided. No wonder such a flight seems
"suicidal."

Whether such a fate is in fact inscribed in Plath's poetry is a
question without an answer. Certainly the work of her last
months does not record an uninterrupted downward spiral, as
though tracing a graph of suicidal despair. In fact, several of the
poems written in January 1963, Plath's last month, mark a definite step back from the brink she seemed to approach the previ-

ous fall. "Mystic," "Paralytic," and "Gigolo" attempt to channel her voice into dramatic monologues or character studies, as though to shield the poet herself from exposure. And poems like "Child" and "Balloons" are lovingly addressed to her children, who offer a respite from the surrounding desolation: "Your clear eye is the one absolutely beautiful thing."

Yet the fact that Plath took her own life shortly after writing the *Ariel* poems cannot but seem more than accidental. The extreme daring of her best poetry, its voicing of the most forbidden desires and fears, its appalled fascination with violence—all this seems part of what Robert Lowell called, in a review of *Ariel,* "a game of 'Chicken,' the wheels of both cars locked and unable to swerve." It is not that Plath's late poems simply document her progress toward suicide. Rather, it seems, Plath's fascination with the ingredients of suicide—solipsism and despair—began in her poetry: they were her major themes from "Soliloquy of the Solipsist" through "Full Fathom Five," "Electra on Azalea Path," "Tulips," and "Lady Lazarus." No life demonstrates more savagely than Plath's that the poetry shapes the poet, at least as much as it is shaped in return. Certainly it is impossible to read "Edge," written six days before Plath's suicide, without feeling that she is not the victim but the author of her fate—that legendary death, which four decades later still "wears the smile of accomplishment."

NOTES

The books listed here do not represent a complete bibliography of the poets discussed in *The Wounded Surgeon*, much less a comprehensive guide to the large critical literature they have inspired. Instead, for each chapter, I list the editions of the poet's works that I consulted, along with a few biographical resources that I found indispensable. Verse quotations are annotated, with the title of the poem only, when the source is not identified in the text.

INTRODUCTION

page

x   "some kind of therapeutic": *The Unabridged Journals of Sylvia Plath*, edited by Karen V. Kukil (Anchor, 2000), p. 355.

x   "the speaker can never be": John Berryman, *The Freedom of the Poet* (Farrar, Straus and Giroux, 1976), p. 321.

x   "more and more anguish": Brett C. Millier, *Elizabeth Bishop: Life and the Memory of It* (University of California Press, 1993), p. 361.

xi   "the whole balance": Robert Lowell, *Collected Prose* (Noonday/Farrar, Straus and Giroux, 1990), p. 246.

xi   "I am obliged": Dream Song #67.

xii   "The generation of American poets": Randall Jarrell, *The Third Book of Criticism* (Farrar, Straus and Giroux, 1969), p. 296.

xii   "never before or since": Lowell, *Collected Prose*, p. 17.

xii   "take a man's full weight": ibid., p. 43.

xiii   "the poet is a maker": Cleanth Brooks, *The Well Wrought Urn: Studies in the Structure of Poetry* (Harvest, 1956), p. 74–75.

xiii   "a structure of meanings": Brooks, *The Well Wrought Urn*, p. 195.

xiv   "a pattern of resolved": Brooks, *The Well Wrought Urn*, p. 203.

xiv   "Judging a poem": W. K. Wimsatt, *The Verbal Icon: Studies in the Meaning of Poetry* (University Press of Kentucky, 1967), p. 4.

xiv   "a good poem . . . was simply": Lowell, *Collected Prose*, p. 59.

xiv   "What the literary methods": *Selected Essays of Delmore Schwartz*, edited by Donald A. Dike and David H. Zucker (University of Chicago Press, 1970), p. 140.

xiv   "amusing theory": Berryman, *The Freedom of the Poet*, p. 230.

xv   "The kind of poet I am": Ian Hamilton, *Robert Lowell: A Biography* (Vintage, 1983), p. 57.

ROBERT LOWELL

Collected Poems by Robert Lowell, edited by Frank Bidart and David Gewanter (Farrar, Straus and Giroux, 2003)

Notebook by Robert Lowell (Noonday/Farrar, Straus and Giroux, 1971)

Collected Prose by Robert Lowell, edited by Robert Giroux (Noonday/Farrar, Straus and Giroux, 1990)

Robert Lowell: A Biography by Ian Hamilton (Vintage, 1983)

Lost Puritan: A Life of Robert Lowell by Paul Mariani (W. W. Norton, 1994)

1   "My heart, beat faster, faster": "Colloquy in Black Rock."

3   "on the old nineteenth-century scale": Edmund Wilson, "An Interview with Edmund Wilson," *The Bit Between My Teeth* (Farrar, Straus and Giroux, 1965), p. 548.

3   "the line from King David": "In the Back Stacks."

3   "full of Miltonic": "Visiting the Tates," *Prose*, p. 58.

4   "saying the start of *Lycidas*": "Anne Dick 1. 1936."

4   "When I began to publish": "After Enjoying Six or Seven Essays on Me," *Poems*, p. 992.

4   "poetry must be burly": *Prose*, p. 60.

4   "intellectual style": Introduction to *Land of Unlikeness*, *Poems*, p. 859.

6   "I used to lie": "Antebellum Boston," *Prose*, p. 300.

12   "Wasn't the Jamaican rum": "Cotton Mather," *Prose*, p. 183.

18   "five messy poems": "A Conversation with Ian Hamilton," *Prose*, p. 269.

18   "It's hell finding": Hamilton, p. 196.

18   "I wish rather in vain": Hamilton, p. 181.

18   "spontaneous, open": Randall Jarrell, "An Introduction to the Selected Poems of William Carlos Williams," *Poetry and the Age* (Faber & Faber 1996), p. 208.

19   "seemed distant": "On 'Skunk Hour,' " *Prose*, p. 227.

19   "human richness": "An Interview with Frederick Seidel," *Prose*, p. 241.

19   "And Uncle Devereux stood": "Near the Unbalanced Aquarium," *Prose*, p. 361.

25   "I feel I could write": Hamilton, p. 233.

33   "*All* the poems about": Hamilton, p. 237.

34   "The kind of poet": Hamilton, p. 57.

34   "You leave out a lot": *Prose*, p. 246.

37   "early personal memories": *Poems*, p. 1065.

42   "say almost anything": *Prose*, p. 270.

42   "I did nothing": *Prose*, p. 272.

43   "I don't believe": *Prose*, p. 248.

44   "I hope this jumble": Note to *History*, *Poems*, p. 1074.

44   "It's somewhere, somewhere": "Cicero, The Sacrificial Killing."

46   "Stephen Decatur": "Old Prints: Decatur, Old Hickory."

46   "the white glittering": "Coleridge and Richard II."

46   "he haws on the gristle": "Charles V by Titian."

46   "the ant's cool": "Before Repeal."

48   "What raised him": "Stalin."

48   "No one was like him": "Death of Alexander."

49   "He knew the monster" "Clytemnestra 3."

49   "What does he care": "Bosworth Field."

49   "Dare we say": "Napoleon."

49   "a blindman": Marcus Cato 234–149 B.C."

49   "You must die": Achilles to the dying Lykaon."

50   "unlocking to keep": "The March 1."

50   "bites his own lip": "Life and Civilization."

50   "What is history?": "Mexico 4."

51   "one man, two women": "Exorcism 2."

52   "prickly hedgehog": "New York 3."

52   "Dr. Johnson": "Late Summer 8."

52   "shouldn't I ask": "Harvard 3."

52   "Woman, so small": "The Charles River 2."

52   "the soul groans": "Mexico 8."

52   *"all flesh is grass"*: "Harvard 2."

53   "I draw a card": "Doubt 1."

53   "find their kittens": "Summer Between Terms 1."

53   "drop in the beercans": "Fall Weekend at *Milgate* 3."

54   "One can use one's life": Elizabeth Bishop, *One Art: Letters,* edited by Robert Giroux (Farrar, Straus and Giroux, 1994), p. 562.

54   "not avoiding injury": "Dolphin."

56   "Do I romanticize": "New York 7."

56   "the fiction I colored": "Marriage 9."

57   "eelnet made by man": "Dolphin."

59   "What is won": To Frank Parker."

59   "We are things": "Our Afterlife I."

59   "we learn the spirit": "Jean Stafford, a Letter."

59   "if we see a light": "Since 1939."

ELIZABETH BISHOP

The Complete Poems 1927–1979 by Elizabeth Bishop (Noonday/Farrar, Straus and Giroux, 1983)

The Collected Prose by Elizabeth Bishop, edited by Robert Giroux (Noonday/Farrar, Straus and Giroux, 1984)

One Art: Letters by Elizabeth Bishop, edited by Robert Giroux (Farrar, Straus and Giroux, 1994)

Becoming a Poet: Elizabeth Bishop with Marianne Moore and Robert Lowell by David Kalstone, edited by Robert Hemenway (Noonday/Farrar, Straus and Giroux, 1989)

Elizabeth Bishop: Life and the Memory of It by Brett C. Millier (University of California Press, 1993)

Conversations with Elizabeth Bishop, edited by George Monteiro (University Press of Mississippi, 1996)

Remembering Elizabeth Bishop: An Oral Biography, edited by Gary Fountain and Peter Brazeau (University of Massachusetts Press, 1994)

63   "Everything only connected": "Over 2,000 Illustrations and a Complete Concordance."

64   "I have met few people": *One Art,* pp. 276–77.

65   "In general, I deplore": *One Art,* p. 562.

65   " 'I' counting up": Kalstone, p. 32.

66   "When they had": "Primer Class," *Prose,* pp. 10–11.

70   "with the roosters": Millier, p. 158.

70   "to be good": "Efforts of Affection," *Prose,* p. 137.

72   "ELIZABETH KNOWS BEST": *One Art,* p. 96.

75   "In her long, descriptive": Anne Stevenson, *Elizabeth Bishop* (Twayne Publishers, 1966), p. 51.

80   "there is an element": *Prose,* p. 144.

83   "I'm going to turn": *One Art,* p. 385.

92   "it is fun to be": Millier, p. 62.

99   "It seems to me": *One Art,* p. 350.

JOHN BERRYMAN

The Dream Songs by John Berryman (Noonday/Farrar, Straus and Giroux, 1969)

Collected Poems 1937–1971 by John Berryman, edited by Charles Thornbury (Noonday/Farrar, Straus and Giroux, 1991)

The Freedom of the Poet by John Berryman (Farrar, Straus and Giroux, 1976)

Berryman's Shakespeare by John Berryman, edited by John Haffenden (Farrar, Straus and Giroux, 1999)

We Dream of Honour: John Berryman's Letters to His Mother, edited by Richard J. Kelly (W. W. Norton, 1988)

The Life of John Berryman by John Haffenden (Ark, 1983)

Dream Song: The Life of John Berryman by Paul Mariani (Paragon House, 1992)

Poets in Their Youth by Eileen Simpson (Noonday/Farrar, Straus and Giroux, 1990)

101   "To become ourselves": Sonnet #45.

101   "it was far from agreeable": *Honour,* p. 335.

102   "my orders were sealed": Dream Song #369.

103   "I didn't so much wish": "One Answer to a Question: Changes," *Freedom,* p. 323.

103   "to keep free": *Honour,* p. 94.

103   "I shut my eyes": *Honour,* p. 93.

104   "writes to express": R. P. Blackmur, "W. B. Yeats: Between Myth and Philosophy," *Form and Value in Modern Poetry* (Doubleday Anchor, 1957), p. 61.

104   "Let us take 'ritual'": "The Ritual of W. B. Yeats," *Freedom,* p. 248.

105   "This night I have seen": *Honour,* p. 56.

106   "More and more I hate": *Honour,* p. 63.

106   "Given life and tenacity": Haffenden, p. 98.

106   "slavishly Yeatsish": Randall Jarrell, *Kipling, Auden & Co.* (Farrar, Straus and Giroux, 1980), p. 152.

109   "Analysands all": "The Lightning."

109   "Somebody slapped": "New Year's Eve."

110   "If Miss Gonne": Simpson, p. 156.

111   "pieces of living": "Shakespeare at Thirty," *Shakespeare,* p. 42.

111   "the poet's effort": "The Sonnets," *Shakespeare,* p. 287.

112   "the mild days": Sonnet #1.

112   "the SS woman": Sonnet #110.

113   "the truth is": Haffenden, p. 177.

114   "swine- / enchanted": Sonnet #4.

114   "mutinous": Sonnet #12.

114   "a clown": Sonnet #58.

114   "my leer": Sonnet #100.

114   "Muffled in capes": Sonnet #15.

114   "monk / Of Yeatsian order": Sonnet #5.

115   "I am this strange thing": Sonnet #45.

115   "I have never tried": Simpson, p. 228.

115   "I have always failed": *Honour,* p. 244.

115   " 'You've never written' ": John Haffenden, *John Berryman: A Critical Commentary* (NYU Press, 1980), p. 25.

115   "the most distinguished": Haffenden, p. 3.

116   "something spectacularly NOT": *Freedom,* p. 327.

116   "a lifetime's study": *Freedom,* p. 328.

119   "a poem means more": "Dylan Thomas: The Loud Hill of Wales," *Freedom*, p. 283.

120   "interested in craft": "The Poetry of Ezra Pound," *Freedom*, p. 264.

120   "amusing": "Song of Myself: Intention and Substance," *Freedom*, p. 230.

120   "intolerable": "Thomas Nashe and *The Unfortunate Traveller*," *Freedom*, p. 12.

120   "One thing critics": "Despondency and Madness: On Lowell's 'Skunk Hour,'" *Freedom*, p. 316.

121   "not as *maker*": *Freedom*, p. 230.

121   "The poet—one would say": *Freedom*, p. 232.

121   "If I take 1938": *Honour*, p. 271.

122   "I am engaged": *Honour*, p. 276.

122   "I'm . . . literally out": *Honour*, p. 291.

122   "Some of my simplest": *Honour*, p. 282.

123   "The reflective man": *The Basic Writings of Sigmund Freud*, trans. A. A. Brill (Modern Library, 1938) p. 192.

125   "editors and critics": *Freedom*, p. 330.

125   "the construction of a world": *Freedom*, p. 330.

125   "the speaker can never": *Freedom*, p. 321.

128   "hopeless, inextricable lust": Dream Song #6.

128   "Love her he doesn't": Dream Song #69.

128   "Bats have no bankers": Dream Song #63.

129   "tragic, yet funny": "The Mind of Isaac Babel," *Freedom*, p. 118.

130   "I have a style now": *Honour*, p. 319.

131   "The Garden Master": Dream Song #18.

131   "the quirky medium": Dream Song #38.

131   "The high ones die": Dream Song #36.

132   "They blew out": Dream Song #8.

134   "God's Henry's enemy": Dream Song #13.

134   "at odds wif de world": Dream Song #5.

135   "while Keats sweat' ": Dream Song #6.

136   "If something happened to Henry": Mariani, p. 443.

137   "I sh[ould]n't be surprised": Mariani, p. 398.

137   "are partly independent": Haffenden, p. 327.

137   "to stop writing": Mariani, p. 386.

137   "the threat of mannerism": Mariani, p. 406.

138   "the boldest and most brilliant": Mariani, p. 416.

138   "Henrify": Haffenden, *John Berryman: A Critical Commentary*, p. 58.

138   "I write with my stomach": Dream Song #328.

140   "Miss Dickinson": Dream Song #187.

140   "no deadline": Dream Song #83.

140   "Not Guilty by reason": Dream Song #86.

142   "marvellous faculties": "At Chinese Checkers."

142   "Ten Songs, one solid block": Dream Song #157.

142   "fighting for air": Dream Song #156.

142   "His mission was obscure": Dream Song #155.

142   "I'm cross with god": Dream Song #153.

142   "long experience": Dream Song #256.

143   "If all must hurt": Dream Song #194.

143   "let's exchange": Dream Song #200.

144   "Naked the man": Dream Song #370.

145   "giving specific instances": *Honour*, p. 372.

145   "the poet speaks": Haffenden, p. 414.

145   "the speaker can never": *Freedom*, p. 321.

145   "International art": "Antitheses."

146   "Impressions, structures": "Message."

149   "Do you not know": *A Kierkegaard Anthology*, edited by Robert Bretall (Princeton University Press, 1973), p. 99.

150   "A religious poet": *The Living Thoughts of Kierkegaard*, edited by W. H. Auden, (New York Review Books, 1999), p. 96.

RANDALL JARRELL

The Complete Poems by Randall Jarrell (Farrar, Straus and Giroux, 1969)

Poetry and the Age by Randall Jarrell (Faber & Faber, 1996)

A Sad Heart at the Supermarket: Essays and Fables by Randall Jarrell (Atheneum, 1962)

The Third Book of Criticism by Randall Jarrell (Farrar, Straus and Giroux, 1969)

Kipling, Auden & Co.: Essays and Reviews 1936–1964 by Randall Jarrell (Farrar, Straus and Giroux, 1980)

Randall Jarrell's Letters: Expanded Edition, edited by Mary Jarrell (University of Virginia Press, 2002)

Randall Jarrell 1914–1965, edited by Robert Lowell, Peter Taylor, and Robert Penn Warren (Farrar, Straus and Giroux, 1967)

Randall Jarrell: A Literary Life by William H. Pritchard (Farrar, Straus and Giroux, 1990)

Remembering Randall: A Memoir of Poet, Critic, and Teacher Randall Jarrell by Mary von Schrader Jarrell (HarperCollins, 1999)

153   "Oh, bars of my own body": "The Woman at the Washington Zoo."

153   "was so overwhelmed": *Letters,* p. 380.

154   "goes beyond the standards": *Randall Jarrell 1914–1965,* p. 189.

155   "'Modern' poetry is, essentially": "A Note on Poetry," *Kipling,* p. 48.

156   "post- or anti-modernist": "From the Kingdom of Necessity," *Age,* p. 189.

156   "the marionette looks": *Kipling,* p. 50.

157   "About 2/3 are poems": *Letters,* p. 277.

157   "The future already": "Up in the sky a star is waiting."

157   "unusual punctuation": "Changes of Attitude and Rhetoric in Auden's Poetry," *Third Book,* p. 132.

163   "I've never written": *Letters,* p. 151.

163   "The real war poets": "Poetry in War and Peace," *Kipling,* p. 129.

169   "If you met your proconsuls": *Letters,* p. 124.

170   "written on a typewriter": *Kipling,* p. 137.

170   "baby critics": "Some Lines from Whitman," *Age,* p. 114.

171   "I *like* liking poetry": "Recent Poetry," *Kipling,* p. 260.

171   "the critic points": *Age,* p. 114.

171   "such an article as this": "To the Laodiceans," *Age,* p. 54.

171   "It might be better": "The Humble Animal," *Age,* p. 156.

171   "the least crevice": "The Other Frost," *Age,* p. 26.

172   "humor and sadness": *Age,* p. 59.

172   "moral and human attractiveness": "An Introduction to the Selected Poems of William Carlos Williams," *Age,* p. 218.

172   "look at the literary quarterlies": "The Age of Criticism," *Age,* p. 70.

172   "Criticism *does* exist": *Age,* p. 62.

173   *"Read at whim!"*: "Poets, Critics and Readers," *Kipling,* p. 318.

173   "it is a pleasure to read": "Poets," *Age,* p. 194.

173   "after thirty or forty": "Three Books," *Age,* p. 220.

173   "life beats art": Pritchard, p. 245.

177   "I feel like the Dickens": *Letters,* p. 299.

177   "is supposed to be *said*": *Letters,* p. 26.

181   "he was, down to the details": *Randall Jarrell 1914–1965,* p. 5.

181   "boyish, disembodied": *Randall Jarrell 1914–1965,* p. 102.

181   "identified with children": *Randall Jarrell 1914–1965,* p. 264.

181   "Sometimes we were brother": *Remembering,* p. 135.

195   "Randall was in thrall": *Remembering,* p. 121.

DELMORE   SCHWARTZ

Selected Poems: Summer Knowledge by Delmore Schwartz (New Directions, 1967)

Genesis: Book One by Delmore Schwartz (New Directions, 1943)

Shenandoah and Other Verse Plays by Delmore Schwartz, edited by Robert Phillips
(BOA Editions, 1992)

In Dreams Begin Responsibilities and Other Stories by Delmore Schwartz, edited by
James Atlas (New Directions, 1978)

Selected Essays of Delmore Schwartz, edited by Donald A. Dike and David H. Zucker
(University of Chicago Press, 1970)

Letters of Delmore Schwartz, selected and edited by Robert Phillips (Ontario Review
Press, 1984)

Delmore Schwartz and James Laughlin: Selected Letters, edited by Robert Phillips
(W. W. Norton, 1993)

The Ego Is Always at the Wheel: Bagatelles by Delmore Schwartz, edited by Robert
Phillips (New Directions, 1986)

Delmore Schwartz: The Life of an American Poet by James Atlas (Welcome Rain,
2000)

197   "Pain is creative": *Genesis,* p. 40.

197   "it is so good that no one": *Laughlin,* p. 147.

197   "In days to come": *Laughlin,* p. 188.

198   "the only genuine innovation": Atlas, p. x.

200   "the first or the typical": "The Isolation of Modern Poetry," *Essays,* p. 9.

200   "Because this private life": *Essays,* p. 11.

200   "bound to be drawn": "Poetry Is Its Own Reward," *Ego,* p. 35.

201   "Nothing could be more peculiar": *Essays,* p. 4.

201   "The artifice of spontaneity": *Letters,* p. 72.

202   "enables me to mention things": *Letters,* p. 64.

202   "to refer, with the least strain": *Letters,* p. 75.

203   "the development of the historical sense": "T. S. Eliot's Voice and His Voices," *Essays*, p. 141.

212   "By 1938, I had read": "The Ego Is Always at the Wheel," *Ego*, p. 2.

216   "obviously personal": *Letters*, p. 107.

218   "He reflected upon his separation": *In Dreams*, p. 19.

219   "this story-succeeded-by-commentary": *Laughlin*, p. 159.

222   "about my long poem": *Laughlin*, p. 109.

222   "I was never so sure": *Laughlin*, p. 149.

222   "disillusion and disappointment": *Letters*, p. 127.

223   "Every time I read": *Letters*, p. 91.

224   "hypnotized by the personal": William Barrett, *The Truants: Adventures Among the Intellectuals* (Doubleday Anchor, 1982), p. 234.

229   "the Atlantic migration": *Laughlin*, p. 149.

231   "Melville went to the grave": *Laughlin*, p. 204.

234   "this / Is supreme": "Vivaldi."

234   "Hide private parts": *Essays*, p. xvi.

SYLVIA PLATH

The Collected Poems by Sylvia Plath, edited by Ted Hughes (Harper Perennial, 1992)

The Unabridged Journals of Sylvia Plath, edited by Karen V. Kukil (Anchor, 2000)

The Bell Jar by Sylvia Plath (Bantam, 1972)

Johnny Panic and the Bible of Dreams: Short Stories, Prose, and Diary Excerpts by Sylvia Plath (Harper Torchbooks, 1986)

Bitter Fame: A Life of Sylvia Plath by Anne Stevenson (Houghton Mifflin, 1989)

235   "I am the magician's girl": "The Bee Meeting."

235   "either Kafka lit-mag": *Journals*, p. 288.

236   "I said I wanted": *Bell Jar*, p. 83.

243   "I need a strong mate": *Journals*, p. 173.

245   "What is more wonderful": *Journals*, p. 8.

246   "As if poetry were": *Journals*, p. 355.

250   "Another title": *Journals*, p. 381.

252   "But her [Woolf's] suicide": *Journals*, p. 269.

254   "My main thing": *Journals*, p. 471.

256   "You are twenty": *Journals*, p. 154.

262   "The chaemeras": *Journals*, p. 424.

INDEX

DATE DUE